Motown and the Making of
Working-Class Revolutionaries

SERIES EDITORS

David L. Brunsma
David G. Embrick

SERIES ADVISORY BOARD

Margaret Abraham
Elijah Anderson
Eduardo Bonilla-Silva
Philomena Essed
James Fenelon
Evelyn Nakano Glenn
Tanya Golash-Boza
David Theo Goldberg
Patricia Hill Collins
José Itzigsohn
Amanda Lewis
Michael Omi
Victor Rios
Mary Romero

Motown and the Making of Working-Class Revolutionaries

The Story of the League of Revolutionary Black Workers

Jerome Scott and Walda Katz-Fishman

The University of Georgia Press
ATHENS

Sociology of Race
and Ethnicity website

© 2025 by the University of Georgia Press
Athens, Georgia 30602
www.ugapress.org
All rights reserved
Set in Garamond Premier Pro by Melissa Buchanan

Most University of Georgia Press titles are
available from popular e-book vendors.

Printed digitally

Library of Congress Cataloging-in-Publication Data
Names: Scott, Jerome, 1945– author | Katz-Fishman, Walda author
Title: Motown and the making of working-class revolutionaries :
    the story of the League of Revolutionary Black Workers /
    Jerome Scott and Walda Katz-Fishman.
Other titles: Story of the League of Revolutionary Black Workers
Description: Athens : The University of Georgia Press, [2025] |
    Series: Sociology of race and ethnicity | Includes
    bibliographical references and index.
Identifiers: LCCN 2025013258 | ISBN 9780820374277
    hardback | ISBN 9780820374284 paperback |
    ISBN 9780820374291 epub | ISBN 9780820374307 pdf
Subjects: LCSH: African Americans—Political activity—
    Michigan—Detroit—History—20th century | African
    Americans—Michigan—Detroit—Social conditions—20th
    century | League of Revolutionary Black Workers | League
    of Revolutionary Black Workers—Biography | Labor unions
    and communism—Michigan—Detroit | Automobile
    industry and trade—Michigan—Detroit—History—20th
    century | Detroit (Mich.)—Race relations—Political aspects
    | Detroit (Mich.)—Social conditions—20th century
Classification: LCC F574.D49 B5367 2025 2025
LC record available at https://lccn.loc.gov/2025013258

*To the fighters turned thinkers and
the thinkers turned fighters.*

*To all those who have been ordained
in revolutionary struggle.*

*And in memory of General Baker, a father first,
a laborer, an educator, and a person whose praxis
has left behind a legacy in motion, being carried
out by all who knew, loved, and learned from him.
Who stand at the ready for when the call is made to
liberate the working class from all which shackles us.*

   General Baker Institute

*On a personal note, to my family and especially my
four children who shared this journey with me.*

   Jerome

CONTENTS

LIST OF ILLUSTRATIONS   IX

LIST OF ABBREVIATIONS   XI

PREFACE   XIII

Part One.   **Black Workers and Auto—the Beginning**

CHAPTER 1.   The League Story in Our Own Words   3

CHAPTER 2.   Our Southern Roots and Radicalization   11

CHAPTER 3.   Workers, Capitalists, and the United Auto Workers in the Auto Industry, Twentieth and Early Twenty-First Centuries   17

Part Two.   **From Our Origins to the Split—the League Story**

CHAPTER 4.   Founding Members of the League of Revolutionary Black Workers Meet Up in the Early 1960s   29

CHAPTER 5.   Working-Class Rebellions in Detroit and the World—the Working Class Takes the Offensive, 1967 to 1968   42

CHAPTER 6.   The League Days, 1968 to 1971   58

CHAPTER 7.   League Women and Students—the Woman Question, the 1960s to 1971   78

CHAPTER 8. Class, Race, and Revolution—Understanding the Real World 97

Part Three.   The Split and Coming to Revolutionary Consciousness

CHAPTER 9. The Split and the Struggle for Education, 1971 103

CHAPTER 10. Becoming Working-Class Intellectuals and Lifelong Revolutionaries, 1971 and Beyond 113

CHAPTER 11. Other Detroiters Join the Journey and the Study 127

Part Four.   Lessons and Possibilities in Revolutionary Times

CHAPTER 12. The Centrality of Education in Revolutionary Struggle 143

CHAPTER 13. Riding the Ebbs and Flows of Class Struggle—Longevity and Lessons for Today's Revolutionaries 151

CHAPTER 14. Revolutionary Possibilities 171

APPENDIX. METHODOLOGY 183

BIBLIOGRAPHY 187

INDEX 195

ILLUSTRATIONS

Figures

1. U.S. auto production, U.S. auto workers, and UAW membership, 1899–2022   18

2. U.S. auto production as a percentage of world auto production, 1950–2019   18

Photos

Volunteer crew and videographers for the League Education and Media Project   xv

League of Revolutionary Black Workers members and family   30

Flyers, posters, communications, and newspapers from the movement   48

League Executive Board members at a protest in Detroit   73

Conversation at Darryl Mitchell's house   94

Comrades who joined the journey   114

ABBREVIATIONS

BEDC	Black Economic Development Conference
BSUF	Black Student United Front
BWC	Black Workers Congress
CCL	California Communist League
CL	Communist League
CLP	Communist Labor Party
Colectiva	Colectiva del Pueblo / Collective of the People
CP	Communist Party of America
DRUM	Dodge Revolutionary Union Movement
GBI	General Baker Institute
LRBW	League of Revolutionary Black Workers
LRNA	League of Revolutionaries for a New America
MCLL	Motor City Labor League
MEChA	Movimiento Estudiantil Chicano de Aztlán / Chicano Student Movement of Aztlán
MLWA	Marxist-Leninist Workers Association
NAACP	National Association for the Advancement of Colored People
NSM	Northern Student Movement
Panthers	Black Panther Party
PAR	People Against Racism
POC	Provisional Organizing Committee
RUMs	Revolutionary Union Movements
SDS	Students for a Democratic Society
SNCC	Student Nonviolent Coordinating Committee
UAW	United Auto Workers

PREFACE

> At the risk of seeming ridiculous, let me say that the true revolutionary is guided by a great feeling of love. It is impossible to think of a genuine revolutionary lacking this quality.
>
> —Ernesto "Che" Guevara,
> *Socialism and Man in Cuba* (1965)

Who We Are and Why We're Writing the League Story—Biography and History

The story of the League of Revolutionary Black Workers (LRBW) in our own words is a labor of life, of love, of continuous struggle, and of necessity. We came to this project through very different paths that connected in the 1980s. From that moment we collaborated on projects of political education and political struggle in many spaces.

We, Jerome and Walda, are your guides on the LRBW journey from then to now, placing biography within history, bringing analysis, context, and continuity. Jerome is a native of Detroit and a Vietnam veteran. He was an auto worker at Chrysler Detroit Forge, became an LRBW member and organizer, and participated in the collective movement from the LRBW to the Communist League (CL), the Communist Labor Party (CLP), and the League of Revolutionaries for a New America (LRNA). He is one of the organizers and coordinators of the League Education and Media oral history project, the basis for this book.

Walda is a scholar-activist and movement organizer. She is a native of New Orleans and grew up in the Jim Crow South. She received her PhD in sociology from

Wayne State University in Detroit, the key link in how she joined the collective journey in the late 1970s as a member of the CLP and later the LRNA. She helped coordinate the LRBW oral history project.

As narrators of the LRBW journey, we are engaged as both actors and observers, and we write in the collective first person—"we," "us," and "ours." We conducted a long and informative interview with Jerome and quote his interview material using the same format as other interviews, though, as narrator, Jerome also brings a big picture frame from theory and from personal and political practice.

Appreciating the Team Who Made the League Project Possible

Marian Kramer, a close friend and comrade across the whole journey, helped organize and coordinate the project on the ground in Detroit. John Williams and Darryl "Waistline" Mitchell joined Marian in that work. Darryl joined the ancestors on April 17, 2024.

We could not have completed this project without the labor, love, and incredible support of several essential people whom we developed relationships with over the years. Can "John" Tuzcu brought his skills as a videographer and filmmaker. Virginia Leavell served as our tech guru and shared coordination and interviewing. Spence Mann and Anna Lee-Popham joined the videography team. Alex Rodriguez helped gather data on auto production, auto workers, and United Auto Workers (UAW) membership and prepare the figures. Annie Armiger joined the team to edit and upload interviews and photographs.

Daymon Hartley, photographer and comrade, took photographs during the interviews and provided historical images. He and David Goldberg, professor at Wayne State University, secured space at Wayne for taping many of the interviews. Charles Ferrell reserved space at the Charles H. Wright Museum of African American History for taping interviews later in the process. Crystal Bernard, who is Gen and Marian's niece, wrote the dedication for this book.

Why the League Story in Our Own Words?

We said for decades that we have to tell our story—for the historical record and to document the truth about our participation in the revolutionary process and the working-class struggle.

In the early 2000s we began meeting in the living room of Marian and General "Gen" Baker in Highland Park, Michigan—preparing to conduct this oral history project. A few LRBW comrades had already joined the ancestors, and we were not

Volunteer crew and videographers—Virginia Leavell, Can Tuzcu, Spence Mann, and Anna Lee-Popham—for the League Education and Media Project. Courtesy General Baker Institute.

getting any younger. When Gen joined the ancestors on May 18, 2014, we knew time was running out. It took us a year to plan and organize the videography team of amazing young movement activists—Can, Virginia, Spence, and Anna—and to reach out to LRBW folks in Detroit and nearby. In December 2015 we met with Marian, John, and Darryl at Marian's house, taped the promo video, and planned the project. We started taping in 2016 and completed most of the taping in 2017. We interviewed forty people in Detroit and elsewhere, including several small groups. We opened with two days of large-group conversations at Wayne State University. (See the appendix for more information on our methodology.)

Virginia established the website for the League of Revolutionary Black Workers Education and Media Project (https://www.revolutionaryblackworkers.org/) and posted videos on Vimeo. Annie picked up the task of uploading the bulk of the interviews. We were also part of establishing the General Baker Institute (GBI), which owns all the media from the project (GBI 2017).

The LRBW journey, the League Education and Media Project, and the GBI all tell the story of the LRBW as family—kinfolk and kids, coworkers, neighbors, close friends, and movement comrades.

Understanding and Acting in the World

This book represents our attempt at applied Marxism. It offers a theoretical and political lens on our lives and analysis—of understanding the world as it is and as it is becoming, of guiding strategic political practice—for over fifty years.

Theory is a tool and a weapon in understanding class struggle. It analyzes the relations between class and race and gender and coming to class consciousness. Many LRBW members, and virtually all of the point-of-production workers, did not enter the process as Marxists. We developed as Marxists through study and struggle.

Motown and the Making of
Working-Class Revolutionaries

Part One

Black Workers and Auto—the Beginning

CHAPTER 1

The League Story in Our Own Words

> We have all read and heard the different analyses by different people in their books where they summarized the history of the League of Revolutionary Black Workers. This time we wanna set a lot of this stuff straight.
>
> —Marian Kramer, LRBW *Extended Promo* (2016)

> How do you become a revolutionary in the 1960s and go through numerous transitions but remain a revolutionary today? That story being told by the people who lived those decades can be very significant for some of the critical questions I hear.
>
> —Jerome Scott, LRBW *Extended Promo* (2016)

Over the centuries, revolutionaries and scholars have analyzed the dialectics of class exploitation and racial and gender oppression within capitalist production relations and social reproduction. We enter this intellectual and political conversation around class, race, and revolution in the United States through the voices of the League of Revolutionary Black Workers, sharing our experiences, our consciousness, our vision, and our strategy (GBI 2017). This conversation takes on renewed urgency in this historic moment. The world is in transition from an industrial base of production to a digital, robotic, artificial intelligence (AI) base that disrupts all society and forces the reorganization of major institutions. This transformation embodies deepening capitalist crises, the polarization of wealth and poverty, intensifying white supremacy, genocide, patriarchy, and xenophobia, and the ruling-class struggle to consolidate fascism. The working class is rising up from below in the interests of humanity and the earth (Caffentzis 2013; Dyer-Withered 2015; W. Robinson 2014, 2022).

The proletarian (working-class) intellectuals of the LRBW brought class analysis to the Black liberation struggle at the point of production—in the Detroit plants for automobiles and related industries and their communities from 1968 to 1971. Within the working class, Black workers represent a concentrated expression of capitalist exploitation, oppression, and alienation. The consolidation of white supremacy within capitalism created the conditions for the genocide of Indigenous peoples and the superexploitation and racial oppression of Black labor and that of other peoples of color across the structures and institutions of society. Beginning from the era of forced chattel slavery and continuing through periods of sharecropping and convict labor, factory production, service-sector work, prison labor, increasing redundancy in the labor force, and state violence, Black workers have been central to capitalist profit and control (Du Bois [1935] 1962; Heagerty and Peery 2000; Roediger and Esch 2014).

White supremacy, rooted in material conditions, created deep divisions among workers based on color and nationality that persist, despite changing form. This ruling-class strategy complicates the motion toward working-class unity and class struggle—even as emerging objective conditions are calling into question this strategy of "divide and conquer."

The story of the LRBW is a largely hidden chapter of the labor movement and revolutionary motion across the globe of the late 1960s. It offers many lessons for today's working-class forces and radical youth-, student-, and scholar-activists, organizers, and emerging revolutionaries. The LRBW embodied the coming together of an ideological compass and a practical compass within one organization. We brought together workers on the shop floor, community organizers, and high school students. The story of the LRBW is also about the deep humanity of Black workers, who, in struggle and study, became self-conscious and class-conscious revolutionaries in Detroit and on the world stage. Our worldview and class consciousness continue to inform our strategy and tactics on the ground for power in America today.

LRBW comrades grasped practically and theoretically the power of the working class. We experienced firsthand the power and the limitations of wildcat strikes—organized by workers but unsanctioned by the union or company—and of disrupting both the union and the capitalist economy at the point of production. Tactically wildcats are more disruptive because they come with no advanced warning or company preparation. We grasped this power concretely because we were in a position to control the struggle at the point of production. We also understood the limitations of wildcats because we would have no "union protection" or a strike fund. We simultaneously understood the fight against the corporations and the unions in the factories within the larger reality of class struggle.

At the same time, LRBW comrades in the plants experienced the early stages of the introduction of automation, the potential for the displacement of workers by robots, and the related implication of shifts in the center of gravity of the working-class struggle.

We explore Marxism as a theoretical and political worldview for analyzing the current crises of global capitalism—economic, ecological, social, and political—and today's rising movement. We ground this analysis in our daily experience and study during the LRBW days and in the years since.

Workers who were at the point of production in the 1960s are today increasingly at the point of dispossession, state violence and fascism, and ecological crisis. Many former LRBW members remain engaged in social struggle. Our lives and political practice provide a focus on workers in relation to shifts in capitalist production, the state, and the revolutionary process (Amin 2011; M. Ford 2015; N. Peery 2001).

LRBW members became working-class intellectuals who deeply analyzed our conditions and the path to power. We were not "lefties" or "seeds" who were sent into the factories to organize, nor did we view theory and study abstractly—outside our concrete struggles and political strategies and tactics.

Part of the journey that we took intellectually and politically was coming to Marxism as an ideology, worldview, and practice. Many in the leadership identified as Marxists. But the base of the LRBW, the rank-and-file workers, largely had not yet been introduced to Marxism. We embraced the philosophy because it explained our experience, as a living theory for understanding class struggle.

Marxism is fundamental to our remaining revolutionaries for more than fifty years of ebbs and flows of social struggle. It is the context for many LRBW members being part of revolutionary organizations—beginning with the League of Revolutionary Black Workers, then the Communist League (CL), the Communist Labor Party (CLP), and finally, today, the League of Revolutionaries for a New America (LRNA). It informs our political work in the present in mass movement organizations dealing with struggles related to the South, political education, welfare and poor people's survival, housing and water, trade unions, health care, the environment, education, and various other ongoing worker and retiree struggles. Marxism provides the framework for our analysis of the LRBW story.

We have witnessed different stages of the revolutionary process that are ongoing. The economic revolution at the base of society is rooted in the technological revolution. Automation, robotics, and AI are labor replacing, not labor enhancing, as were machines in the industrial era. These qualitatively new technologies increasingly disrupt the fundamental social relations of capital and labor—capital accumulation based on the exploitation of labor power—because only human labor creates new value. This reality reveals the dynamics of the labor theory of value at the nexus of commodity production and circulation, capital accumulation, the sale of labor power as a commodity, and the falling rate of profit (Katz-Fishman and Scott 2012, 2019). Global capitalism, markets, and wage labor are being irreversibly disrupted. Current conditions are pushing forward the revolutionary transformation of society. Low-wage and unemployed workers require distribution of the abundance of the basic necessities of life that digital technology makes possible based on need, not on the ability to pay (J. Davis, Hirschl, and Stack 1997; N. Peery 2001; W. Robinson 2020, 2022).

We share lessons for a new generation of workers and revolutionaries reflecting decades of political practice and theoretical study of former LRBW members. We have learned it is easy to be radical in revolutionary times, but it takes theory to be revolutionary in ebb times. An essential question is how much power the working class will have when robots and AI are dominant in the production process. It is imperative that today's movement develop a vision and strategy, including theoretical education, to inform the political struggle.

League Oral History Project—Telling Our Story

> The ideas of the ruling class are in every epoch the ruling ideas.
> —Karl Marx and Friedrich Engels,
> *The German Ideology* ([1845] 1968)

Academic intellectuals and corporate media are busy 24/7 spewing forth myths, lies, and distortions. They do not promote the history of working-class realities and struggle and their relevance for the current moment. At the same time, working-class activists, especially youth, yearn to grasp the lessons contained in this largely hidden chapter of the revolutionary struggle of the late sixties and early seventies. Key among these lessons is understanding the importance of political education and working-class intellectuals within the revolutionary process. Recently activists in labor and housing struggles reached out to us to discuss lessons to be gleaned from *Finally Got the News* (1970), the only video of the LRBW from the early days.

Little historical material on the LRBW exists. Some academics who wrote about the LRBW in the seventies, including Dan Georgakas and Marvin Surkin, who wrote *Detroit: I Do Mind Dying* in 1975, were outsiders to the LRBW journey. At the time the LRBW's point-of-production workers refused to talk to the authors, not trusting academics or the media to accurately tell our story. James Geschwender, also an outsider and academic, wrote *Class, Race, and Worker In-*

surgency: The League of Revolutionary Black Workers in 1977. He interviewed two of the Executive Board members, but no point-of-production workers. Reading these books confirmed that we needed to write our own history.

Ours is a different voice, a different understanding, a different strategic worldview. Central to the LRBW story are our becoming proletarian intellectuals, our southern roots, and our over fifty-year journey as social and political family, industrial workers, and comrades. We had to tell our own story to capture the richness, the reality, and the many dimensions of our political path and longevity.

DETROIT: A MOVEMENT CITY

Place matters in the history of a movement. It is no accident that Detroit, known and celebrated as Motown, was home to the LRBW's evolution. The city was the site of huge migrations of workers from the U.S. South, from Appalachia, from Mexico, and from several Arab countries in the early twentieth century. It became an epicenter of industrial production and, at the same time, worker exploitation, racial oppression, and labor struggles.

The city was the founding home to radical organizations. Detroiter Elijah Poole became Elijah Muhammad, founding and leading the Nation of Islam from the 1930s until his death in 1975. The Shrine of the Black Madonna and the Republic of New Afrika (originally Republic of New Africa) both arose in Detroit in the turbulent 1960s. They later moved to the South—the Shrine of the Black Madonna headquarters to Atlanta and the Republic of New Afrika to Jackson, Mississippi. These organizations represented the nationalist trend and its different branches. The LRBW was formed as a worker organization out of the struggles in the Detroit auto industry.

In the early 1960s, before the Shrine of the Black Madonna, the Republic of New Afrika, and the LRBW were founded, their future leadership came together to form an all-Black chapter of the National Rifle Association (NRA). We shared history and cooperative relationships. The LRBW is rooted in this reality of Black organizations and worker organizing in Detroit. This collective history shaped our political paths and the militancy of our resistance and struggle.

WHY WORKING-CLASS ORGANIZATIONS ARE NOT LIFTED UP

The LRBW, as a working-class organization, was effective and forceful in the plants, in the community, and in the schools. This speaks to why the corporate media and scholars do not want to popularize it. Jerome elaborated,

> When we think about why certain organizations are promoted while others are not, even in terms of their history, the media is motivated by what these organizations could mean for today.

Meaning, "If we promote the Panthers and say that's the way to organize, what if people organized another Panther Party?" They're doing that today. Or, "What if we promote the Student Nonviolent Coordinating Committee (SNCC) and people are organizing a new SNCC?" It's not a coincidence that the media promote organizations that wouldn't have that much of an impact if they were re-created. The moment of the Panthers and the civil rights movement has passed. As long as they promote that, that's cool because it's not going to have any real agency in this moment of history.

In contrast, consider an organization like the League and our history. The League started out as an organization that concentrated on Black workers. We reached a point where we understood that the multiracial working class was the main thrust of the revolutionary process. We were able to successfully make that transition.

The League would be relevant today. Media and ruling-class forces don't want that kind of organization pushed or duplicated or glorified. That's the reason the League is not lifted up and remains relatively unknown today among young revolutionaries, and even movement activists, of all generations.

This is how bourgeois media and propaganda operate 24/7. There's always spin about "who's the leader and who's not," and "what organization is good and what's not." It's part of their creation of a false "reality." In every upsurge of the movement, the ruling class figures out a way to tell the movement what organization is best and who your leader is. They're doing it with the developing movements today. (Scott 2017)

WHY WE HAVE TO TELL OUR STORY—FOR HISTORY AND THIS MOVEMENT MOMENT

The LRBW oral history project has been a labor of love to document and share our story in our own words—our political journey as revolutionaries from the point of production to today's multiracial working class movement. Marian Kramer explained,

> This project is key to the history of the struggle out here. For people to understand, they have to know the conditions that gave rise to the League of Revolutionary Black Workers, and the connection of that to today's struggle. (Kramer in Kramer, Scott, and Williams 2016)

Jerome lifted up the significance of the LRBW project:

> We've heard the story of the League of Revolutionary Black Workers from the different perspectives of people who told that story. But you haven't heard it from

The League Story in Our Own Words

us. This project is very significant because we're gonna be looking at the League not only from the standpoint of what we did historically, but what lessons we are able to draw from that and apply those lessons to the whole political struggle we continue to be involved in today. (Scott in Kramer, Scott, and Williams 2016)

John Williams, a member of the LRBW Executive Board, spoke to the lessons of the project for today:

I'd like to share the educational metamorphosis I went through fifty-odd years ago. Things that went on in the 1960s and errors we made that caused us to go astray. Things have changed. We wanna share that because a lot of the tactics and strategies that were used back then are not relevant today. That does not mean you can't learn from them. (Williams in Kramer, Scott, and Williams 2016)

Darryl, an LRBW member who was part of the student movement and became a production worker, reflected on the importance of former LRBW members sharing our history and stories:

This project has been a long time coming and it's a hell of a historic event. Whatever your perspective, we were birthed in struggle, we bonded, and we're trying to provide education for those who are coming after us. (D. Mitchell in *Wayne State* 2017)

Since we began, everyone is aware of historical threads being tied together in front of us. That's where the League came in. That's where Nelson Peery came in. That's the role of revolutionary Black workers, the role of communist leaders and the Communist Labor Party. (D. Mitchell 2017)

Marian noted the longevity of LRBW comrades in revolutionary development today.

You get an opportunity to see some of the people who played a real role in this development. And, at the same time, to understand why we organized the League at that time. Why some of us have stuck and stayed all this time, to make sure that we're on the right path to being a part of the revolutionary development taking place today. (Kramer in Kramer, Scott, and Williams 2016)

Jerome emphasized the significance of the project and LRBW lessons for creating our future.

I've dreamed of this project for a long time. A lot of people have written the history of our struggle, of the struggles in Detroit, the struggles of the League. But those of us who lived it have not written it. We've been trying to figure out how to tell our story and get it out.

> Most of us started with the League. Some of us made many transitions, some made a few, and some made it all the way through this whole process. We talk about the history, but we talk about what that history meant to us and what we're doing today. (Scott in *Wayne State* 2017)
>
> This project is part of making sure that the lessons we can learn from history will be taught to the people who are living that future history now. (Scott in Kramer, Scott, and Williams 2016)

The truth of our story has to be told by the people who lived it. We're not just celebrating our history but learning from our collective history to help guide our collective future. Political education was and is essential for our longevity. The more we study and understand the environment we're living in, the more we are prepared to deal with the ebbs and flows of the movement.

Black workers have been central to class struggle over the centuries—from abolition to labor, Black liberation, civil rights, voting rights, welfare, environmental racism, and fighting state violence and fascism. Former LRBW members, through new organizations, form a conscious political force within today's multiracial, multinational, and multigendered class struggle for our future. We offer the League of Revolutionary Black Workers' story as critical lessons for today's revolutionary movement.

CHAPTER 2

Our Southern Roots and Radicalization

The context of LRBW comrades and LRBW struggle is personal and political—family, community, school, and point of production. It connects the historic southern and northern struggles against white supremacy and exploitation.

We begin with a narrative of this story as can be told only by Gen, who embodied the southern roots of many Black workers in Detroit and in the LRBW. He experienced the intense superexploitation and oppression of the corporation as well as the union, in part because of his political clarity and leadership. He never lost sight of the strategic direction and future of the working-class struggle.

Gen began his personal and political story this way:

> I was born here in Detroit on September 6, 1941, at Saint Aubin Hospital. Doctor Ossian Sweet delivered me and slapped me on my butt. He gave me my birthright and passed on a legacy of struggle I tried to carry out the rest of my life.
>
> My parents were sharecroppers from Georgia and came following Ford's cry for five dollars a day in auto plants in 1941. I spent forty years working in these auto shops—hired in 1963 and retired in 2003. It took me those forty years to get thirty years' seniority because I got fired so many God damned times, and transferred, switched, and changed my name.
>
> The experience we share we got through struggle. If we're gonna win, we gotta have people to help carry it through. (G. Baker 2016)

Like Gen, many comrades in the LRBW had strong southern ties and were first- or second-generation Detroiters. They escaped the violent white supremacy of the South and brought the passion and fire of southern struggle into the auto plants and communities of Detroit, only to fight the white supremacy of the North.

The southern roots of the LRBW are part of the migration journey of Black labor from the plantations of the Jim Crow South to the factories and cities of the industrial North. LRBW comrades carried the history, consciousness, and militancy of the Black liberation struggle with them.

Jerome framed the southern roots of LRBW leadership and the particular quality of the working-class struggle in Detroit this way:

> We investigated where people in the League were from, and the leadership, in particular. Gen's family was from Georgia, he was a first-generation northerner. Chuck Wooten's family was from Tennessee, and he was first generation too. Ken Cockrel's family was from Arkansas, I think. John Williams's family was from Louisiana, Mike Hamlin's family was from Mississippi, and John Watson's family was from Arkansas. Marian Kramer and her brother Allen Ray Bernard were from Louisiana. My family was originally from Georgia. It became clear that the core of the League was southerners who were first-generation Detroiters.
>
> There was a flood of southerners during the two great migrations. Detroit was a magnet for the South because of the auto industry. Other magnets in Michigan were Flint, Saginaw, and all major cities. In Ohio, folks ended up in Cincinnati, Cleveland, and Akron around industry there.
>
> This is a sidebar. In the 1973 wildcat strike when I got fired, seven or eight white guys got fired too. Four of them were from Appalachia. They talked about Appalachia, and we talked about the South. They said, "Shit man, it's the same. The police harassment was the same. The poor-ass schools were the same." Everything they talked about that was down and dirty and nasty in Appalachia was the same stuff that was down and dirty in the South. This was another interesting fact that we found out.
>
> We began to think, "What does it mean that the core of the League is from the South? The civil rights movement was concentrated in the South? A number of people in the League leadership had families in the South who were involved in the civil rights movement?" We began to look at the resistance that had been born and drilled into people in the South and now was expressed in these northern cities and, in this case, Detroit.
>
> That was one of the reasons Gen constantly said, "You can't just duplicate Detroit." Some folks assumed that if we can do it in Detroit, we can do it in any city. But every other city didn't have the concentration of plants in the inner city like Detroit, the concentration of southern workers who had migrated or were first-generation northerners like Detroit. After the League split, some forces went off to try to build the Black Workers Congress (BWC) in other cities and we stayed in Detroit and concentrated on that. The BWC didn't last a year. I don't know if it took hold in any city. (Scott 2017)

We share the southern stories of some of the central figures who, along with Gen, forged the LRBW. John Williams and Mike, both among founding members of the LRBW and the Executive Board, described their journeys. Marian, whose work was based in the community, spoke to the enduring influence of her southern family history. She reflected on having to move north to marry Dave Kramer, her first husband. Allen Ray shared his take on growing up in Louisiana. Edna Watson, a working-class intellectual and wife of John Watson, another founding Executive Board member, remembered her sharecropping family in Arkansas. Darryl, who went from the Black Student United Front (BSUF) into the auto plants at age sixteen, recalled his southern family ties to the labor movement and the effect of the bloody civil rights struggles during his growing up years. Cassandra "Cass" Bell Ford, who was active in the BSUF and later worked in the Cadillac plant, talked about her mother who came from Louisiana. Marsha Music, known as Lynn Battle in the LRBW days, also came into the LRBW through the BSUF and shared the southern influence in her life.

John was brief.

> My political development began with moving from Louisiana to Detroit, going to school, and wanting a world that was just and was based in religion. (John Williams 2017)

Mike described details of his turbulent childhood and youth growing up in Mississippi.

> I was born in 1935 on a plantation near Canton. We lived in a one-room house with an outhouse and a wood stove. My mother was a biracial woman, the daughter of the plantation owner's son, and became an orphan when she was eleven. When I was five, I would sit on the side of the cotton field babysitting my little sister, and my mother was picking cotton.
>
> The lynch mob would come by our house and water their horses and dogs before they'd go down to the swamps chasing brothers. One time they caught him and did the usual ritual on him, cutting off his genitals, stuff them in his mouth, punch his eyes out. The other time they didn't catch him. It seemed like Black folks had a telegraph. I have no idea how they got that word from one to another.
>
> We came to Detroit in August 1947. We rode the train in, got off a segregated car in Cincinnati and changed to an integrated car to Detroit. I started school in September. My first day everybody laughed at me, including the teacher, because of my southern accent. It was a humiliating experience and made me a really driven student.
>
> I worked during the summer. The second year after graduation I worked eighty-nine days at Ford and they laid me off on the ninetieth day. No jobs then, this was the Eisenhower recession. (Hamlin 2017)

Marian explained her move from the South and the influence of her Louisiana family.

> I came from the South in 1964. I couldn't get married in the South, and had to marry Dave Kramer up here because of anti-miscegenation laws in the South. Dave was white and I was Black. We were in the civil rights movement and all that. (Kramer in *Wayne State* 2017)

> The women in my family and the men, too, influenced and encouraged me. My uncle told me on his dying bed, "Don't give up. We need you to stay out there. People are afraid you're gonna get hurt. But you can get hurt walking down the street." My other uncle said "stay." When I started getting my grandfather the *People's Tribune*, our political movement paper, he said "Keep sending those papers. They're better than any other papers you've sent." (Kramer 2017)

Allen Ray moved to Detroit during the LRBW days and worked at the Goodyear rubber plant. He described the impact of his early years in the South.

> For Black workers before the Civil War it was about slavery. You were in bondage. I'm originally from New Orleans, Louisiana, where the slave blocks were. Four generations back my family were slaves. You had no voice, no nothing. As we came up—I'm a baby boomer—a lot was different. People don't remember what an outhouse was. We didn't have phones, maybe one in a block. When phones came along, you had a party line. Television was out of the question.
>
> Workers prior to and post–Civil War had no rights, period. Even after that, workers had no rights. When I came up in the forties, fifties, and sixties we still had no rights. No voice. Especially Blacks. Lower paying jobs. Last hired, first fired. This was objective reality for the lower skilled workers. (Bernard 2017)

Edna spoke to the importance of her earliest years in Arkansas and of southern Black women making bullets for the war effort.

> I was born January 5, 1944, in Pulaski County, Arkansas. The war was raging. We were living as sharecroppers. We moved north during the big migration of people from the South. Many white southerners went west. More Blacks came to Chicago, Detroit, and the Midwest than anywhere. We came to Detroit in 1948. Detroit was pretty grim and gruesome for Black people, it was Jim Crow.
>
> I went back to Arkansas in the summer of 1955. Emmett Till had been killed in 1954, and I was scared to be down South. We had to get off the street when people walked by. I got interested in labor because my mother had to work and other people took care of me. She said that Hitler would have won without us Black women down in Arkansas making bullets. Women left the cotton fields

and worked in the ammunition plants making bullets. That was my first realization that she had been a laborer outside the house. (E. Watson 2017)

Cass's mother was from Louisiana and had concerns about her political activism:

> I was always at the League office. My mother called and came down there asking "what are y'all doing with my daughter?" Gen explained there wasn't anything going on, which was very true. That helped, but she didn't want me doing political things. Her thing was go to school, get an education, and leave that other stuff alone. She came from the South and didn't even talk about the things she went through. She told me you gotta forget that. I said "I can't. I'm not gonna let this happen and not do anything." (C. Ford 2017)

Marsha reflected on the impact of her southern roots—the lasting impression on her generation of the lynching of Emmett Till and the open casket at his funeral, and the efforts of her parents' generation to shield her generation from the brutal realities of the Jim Crow South.

> My father came from the South and opened a record store on Hastings Street in 1945. Blacks were still coming up from the South and there was quite a southern base of the Detroit African American community.
>
> I was born in 1954. The long-lasting memories of the funeral and Emmett Till's body being displayed for mourners was deep in our consciousness. It was terrifying to look at an old *Jet* magazine and see the mutilated body of this child who had been lynched and grotesquely beaten. We were children in this atmosphere of the tumult coming out of the South, watching it on television and being very aware because our parents had grown up in the South. Many of them did not discuss segregation in the South. They didn't want us—the children they were now raising in the North—to know what it was like to pick cotton and the humiliations and abuses they had suffered. They wanted us to have a new free life.
>
> But we began to absorb this reality from our environment. We were trapped—young African Americans kids, ten, eleven, twelve, thirteen years old. We were realizing that all the things the civil rights movement was fighting about in the South had not been totally eradicated here in the North. We did not have permission to actively confront these things. It was unspoken—it is really bad in the South and we're doing the best we can up here. We didn't have the ability to articulate our feelings of angst about the fact that we were not being treated the same as other people. (Music 2017)

Darryl shared personal history and what being a worker in the North, as compared to the South, meant.

> Back in those days the climate in the country was part of the civil rights movement—Emmett Till, Selma, bussing in Montgomery. These things were in our head as we took our place in the workforce.
>
> Growing up, my family revered Walter Reuther and the union movement. Being sharecroppers in Georgia, when they went to tally at the end of the season, their tally was always different than the man's tally. When they came up here and got jobs, they made more money and they got to keep it. It wasn't like the South and sharecropping and the boss. (D. Mitchell in Chandler et al. 2017)

Edna captured the mood of Black workers in Detroit.

> The people who came here from Europe, the people who came here from the South created Detroit into a kind of mecca for the left. We had a Black intelligentsia, a white intelligentsia, a media intelligentsia. But we didn't have any power or control over jobs or money. (E. Watson 2017)

The personal and political histories of Black workers at the point of production and during the 1960s movement moment set the stage for the Dodge Revolutionary Union Movement (DRUM) and the emergence of the LRBW. Many LRBW members had working-class southern roots nurtured in struggles against the slave system, white supremacy, and Jim Crow terror.

The deep influence of southerners in the LRBW is expressed in the leadership. Six of the seven Executive Board members—General Baker, John Williams, Mike Hamlin, Chuck Wooten, John Watson, and Ken Cockrel—were from the South. They brought militancy and clarity to their struggles in the industrial North. They also brought an understanding of the country's horrors—Indigenous genocide, chattel slavery, and Jim Crow state terror and violence. This southern influence helped create Detroit as the movement city it became. It also informs our understanding of the role of the South in political struggles today.

CHAPTER 3

Workers, Capitalists, and the United Auto Workers in the Auto Industry, Twentieth and Early Twenty-First Centuries

To fully grasp the conditions that gave rise to the LRBW, we have to understand the interrelations of the history of the working class—especially the Black section of the class, the history of the industrial capitalists in Detroit, and the history of the United Auto Workers (UAW). A short sketch of the rise and decline of the U.S. auto industry contextualizes that history, highlighting the shifting economic and technological conditions confronting workers generally and Black workers particularly. Technological change—from the introduction of the assembly line in 1913 to the introduction of robots and automation in the sixties and seventies—is the underlying force driving shifts in production, distribution, and communication. This technological change also drives shifts in the relations between capitalists and workers over the twentieth and twenty-first centuries.

A Brief History of U.S. Auto Employment and Productivity

Auto production in the United States began at the turn of the twentieth century. Units produced rose from fewer than 3,200 cars in 1901 to 130,000 by 1910. With Henry Ford's introduction of the assembly line in 1913 and 1914, auto production took off, rising to 1.3 million cars in 1916 and to 3.1 million cars by 1925 (Consumer Guide 2004). The UAW was formed in 1935, and the following year 27,000 UAW members produced 3.3 million cars (UAW Secretary-Treasurer's Office 2016; Consumer Guide 2004). By 1950, 1 million auto workers made 6.3 million cars, with U.S. production representing 75 percent of world auto production (UAW Secretary-Treasurer's Office 2016; Office of Energy Efficiency & Renewable Energy 2009; Consumer Guide 2001a).

The assembly line and an expanding market drove U.S. auto production,

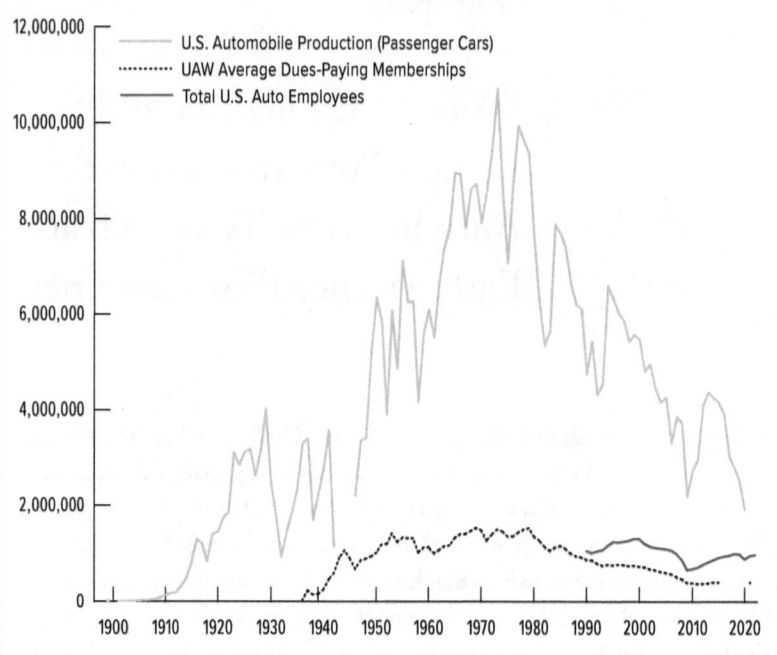

FIGURE 1
U.S. Auto Production, U.S. Auto Workers, and UAW Membership, 1899–2022
Sources: Various

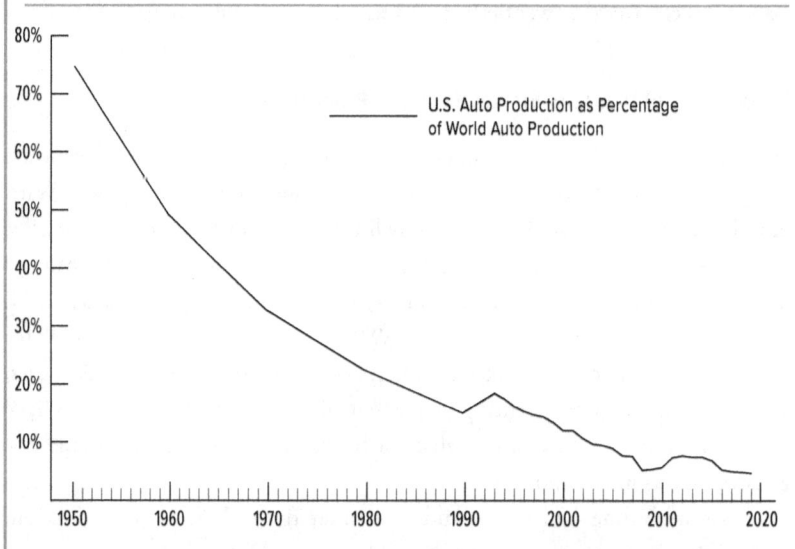

FIGURE 2
U.S. Auto Production as a Percentage of World Auto Production, 1950–2019
Sources: Various

UAW membership, and labor productivity in the first half of the twentieth century. This massive expansion of the U.S. auto industry brought to Detroit workers from throughout the United States and the world, including many Black workers from the South and Arab workers from the Middle East. In 1968, the year of DRUM, and 1969, when the LRBW was formed, 1.5 million auto workers produced 8.7 million cars each year. Only four years later, in 1973, the same number of auto workers—1.5 million—produced 10.7 million cars, an increase of 2 million (UAW Secretary-Treasurer's Office 2016; Office of Energy Efficiency & Renewable Energy 2009).

Henry Ford's assembly line and other labor-enhancing technologies and techniques increased labor productivity and employment and defined mass production in the auto industry for much of the twentieth century. The 1970s marked a break in those processes. The use of automation and robotics in auto production drove a further increase in labor productivity, but with fewer workers producing more cars. As labor-replacing technology eliminated workers from production, that same technology helped push forward a new and different round of globalization in production—shrinking overall U.S. auto production and the U.S. share of the global auto market and shifting some U.S. auto production to the nonunion U.S. South with a declining UAW membership (Greenhouse 2019).

These new processes of automation, robotization, and global production accelerated throughout the late twentieth and into the twenty-first century (Greenhouse 2019). In 1980, 1.4 million auto workers—including UAW members—produced 7.6 million cars in the United States, representing 23 percent of global production. By 1990, annual auto production had declined to 4.7 million cars produced by 1.1 million auto workers—including UAW members. This represented 15 percent of world production. In 2000, 1.3 million auto workers, including UAW members, produced 5.5 million cars, representing 4.6 percent of world production (UAW Secretary-Treasurer's Office 2016; Office of Energy Efficiency & Renewable Energy 2009; U.S. Department of Transportation, Bureau of Transportation Statistics 2018).

Following the Great Recession, in 2010, 678,000 auto workers—including UAW members—produced 2.7 million cars, representing 5.7 percent of world production. By 2022 (during the COVID-19 pandemic), 974,600 auto workers, including UAW members, produced 1.8 million cars, representing 2.7 percent of world production (UAW Secretary-Treasurer's Office 2016; Office of Energy Efficiency & Renewable Energy 2009; U.S. Department of Transportation, Bureau of Transportation Statistics 2020; Statista 2023; Geography of Transport Systems 2023).

The arc was complete—from the height of U.S. auto production through the decline that persists today. Detroit fell from the epicenter of capitalist prosperity to the epicenter of capitalist crisis and massive disruption and destruction of working-class life.

Black Workers, the Auto Industry, and Class Struggle in Detroit

Central to the LRBW's political journey was General Baker, a practical and theoretical leader of the class struggle in Detroit. He brought a working-class worldview to the analysis of Detroit's rise as epicenter of the auto industry and capitalist profit in the mid-twentieth century and to its economic decline and the ensuing social destruction and dispossession of Detroit's multiracial and multigendered working class in the late twentieth and twenty-first centuries.

HENRY FORD AND THE CONTROL OF LABOR IN AUTO—THE RISE OF MASS PRODUCTION

Gen offered the following class analysis of the history of the auto industry, state violence, labor organizing, and Black labor in Detroit. He lifted up Henry Ford's role in shaping the auto industry and labor force in Detroit in the early 1900s.

> Detroit is an auto town. At one point, Chrysler Corporation (now owned by Stellantis Corporation) had twenty-nine plants in the greater Detroit area, General Motors (GM) had another fifteen, Ford had another ten, and they had part suppliers. In 1966, Chrysler Corporation had 66,000 employees. It was the largest employer in Detroit. In 2010 Chrysler Corporation had about 20,000 employees nationwide. You can see how much it's failed.
>
> The auto industry came in the early 1900s and is just over a hundred years old. Things changed rapidly. The horseless carriage paved the way with Henry Ford and his moving assembly line. Detroit grew based on the demand for labor. Ford decided to pay five dollars a day—which wasn't really true. That story is out there, but you had to fit into a special category to get the five dollars. But just a cry for five dollars a day when people made six dollars a week drew people from foreign lands, from Appalachia, from the Deep South, from all over. People poured into Detroit looking for work. It was a booming town. (G. Baker 2016)

THE PUSH TO ORGANIZE LABOR IN AUTO— MASSACRE AT FORD MOTOR COMPANY

In the 1920s and 1930s a confluence of forces propelled union organizing within the expanding U.S. auto industry. Labor in the early twentieth century experienced unfettered capitalism and the extreme exploitation and power of capital over labor as well as worldwide depression. Workers confronted capital with growing working-class consciousness and labor organizing in the United States and globally in the wake of the 1917 Russian Revolution. The Roosevelt administration's response to the Great Depression and preparations for fighting fascism in Europe included major New Deal legislation. The National Labor Relations Act went into effect in 1935. That same year the Congress of Industrial Organizations was founded to organize workers in industrial organizations, as opposed to craft-based organizing, and the UAW was formed in Detroit. By the 1940s, World War II had engulfed the world and the Detroit auto industry shifted to war production (Greenhouse 2019; Roediger and Esch 2014).

In Detroit in 1932, the government's unbridled use of state violence against the Depression-era march organized by the Unemployed Councils was a major provocation. The murder of auto workers at the Ford River Rouge plant propelled the labor movement and union organizing forward.

Gen described the march, the massacre, and the funeral for the workers murdered by the police.

> As the workers marched up Miller Road, the Dearborn Fire Department hit them with fire hoses and watered them down. It was March 11, 1932, so it was really cold. They marched further and the Dearborn Police sent horses after them and started stomping them. By the time the marchers got to the gate at Ford, the police opened up with machine gun fire. Five workers were shot and killed, and another twenty-five or so were wounded. The hunger march stopped.
>
> The largest mass funeral ever held in Detroit grew out of this. Sixty-five thousand people participated in the funeral procession for four of the workers. Five were killed. But one, who was Black, died later. The Black worker was cremated and his ashes were spread over the Rouge plant. They couldn't bury him in the same cemetery with the white guys who were killed because cemeteries were segregated.
>
> Nobody was brought to trial or charged with anything. Ford was never held accountable for this murder in the streets. The seeds for organized labor to organize the shops in the city came out of the anger and mass action that grew out of the massacre at Ford Motor Company. (G. Baker 2016)

WAR PRODUCTION AND THE RISE OF DETROIT—
A MASSIVE SEA OF HUMANITY

War production catapulted Detroit to the center of U.S. capitalist production. World War II also transformed U.S. industry in relation to the composition of the labor force, bringing Black and women workers into jobs at the point of production, where they previously had not been employed in significant numbers (Roediger and Esch 2014).

Gen discussed war production and the growth of Detroit as central to labor, including Black and women workers, and capital.

> In 1941 things changed rapidly. World War II broke out. Ford was organized in April 1941. Pearl Harbor Day was December 1941. There wasn't a single new car built between 1941 and 1945. The entire auto industry was transformed into war production. The government covered the costs of production plus 10 percent. So, the companies didn't care how many people they hired.
>
> Detroit became a massive sea of humanity. People came from everywhere. Streetcars ran all night and all day. The plants ran 24/7, massive amounts of production. The Ford plant built in Willow Run hired 42,000 people. That's why we saw Rosie the Riveter out there riveting airplanes together. We ran PT boats at the plant that I worked in later. Armaments and tanks were made all over the city.
>
> The whole character of production changed. That's an important part of the history of the early development of the auto industry and the organization of labor in this country. (G. Baker 2016)

WHITE SUPREMACY DURING WAR PRODUCTION

White supremacy is part of the organization of U.S. capitalism and is located in every structure, institution, and workplace—North and South. It is not surprising, then, that racism continued throughout industry during the years of war production.

Gen described the white supremacy in the plants and the union during the war.

> We had all kind of conflicts in the midst of the war. An old guy I ran with, Dave Moore, told me when they were building all these trucks, the Teamsters Union would not allow Blacks to drive the trucks. Army trucks were parked all over Livernois Avenue and other streets. White workers were killing themselves trying to drive the trucks to the army bases. Black workers tried to figure out how to break through, and had lots of resistance from the Teamsters. The Black workers had to appeal to Eleanor Roosevelt to get the Teamsters to break their discrimination and allow Blacks to drive the trucks to the army bases.
>
> In the middle of the war race riots broke out in Detroit. When Black workers first entered the Packard plant in assembly positions, all the whites walked out. Same thing happened at Timken Axle. This strife existed in the plants where Blacks were supposed to stay in janitorial jobs or foundries, and were not supposed to integrate into final assemblies. (G. Baker 2016)

CLASS AND RACE IN THE AUTO INDUSTRY AND THE UNION

The deep contradictions of capitalism and the social relations of capital and labor, including Black labor, were on full display in the Detroit auto industry and in the

UAW in the mid-twentieth century. The nexus of capital accumulation is that capitalists hire workers and pay wages less than the value the workers produce—creating profit and wealth for the capitalists. Workers, though exploited in this way, and Black workers, who were also racially oppressed, were still employed, earning wages and spending them on the necessities of their lives. Despite the class exploitation and racial oppression of auto workers in Detroit, they were among the best paid workers in the United States during the post–World War II period. The automotive sector was a powerful engine of work, wages, and the working-class standard of living, including for Black workers (Greenhouse 2019; Roediger and Esch 2014).

Gen analyzed the significance of the large number of Black workers and the irony of Henry Ford's role in hiring Black workers to prevent multiracial working-class organizing.

> The struggles against racism developed early on, lasted throughout the war years, and continued. At that period, over half of the factory workers in Detroit worked for Henry Ford. That's how Detroit became a Black city—because of all the factory workers.
>
> That was not the intent of Ford. He was hiring Blacks to keep them from building a union and uniting with the white workers. But the end result was building a huge Black "middle class" in Detroit that grew on the basis of the auto industry.
>
> That's important in terms of understanding how Detroit became what it is. It wasn't accidental. It wasn't magic. Hell, Henry Ford was trying to keep workers from organizing and he got different results than what he angled for.
>
> Those are the early struggles, but Detroit prospered. It is a city of 139 square miles and we had all these single homes—not a lot of apartment buildings or brownstones. Everybody had a single home. I knew factory workers so proud of their homes, they'd carry pictures in their wallets. "Ain't that something? I'm so glad this is mine." Pride in the fact that they were homeowners. (G. Baker 2016)

Changing Conditions in the 1950s and 1960s—
Post–World War II Strikes and Restructuring Capital and Labor in Auto

The end of World War II set the basis for the great expansion of capitalist globalization. The U.S. capitalist class was positioned for the consolidation of U.S. imperialism on the world stage—economically, politically, and ideologically. The U.S. industrial infrastructure emerged from war unscathed and technologically developed, putting the United States in a dominant position globally. At the same time, the wartime destruction of Europe and Japan put them in a dependent position in relation to U.S. capital. The Bretton Woods institutions—the International Monetary Fund and World Bank—and the Marshall Plan established the global financial framework and legal foundation for the post–World War II world and for rebuilding Europe and Japan as "junior partners" of the United States. U.S. finance, technological innovation, and productivity held sway over the global market (Greenhouse 2019; W. Robinson 2014, 2022; W. Robinson and Fuentes 2023).

The U.S. ruling class and its state apparatus became a powerful force on the global stage. The mushrooming U.S. military-industrial complex and the formation of the North Atlantic Treaty Organization (NATO) consolidated and ensured U.S. political and military dominance globally. Ideologically and politically, the containment of communism was expressed through McCarthyism in the United States, in the Cold War on a world scale, and in the Korean War. U.S. intervention in anticolonial movements helped install procapitalist forces to power in national liberation struggles and in postcolonial governments. COINTELPRO—the U.S. counterintelligence program—and other U.S. government programs of surveillance and repression of social movement, Black liberation, and civil rights forces were the domestic expressions of these global dynamics.

The growth of commodity production for the consumer market after years of war production, the coast-to-coast expansion of the Interstate Highway System, and the suburbanization of America fueled the auto industry and new realities on the ground in Detroit.

Gen laid out the consolidation of the auto industry—first the big four and later the big three—and growing labor repression.

> The plants began to break up in the 1950s and move to suburban areas—because the corporations were afraid of union organizing. During the war we had "no strike" clauses because striking would affect the war production. As soon as the war was over and soldiers came home, there was a strike wave. Workers started striking everything. That set the groundswell for the passage of the Taft-Hartley Act in 1947 that led to "right-to-work" states in the U.S. South and other repressive measures on labor organizing.
>
> By 1953 the corporations were building suburban plants and sending the plants to other places to try to minimize union power inside the plants. Packard left, Studebaker closed, and Kaiser and Frazer went out of business. Those old cars were made in Detroit. We ended up at that time with the big four. Chrysler, Ford, General Motors, and American Motors—which made the Nash, the little Henry J, and Jeeps.
>
> Since then we've been in a crisis in Detroit with overproduction and companies moving and leaving. Some went to the U.S. South, others closed altogether. The city began to change. (G. Baker 2016)

It's the 1960s—Plants Were Hiring and Racial Discrimination Persisted

In the 1960s Europe and Japan had not yet recovered from the devastation of World War II in terms of competing with U.S. economic and political dominance. The U.S. economy remained the engine of the world capitalist system; the country's auto industry was still expanding into the global marketplace while filling the void created during the war.

In Detroit, Motown, at one time the number-one producer and distributor of rhythm and blues in the country, became a cultural center. Berry Gordy, a former auto worker and founder of Motown, brought the factory concept of the assembly line to music production. It was both a reflection and a shaper of working-class life on the national scene. At the same time, racial oppression persisted as a reality of capitalism and U.S. working-class life, despite changes in the law and forms of expression (Roediger and Esch 2014).

Gen lived that reality:

> The 1960s saw the development of work inside the shops expanding. Back then jobs were so plentiful, you could work day shift here, get fired or quit, and go over there and work afternoons at the next plant. It was that easy. When I got hired at Dodge Main in 1964, the plant had ten thousand employees. They put a whole second shift on, hired five thousand people at a time. Hiring was massive and things were lucrative. That was the mood of the city then.
>
> Other things about the plants hadn't changed. We had all kind of discrimination inside the shop. When I got hired at Dodge Main, I'd go in with a white buddy. I end up in the foundry, hardest and most dangerous job, and he ends up my foreman. Or I end up at the spot welding and body shop, and he ends up in skilled trades. Discrimination was that tough. You couldn't get the kind of positions that were held open mainly for whites. A lot of the Chrysler and General Motors plants were real discriminatory, and that's what set the basis for us to begin organizing inside the shops. We began to do organizing work inside the factories after the 1967 Detroit Rebellion. (G. Baker 2016)

Gen lifted up the 1967 Detroit Rebellion as the spark that ignited the formation of DRUM and the LRBW among Black workers at the point of production. It set in motion our political journey of over fifty years. Our journey took us from the LRBW, a revolutionary organization of Black workers, to the League of Revolutionaries for a New America, a multiracial, multigendered, multinational revolutionary working-class organization.

Part Two

From Our Origins to the Split—the League Story

CHAPTER 4

Founding Members of the League of Revolutionary Black Workers Meet Up in the Early 1960s

The founding members of the LRBW and others had long-standing relationships. We share their personal and political history as context. Detroit was in motion, and the movement activists who would form the LRBW Executive Board—General Baker, John Williams, Luke Tripp, Mike Hamlin, John Watson, and Ken Cockrel—crossed paths at Wayne State University, at the *Detroit News* warehouse, and in the larger struggle. Chuck Wooten joined the process later.

They were caught up in the tumultuous sixties and were drawn to the study of Marxism. They wanted to deeply understand the realities of class, race, and labor in auto, the police and state-led violence in their communities, and the Cuban Revolution and global anti-imperialist and anticolonial movements.

They traveled to Cuba in 1964, met with revolutionaries, including Rob Williams—who was living in exile from the United States for armed self-defense in North Carolina (see R. Williams [1962] 1998). Back home they helped organize community resistance to police violence and took up the Cynthia Scott case.

They came to the strategic understanding of the centrality of workers at the point of production in the working-class struggle against capitalism and the power of the state. They concluded that it was strategic for organizing in Detroit that at least one of them work in the plants permanently and chose Gen, a second-generation auto worker and working-class organizer at the point of production.

Though some were students at Wayne, they were working-class Detroiters and all spent time working in the auto plants or in the *Detroit News* warehouse. Several pursued different paths—teacher, lawyer, social worker, and professor.

We share short excerpts from the personal and political stories of the LRBW founders we interviewed—John Williams, Mike, and Luke. Mike joined the ancestors April 18, 2017, not long after our conversation. With his last words to us he

League of Revolutionary Black Workers members and family who share our stories from the LRBW origins in 1968 to the split in 1971. Courtesy General Baker Institute.

shared, "I'm really glad you guys are doing this, anything you can do that helps the next generations. It's not going away. It's getting worse" (Hamlin 2017).

We had already lost Gen, Chuck, John Watson, and Ken. Gen left an extensive archival record we draw upon to bring his analysis and life struggle to the LRBW story. Other LRBW founders and members have recollections of Chuck, John Watson, and Ken that we share along with short excerpts from previous interviews and writings.

John Williams elaborated on the early years—meeting at Wayne, studying Marxism, student, worker, and community organizing, the Cuba trip, and Gen's draft refusal.

> I went to Wayne State University in 1961 after a two-year stint in the military. I was introduced to *The Communist Manifesto*. I had never been in a situation where the class question was put in such a clear way. I was enamored by it. I ran into Luke, another student, and John Watson came the following year as a student.
>
> I had met Gen, who was working at Woolworth and was a student at Highland Park Community College. I said, "Why don't you come on down to Wayne?" The next year, in 1962, Gen came over to Wayne State.
>
> What stood out in the city were police relations with the community and police brutality, and the fact that not many Blacks were being hired in the banks and stores. We were pissed. We formed the Negro Action Committee to try to fight some of these struggles. Later UHURU was born.
>
> We talked about understanding Marx and Lenin, without any guide. And we read Stalin, Trotsky, and all those Marxists. We read Lenin's *Where to Begin* and *What Is to Be Done*. That was our guide. We set up two newspapers—the *Razor* for students and the *Vanguard* addressed to workers. We always thought the workers, and Black workers in particular, were the vanguard. It was in our heads that we needed to develop this vanguard and students would follow them. We turned the Wayne State *Collegiate* (campus newspaper) into *The South End*, something totally different, to deal with critical issues.
>
> In 1964 Gen, Charles Simmons, Luke, and Charles Johnson went down to Cuba and ran into Robert Williams, who was in exile there. When they came back, we started putting out the *Crusader*, and used Williams's book, *Negroes with Guns* (1962), in some of our study sessions.
>
> The next year Gen got his induction notice and wrote a beautiful piece to the draft board. We used Gen's refusal statement to show what we were trying to do and why anybody who's oppressed and exploited should refuse to be drafted. Nine of us showed up and protested at the draft board office. Gen went in for a few minutes, turned, and came back out. We celebrated. The protest worked. Gen was out of the military. (John Williams 2017)

Below is Gen's powerful letter dated September 10, 1965, to the Wayne Country local draft board:

TO WHOM IT MAY CONCERN
Gentlemen:
This letter is in regards to a notice sent to me, General Gordon Baker, Jr., requesting my appearance before an examining station to determine my fitness for military service.

How could you have the nerve knowing that I am a black man living under the scope and influence of America's racist, decadent society??? You did not ask me if I had any morals, principles, or basic human values by which to live. Yet, you ask if I am qualified. QUALIFIED FOR WHAT, might I ask? What does being "Qualified" mean: qualified to serve in the U.S. Army? . . . To be further brainwashed into the insidious notion of defending freedom?

You stand before me with the dried blood of Patrice Lumumba on your hands, the blood of defenseless Panamanian students, shot down by U.S. marines; the blood of my black brothers in Angola and South Africa who are being tortured by the Portuguese and South African whites (whom you resolutely support) respectively; the dead people of Japan, Korea, and now Vietnam, in Asia, the blood of Medgar Evers, six Birmingham babies, the blood of one million Algerians slaughtered by the French (whom you supported); the fresh blood of ten thousand Congolese patriots dead from your ruthless rape and plunder of the Congo—the blood of defenseless women and children burned in villages from Napalm jelly bombs. . . . With all of this blood of my non-white brothers dripping from your fangs, you have the damned AUDACITY to ask me if I am "qualified." White man; listen to me for I am talking to you!

I AM A MAN OF PRINCIPLES AND VALUES: principles of justice and national liberation, self-determination, and respect for national sovereignty. Yet you ask me if I am "physically fit" to go to Asia, Africa, and Latin America to fight my oppressed brothers (who are completely and resolutely within their just rights to free their fatherland from foreign domination). You ask me if I am qualified to join an army of FOOLS, ASSASSINS, and MORAL DELINQUENTS who are not worthy of being called men! You want me to defend the riches reaped from the super-exploitation of the darker races of mankind by a few white, rich, super-monopolists who control the most vast empire that has ever existed in man's one million years of History—all in the name of "Freedom"!

Why, here in the heart of America, 22 million black people are suffering unsurmounted toil: exploited economically by every form of business—from monopolists to petty hustlers; completely suppressed politically; deprived of their social and cultural heritage.

> But all men of principle are fighting men... MY FIGHT IS FOR FREEDOM: UHURU, LIBERTAD, HALAUGA, and HARAMBEE!
>
> THEREFORE: when the call is made to free South Africa; when the call is made to liberate Latin America from the United Fruit Co., Kaiser and Alcoa Aluminum Co., and from Standard Oil; when the call is made to jail the exploiting Brahmins in India in order to destroy the Caste System; when the call is made to free the black delta areas of Mississippi, Alabama, South Carolina; when the call is made to free Harlem, New York, to free 12th Street here in Detroit and all the other 12th streets around the country.... Yes, when these calls are made, send for me, for these shall be historic struggles in which it shall be an everlasting honor and pleasure for me to serve.
>
> Venceremos! (G. Baker 2015)

Gen was the first Black working-class activist to publicly protest the Vietnam War and declare that oppressed and exploited people should support each other globally by refusing to serve in imperialist wars.

John concluded,

> That was the beginning and how I got involved. The collective—Gen, Luke, myself, Watson—had been together for at least six or seven years when we got into the League. (John Williams 2017)

Mike recalled the early years working, connecting with John Watson and Ken and studying Marxism—which he said probably saved him from an adventurous death.

> I came back from the army and didn't care whether I lived or died. What saved me was finding John Watson and being introduced to Marxism. John had been studying Marxism and turned me onto it.
>
> It was 1960 and I got a job at the *Detroit News*. I was the third Black hired. Three of us worked there—Ken, John Watson and myself—all very studious. John was a great student of Marxism and, as a teenager, studied with all kinds of people renowned for their Marxism—the SWP (Socialist Workers Party), the CP (Communist Party), with Marty Glaberman, Blacks like Conrad Mallett, and others. Ken and I were like brothers and talked all the time. Nobody messed with us.
>
> In newspaper work, you work between editions. You sit in a room waiting on them to print the paper, then you distribute them to the trucks. We had a lot of time to talk. We'd be loading trucks at night on the dock, and we'd be rapping loudly.
>
> Marxism was the tool I needed and we decided to study people who had

made revolutions. We studied the Algerian Revolution, Ho Chi Minh, Mao and China. We had a link with China. They sent us thousands of books which we distributed. We got a lead to link with the Cubans and they sent us materials. (Hamlin 2017)

Mike had much more to say about studying Marxism, McCarthyism, and the left:

> Everybody who was a leftist came to Detroit because we were drawing workers to Marxism. We were very explicit and very clear that we were Marxists. This is in the aftermath of McCarthyism. We did not give a damn about McCarthyism. In fact, I believe we made a major contribution to destroying it.
>
> Students for a Democratic Society (SDS) was in a battle over who was the revolutionary force and they said it was students. Most of them were children of leftists. We were advancing from a position that Black workers were the vanguard of the struggle, had a revolutionary potential, and had power at the point of the production. We began to attract all kinds of people. Young whites—a lot of them were still struggling, still carrying on. They had risen to high positions, but their politics were still the same.
>
> In the aftermath of McCarthy we had to start all over again. We had to rebuild communist ideas and ideology. We attracted a lot of people, some of whom are still here. (Hamlin 2017)

Luke explained his coming to revolutionary consciousness and embracing the dialectic of Black liberation and Marxist anticolonial struggles around the world.

> The terrain in the 1960s was such that it was possible for something like the League to emerge. In 1967 the Black rebellion was at its height. We had a group with a high consciousness of class struggle, with a revolutionary orientation in relation to Black liberation struggles, and a Marxist orientation all around the world. Sort of a global Marxist movement—China, the Soviet Union, struggles in Africa led by Africans who were Marxist loyalists in Mozambique, even in South Africa. They were socialist orientated and there was a similar orientation in Latin America. (Tripp 2017)

Luke brought his analysis and skills to teaching in high school and college:

> I was a math and science teacher, teaching Black students who were pushed out of the traditional school system. Later I enrolled in the University of Michigan in Ann Arbor and earned a PhD in higher education. Many of my friends and comrades outside of Detroit were taking positions in various departments as part of our struggle to kick in the door. (Tripp 2017)

Edna Watson spoke extensively of her own experience in the early years leading up to the LRBW and at Wayne State and her recollections of John Watson, her husband for a time.

> I came back to Detroit in 1962, became a nurse, and worked at Hudson Hospital with Dr. Charles Wright, one of the founders of the Medical Committee for Human Rights. In 1964 I met Charles Simmons, who was an orderly at Hudson.
>
> In 1965 I went to Wayne State. It was a hotbed of activity around Black rights, Black everything. The Cuban Revolution had occurred. You had the Revolutionary Action Movement (RAM) and Max Stanford [Ahmad 2008], and lots of competing movements.
>
> We had study groups and studied with notable people. They seeded a lot of leftists and empowered us. We got to take over *The South End* because David Herreshoff was the faculty advisor. He showed us how to stack the voting committee and get the votes so John could be editor. In late 1966 and early 1967, we created the *Inner-City Voice*—me, Mike, and John Watson. We couldn't get any printing house to help us print, so we did everything ourselves and took the paper to Chicago to get printed.
>
> I met people like Justin Ravitz, the first open communist elected as a judge in Detroit, and Gen. I had met John in kindergarten. We lived in the same neighborhood on the same street and were born in January 1944. We ran across each other again at Wayne in 1966. Ken and others lived there in student housing. We instituted the first of the notorious Detroit crash pads there because people needed a place to be. Homeless people back then were mistreated and locked up like vagrants.
>
> That was 1967, and we had already become a force to be reckoned with. The street kids came to us, they knew we were radical. They were attacking the police because the National Guard had come in. We told them you really don't wanna attack the police. We thought they would be slaughtered, maybe not, but that wasn't the best idea.
>
> John and I hooked up in 1967 and we stayed together seven years. He was elected editor of *The South End*, probably the same year we had the Black Economic Development Conference (BEDC). BEDC was aimed at getting money into the Black community for economic development. Out of BEDC came a *Black Manifesto*. The *Black Manifesto* was a demand to the Christian churches and Jewish synagogues for reparations for slavery. One of the big omissions was they didn't demand reparations from the Islamic world which had participated in slavery, too, and had engineered way more of it than anyone knew.
>
> We were very much enamored with the Palestinians in that period. We sided

with them during the Six-Day War with Israel and brought the wrath of the world on us. Palestinians lived with us in Highland Park, they worked in the plants with us. They were brethren, friends, comrades, and neighbors. We were naive leftists. We didn't understand that when you step into the global arena, the global arena bites back. We put ourselves up against COINTELPRO and the CIA. (E. Watson 2017)

Jerome asked Edna about John's trip to the Middle East and what happened after that. Edna offered this cryptic response:

> No one ever talked to me about it. Some things, if you're in a cadre organization, are "need to know." When John died six weeks after 9/11, I got a call from an Arab who I considered a longtime friend. This person said, "They probably got to him, and we should never talk again." So I'm never gonna talk about that again, unless I'm eighty-five and on death's door. (E. Watson 2017)

Gracie Wooten and Marian shared their recollections of Chuck, who joined the ancestors October 27, 2011. Gen and Chuck became a powerful team working at Dodge Main in the years leading up to the formation of DRUM and the LRBW. Gracie, who was married to Chuck and powerful in her own right, remembered those years:

> I came into the League as a result of General Baker and Charles, my husband. You all know him as Chuck. I refer to him as Charlie. He grew up in the projects when it was full of gangs. He had a good mother and father, but he gravitated towards the street. He sold bricks as a child to workers in the neighborhood who were doing construction. He told our kids, "I've been working since I was eight years old."
>
> Gen was persistent in trying to get Charlie involved in DRUM. I remember the knock on our apartment door and Gen would ask if Chuck was home. I'd say no. He was at the race track most often. It was early 1968—at the very beginning. Charlie had a totally different lifestyle before he became involved in DRUM. Eventually, he became involved in DRUM and I became involved as a support person. (G. Wooten 2017)

Marian added her remembrances of Chuck:

> Chuck was an interesting person, smart, and a lot of fun. Thank God Gracie stuck with him, because she kept him alive. And Gracie's smart too. The talent that was in the League was tremendous. Chuck was one of the seven founders of the League, and one of the original people who formed DRUM. His brother was in here too.
>
> Chuck was always clear. He learned the science, and applied the science to the

conditions at Dodge Main where they worked. He and Gen were tight. It hurt Gen so much, and all of us, when Chuck passed away. We said, "One of the greatest minds that has ever lived has gone away." (Kramer 2017)

Others Join the LRBW Journey in These Early Years

Charles Simmons, Wylie Rogers, Leah Rogers, Alonzo Chandler, William "Mitch" Mitchell, and Allen Ray Bernard shared how they connected with the LRBW founders and their coming to class consciousness in these early years.

Charles Simmons brought another lens to the early years leading toward LRBW formation. He recalled meeting up in 1963 in UHURU, protesting the brutal Detroit police murder of Cynthia Scott, the Olympics, and the police raids at Wayne State.

> My connection with the League evolved, beginning with my meeting Gen, Luke, and John Watson and all the group in UHURU around 1963. The League was an evolution that began in previous organizations, and Gen and I were close personally.
>
> We were together in major struggles—the Cynthia Scott demonstration and the anti-Olympics demonstration. In response to the demonstrations, the police came onto the Wayne State campus, came into the classrooms, and arrested people. I can't recall if they had warrants. But these tactics were vestiges of the whole McCarthy era we were still in. I think we're back in that now. (Simmons 2017)

Charles spoke of the importance of their Cuba trip in 1964, their coming to international revolutionary consciousness, and going from the "hood in Detroit to meet with world revolutionary leaders":

> Four of us from Detroit, Luke, Gen, Charlie Johnson, and myself, went to Cuba together—gaining an international consciousness and being part of the world revolution. Going from the hood in Detroit to meet with and learn from world revolutionary leaders in their countries was a major step. We jumped generations in political consciousness.
>
> We also met Robert Williams, who was involved in the anti-Klan struggle in the United States and the international struggle. Rob had spent time with Mao Zedong, Ho Chi Minh, and various African leaders. We inherited that thinking and the ideas and the passion from these movements and leaders that followed us through to the League and beyond. (Simmons 2017)

Charles continued with two other takeaways—the importance of youth and intergenerational sharing and the intense state repression of movement forces in those years:

> When we came back from Cuba, the four of us were subpoenaed to go before a federal grand jury in New York over a frame-up of a Black Panther, Bob Collier, who was accused of plotting to blow up the Statue of Liberty and Washington Monument. This was the high point of COINTELPRO. They did convict him with nothing, and they tried to bring us into this net.
>
> We were kids when we traveled to Cuba and did most of these things. Young people have the courage and the innocence, they haven't been corrupted yet. They've got challenges. Cultural imperialism is much stronger and more pervasive than ever before. It's on their shoulders now, but we elders have to give advice or encouragement whenever we can. (Simmons 2017)

Charles also explained why folks from UHURU, the Cuba trip, and international work made the strategic decision to organize Black workers in the Detroit auto plants. He shared their understanding of the role of Black labor in the struggles of the sixties.

> Black labor was concentrated in heavy industry at that time. It was clear—in any plant—that most workers were Black where the work was most difficult, hot, and dangerous. We were mostly located in the foundry, but were throughout the plants in heavy industry. If you met a Black man in Detroit in the 1950s and 1960s, after you introduce yourself and ask "what's your name?," the next thing was "what plant do you work at?" (Simmons 2017)

Wylie Rogers and Leah Rogers, married for decades and living in Flint, Michigan, explained their connection to the LRBW before it was formed through John Williams. Wylie was a social worker and Leah was a teacher. Wylie opened,

> I was involved with the League before it came into existence. I met John, a founder, at the University of Michigan. I was in graduate school in social work in 1966—confused, but trying to start the Association for Black Social Workers. I hooked up with John reaching out to other Black students. It was eye-opening to hear about Detroit—UHURU, the activity at Wayne State, and what was going on with Black workers. (W. Rogers 2017)

Leah shared her experience in student activism in the early 1960s.

> I was involved in student activity around civil rights and social rights as a student in junior college in Flint. I went to Wayne State for a Northern Student Movement (NSM) conference, probably in 1963. It was affiliated with the Student Nonviolent Coordinating Committee (SNCC) and was SNCC's way of organizing support among students in the North. It was a multinational group, a new experience for me that made quite an impact. (L. Rogers 2017)

Wylie spoke to the motion in the North, the earth-shattering impact of the 1967 Detroit uprising and the federal military response to crush the rebellion, the Algiers Motel police killings, his life swirling, and the hope from the LRBW in the midst of chaos, state murder, and repression:

> It was a tumultuous time. It seemed distant because it was taking place in the South. But activities were bubbling up in the North. I encountered SDS and Tom Hayden, and Julian Bond at the University of Michigan. When I met John and got an understanding of what was going on in Detroit—that opened my eyes.
>
> I had a field placement in Detroit and worked on the East Side where the 1967 uprising popped. I lived in Ann Arbor and will never forget driving back to my place in Detroit. During the uprising President Johnson called out the 101st Airborne. I was driving and seeing all that ordinance, the tanks, and the troops along I-75 poised to go into Detroit. It was scary.
>
> Meeting John when the League was in the process of formation united us in conversation. Seeing all that power situated to crush what was gonna happen in Detroit shaped my life. It turned my world upside down in a short period, October 1966 to April 1967. What the hell was I thinking about before then?
>
> I was with Ken Cockrel, a founding member of the League, at the Department of Social Service in Detroit where we both worked. We were angry. Things happening so fast, people getting killed. I didn't know what the hell to do, but we had to do something. Leah was home with our son who had just been born.
>
> There was an incident where the police killed three guys in the old Algiers Motel. I was driving, I stopped and broke into uncontrollable tears. There was an organized police violence operation, a campaign of terror. It was a time of anger, of despair, but it was hopeful. The effort to form the League at the time was a very hopeful sign, there were people ready to fight. (W. Rogers 2017)

William "Mitch" Mitchell met Ken, Mike, and John Watson at the *Detroit News*. They introduced him to Gen, and the rest is history. Mitch worked with Gen at Dodge Main and helped organize the wildcat strikes. He explained his coming to consciousness during his growing up years:

> I was born in 1947 and grew up in the mid-1950s. The civil rights struggle was raging throughout the country. My friend and I looked at *Jet* and we found a picture of Emmett Till. It shook me up and I would never forget. His face was torn up, and I couldn't understand how anyone could do this to another human being. That got me thinking. My mother was active in sit-down strikes at Woolworth's and she dragged me along. When Martin Luther King came, she insisted I go hear his speech.

> I was a doubting Thomas on religious things. When they blew up the church in Birmingham in 1963 that finished it. I told my mother, "If He can't protect little girls singing hymns in church, I can't use Him." I was looking for something. I tried Reverend Cleage, minister at the Shrine of the Black Madonna—the whole religious thing with a Black face. I tried the Muslims, but that didn't work out. I kept searching. The Detroit Rebellion in 1967 had that effect.
>
> After that, I had a job at the *Detroit News* and met Ken, Mike, and John Watson. They were printing a newspaper, the *Inner-City Voice*. They said to come by their office and they introduced me to General. I was so taken by Gen. He could sit down and edit a dissertation, but he was just as quick to mop the floor—whatever job had to be done. I became his helper, left home and moved in. During the early days of organizing I was there. For the RUMs, for DRUM, ELRUM (Eldon Revolutionary Union Movement), FRUM (Ford Revolutionary Union Movement) and so on down the line. (W. Mitchell 2017)

Alonzo Chandler worked at Chrysler Eldon and Jefferson and was drawn to the LRBW through his understanding of the power of Black workers from slavery to the plants.

> When I was a kid, my grandmother told me, "Whenever the white man gets in trouble, he looks to us to pull him out." Everything has a duality. The Constitution was probably one of the best documents at that time. But it was set in conditions of slavery, of slavocracy. Most of the first fourteen presidents came from the South with a southern perspective. When Lincoln was assassinated, Andrew Johnson, who became president, was a "slaver."
>
> Black workers have always been at the forefront of whatever progressive movement happened in the United States. (Chandler in Chandler et al. 2017)

Marian introduced Allen Ray to the LRBW when he moved from Dallas to Detroit around 1967. He explained,

> I was recently discharged from the military and my sister, Marian, lived in Detroit. I had a background as a machinist and ended up at Uniroyal. I didn't have any history with the union.
>
> Marian was involved with different organizations and I became involved with them—the League, the Black Panthers, the Communist Labor Party (CLP). We got educated. I had no knowledge of any form of organization other than the military. After being in the plant for a short time, I learned what unions were and how the workers didn't have any rights or voice, particularly Black workers. I met Gen, Luke, John Williams, and Jerome and all of us started organizing the League. Fighting back, trying to get recognition for workers. (Bernard 2017)

Founding Members of the LRBW

There were two groupings of folks who met up and were part of a number of organizations before they became the LRBW Executive Board. The grouping at Wayne State University included John Williams, General Baker, Luke Tripp, and John Watson. The *Detroit News* warehouse group included Mike Hamlin, Ken Cockrel, and John Watson, who was in both groups and connected them up. Gen brought Chuck Wooten into the process a bit later.

Folks in these groups knew each other and worked together beginning in the early sixties. They developed the ability, through the study of Marxism and practice, to make strategic decisions collectively. What held them together as they moved into the plants and onto the world stage was their unity around two strategic points. One was the strategic importance of organizing at the point of production. The other was the strategic importance of working-class internationalism linking U.S. working-class struggles with global anticolonial struggles, especially in Palestine and the Middle East. They were not prepared for the state repression resulting from stepping onto the world stage.

CHAPTER 5

Working-Class Rebellions in Detroit and the World— the Working Class Takes the Offensive, 1967 to 1968

> Labor in the white skin can never free itself as long as labor in the black skin is branded.
> —Karl Marx, *Capital* ([1867] 1887)

> Here is the real modern labor problem.... The emancipation of man is the emancipation of labor and the emancipation of labor is the freeing of that basic majority of workers who are yellow, brown and black.
> —W. E. B. Du Bois, *Black Reconstruction in America 1860–1880* ([1935] 1962)

In Detroit, the violent state repression by the police, National Guard, and army to quell the working-class uprising during the 1967 Detroit Rebellion and the wildcat strike at Dodge Main in 1968 together sparked a critical working-class reaction.

The 1967 Detroit Rebellion and Lessons Learned for Working-Class Organizing

Uprisings within twentieth-century Black liberation struggles against Jim Crow policies and centuries of Black poverty and oppression were a U.S. expression of the global anticolonial movement. The 1967 Detroit Rebellion and working-class resistance to the state violence sweeping the country set in motion a wave of wildcat strikes. The wildcats set the basis for the formation of Revolutionary Union Movements (RUMs) at various auto and related industry plants and for community and student organizations that culminated in the LRBW (Roediger and Esch 2014).

Workers in Detroit in the post–World War II period, though exploited and oppressed, still had the "best that capitalism had to offer." The ruling class never thought the working class would rise up in opposition, so ruling-class forces were confused when the Detroit Rebellion jumped off in 1967 and reacted by calling in the National Guard and U.S. Army to quell the rebellion.

The rebellion, wildcat strikes, and formation of the LRBW were expressions of Black workers achieving class consciousness through their experience of power as workers at the point of production in a moment when U.S. industrial power was still at its apex. Of the Black workers who formed the LRBW, several were working-class intellectuals, Marxist theoreticians and political strategists. They embodied the consciousness, heart, and soul of the revolutionary struggle.

The LRBW story continues with Gen as a leader and narrator. He described the rebellion from the inside.

> The Detroit Rebellion in 1967 is a defining moment in this city's history. I was working at the Dodge Main plant—twelve hours, seven days a week. We got off work on the afternoon shift at three A.M. and went to various blind pigs (unlicensed after-hours joints) all over the city, because the bars were closed. That was part of our daily activity. So when the rebellion broke out about six A.M. on Sunday, July 23, on Twelfth Street (now Rosa Parks Boulevard) and Clairmount Avenue, I was right there. I lived three blocks away on Gladstone.
>
> The police came and tried to raid the blind pig. It was surrounded by about a hundred workers on the street who started throwing bricks at the police. Then people broke down the street and went to the pawn shops. Almost everybody back then lived off the pawn shop. You work and get paid on Friday, go buy some stuff. By Wednesday the next week, you had to put it in the pawn shop to have enough to eat the next two days. If you ever pawned anything, you know on the back of your pawn slip it says in great big letters, "Not responsible for fire, theft, or other unavoidable accidents." Everybody who went into the pawn shops had to go in there to get their own stuff back. Obviously, the first ones took somebody else's stuff too. (G. Baker 2016)

RACIAL INTEGRATION, POLICE ASSASSINATION, AND MORE ARRESTS

The rebellions of the 1960s, especially in Watts and Detroit, have often been portrayed as "race riots." They were, in fact, among the long history of rebellions in the United States in which Black participation and working-class Black leadership stepped up. The Detroit Rebellion clearly expressed this dialectic of exploitation and oppression of U.S. workers. Historians and the media have a strategic predisposition to present these class uprisings as "race riots." But we have an even more important and strategic task to put forward the reality that these were class-based, multiracial rebellions.

Marsha, a high school student at the time, shared what the rebellion meant to her generation and affirmed its multiracial and working-class character.

> In 1967 the social anxiety and oppression boiled over. It started with a Vietnam veteran who had come home. To celebrate, he and some friends went to an after-hours joint on Twelfth Street. The police raided the place. On that day in July it boiled over into a conflagration. People began expressing their rage at all the police brutality and racial oppression we were dealing with.
>
> My dad was not feeling it. He was from the older, more conservative people who were afraid of reprisals for people fighting the power. We refer to the "riot" as the rebellion because we were rebelling against what was going on. It was spontaneous, but engaged many people. There were many whites, poor whites that still lived in the city, and many of them were engaged in this looting and protesting in the street. People don't realize how many white people were also engaged in the rebellion. It wasn't a race riot, it wasn't Black against white. (Music 2017)

Gen, a leading actor in this historic moment, shared his experience:

> I was arrested on the first night for violation of curfew and did fifteen days in Ionia State Penitentiary, waiting to come back to trial. A lot of characteristics of the Detroit Rebellion were different than other rebellions. Everybody proclaims that the Detroit Rebellion was integrated. The first person killed in the rebellion was a white worker who was looting a store down on Trumbull Avenue. When they carried me to Ionia, two white guys arrested for sniping were on my bus. (G. Baker 2016)

John Williams added his observations:

> In 1967 we had the uprising. A lot of people called it a "riot." We called it a civil disobedience. It was an expression of years of frustration with the police. (John Williams 2017)

ALGIERS MOTEL INCIDENT

The Detroit Rebellion was unique in its extreme expression of state violence against the working class of Detroit. This included the police assassination of Carl Cooper, a seventeen-year-old Black man, in what is known as the Algiers Motel incident. After the rebellion, ruling-class forces perpetrated an intentional removal of the incident and the Algiers Motel itself from the historic memory of

Detroiters. They went to great lengths to remove accounts and books about the Algiers Motel incident from Detroit libraries and schools, ensuring that knowledge of this explosive confrontation of deadly state power and working-class rebellion be hidden from the people (Hersey 1968).

Gen spoke directly to this reality:

> The Detroit Rebellion is the only one that had an assassination that took place during the course of the rebellion—the Algiers Motel incident. The Algiers Motel no longer exists. They renamed it the Desert Inn, and that lasted a few years. Then they closed it. When you get to Virginia Park Street and Woodward Avenue, it's a gated community with a brick wall. The Algiers Motel has been wiped off the pages of history. When you go to the Detroit school system you can't find a book on the Algiers Motel incident. They don't want kids to know about it. (G. Baker 2016)

OVER SEVEN THOUSAND PEOPLE ARRESTED

Other expressions of state power and state violence directed against the Detroit working class included mass arrests and imprisonment and the National Guard's unbridled use of live ammunition in the streets of Detroit. There were so many arrests that the prisons across Michigan filled up. Officials had to turn Belle Isle, a small park in the Detroit River usually used as a recreational space, into a prison—dubbed "Bellecatraz" by Detroiters.

Gen described his own arrest and imprisonment along with seven thousand other working-class Detroiters.

> The Detroit Rebellion was also different because they arrested so many people—over seven thousand people. They sent us to Marquette, Milan, Jackson, and Ionia. They filled up all the prison systems in the state. When they were finished with that, they sent the rest of the people to Belle Isle. You usually talk about Belle Isle as a place for leisure, but it became a jail. We called it "Bellecatraz." (G. Baker 2016)

Gen brought firsthand knowledge of the 150,000 rounds of ammunition the National Guard used to shoot up Detroit. Detroiters made necklaces from the shell casings.

> Another factor is that the National Guard shot up Detroit. Anybody who went into the rebellion who didn't hate the police, had to hate them when the rebellion was over. They shot over 150,000 rounds of ammunition with fifty-caliber machine guns all over the city. So many shell casings were laying on the ground.

> We picked up the empty fifty-caliber machine gun shells, put rawhide on them, and wore them for necklaces as a symbol to the rebellion. (G. Baker 2016)

The violence of the state in pursuing the interests of capital over labor continues to inform revolutionaries across time and place.

Dodge Revolutionary Union Movement (DRUM)—How Did It Happen?

> Dare to fight! Dare to win! Fight, fail. Fight again, fail again. Fight on to final victory!
>
> —LRBW slogan

The working class struck back against capitalism and imperialism the world over across 1968, a year that witnessed the culmination of over a decade of social struggle. It was a tumultuous time for movement development and progressive and revolutionary forces organizing. Social motion broke out—from the Tet offensive against U.S. imperialism to the protest of Black athletes at the Mexico City Summer Olympics and the Palestinian liberation struggle. Student movement forces, including the South African Student Association spearheaded by Steve Biko, took to the streets of Paris, Mexico City, and other cities around the globe. In the United States the assassination of Dr. Martin Luther King Jr. sparked urban uprisings across the country. The rebellion of diverse forces against the Democratic Party machine erupted into a major confrontation outside the party's convention in Chicago in August.

The environment was ripe for the outbreak of working-class organizing, including wildcat strikes led by Black workers. DRUM emerged out of this massive worldwide class struggle. DRUM laid the basis for RUMs in auto and related industry plants as well as community and student organizing across the Detroit region during 1968 and 1969. The LRBW was formed in 1969 out of the turbulent resistance to the exploitation and oppression of Black workers in relation to auto and other industries, the United Auto Workers (UAW), the state, and their struggle to transform their lives and communities.

To the best of our knowledge, the LRBW was the only popular sixties Black liberation organization—among SNCC, the Black Panther Party, Deacons for Defense, and others—that was firmly grounded within working-class struggle and located at the point of production. This reality was not accidental or happenstance. Rather, it was the very intentional and class-conscious decision of a section of working-class freedom fighters who fought state power in the streets of Detroit during the 1967 rebellion. The auto workers learned a strategic lesson during the rebellion around the curfew that led them to organize in the plants.

Gen shared this lesson in his own words:

> The struggle to organize the workers grew out of the rebellion. We learned a fundamental lesson—the only place that Black people had any value in the society was at the point of production, making profit for the corporations. That's why we turned our efforts toward organizing in the factory. Within a year's time after the Detroit Rebellion, DRUM was born. (G. Baker 2016)

John Williams brought additional context and detail to Gen's work in the plant and the origins of the LRBW:

> When DRUM was formed, various plants—Ford, Chrysler Detroit Forge, Jefferson Assembly, and more—were forming Revolutionary Union Movements (RUMs). We needed an umbrella organization under which they would all fit, and that's how the League was formed.
>
> In terms of the history and the leadership of DRUM, it started back in 1961. That's important because Gen didn't go into DRUM blind. He didn't go into the plant like the average worker going to get a job. He had a clear understanding of what he wanted to do, and he let it flow to him. We met people like Ron March, and they all started coming around. We discussed how we would move from there. They loved Gen, no question about that. (John Williams 2017)

ECONOMIC AND RACIAL VIOLENCE INTENSIFIED
THE MOTION TOWARD DRUM

Black workers in Detroit in the late sixties continued to experience the effects of white supremacy in the corporations and in the UAW. Their struggle against economic exploitation and racial oppression on both fronts drove their organizing in plants, communities, and high schools. The organizational form this took in the period from 1968 to 1971 was the RUMs and the LRBW.

Gen explained the spark that ignited the motion toward DRUM:

> DRUM started from a grievance that Black workers had. The corporation was running fifty-six units an hour for automobiles on the line. There was no additional help. Workers were doing almost twice as much work one day as they did the day before. The foreman on the line had to see that their section ran smoothly. Many times they didn't notice defective automobiles going down the line. All they wanted to do was get them the hell out of their area and out on the street—by any means necessary.
>
> We realized we were in two struggles at the same time. We started making demands that the UAW should have been making—demands about production standards and overtime. Workers began to question just who the UAW represented—the workers or the corporation. (G. Baker 2016)

Flyers, posters, communications, and newspapers from the early days of the Dodge Revolutionary Movement (DRUM) and wildcat strikes in 1968 through the LRBW days. Courtesy League Collective.

John Watson was an LRBW Executive Board member who left to become a leader in the Black Workers Congress (BWC) as part of the split. He joined the ancestors in October 2001. In a 1969 interview with the *Fifth Estate*, he offered his take on the origins of DRUM:

> The organization of DRUM was in direct response to numerous attempts by black workers over the last several years in the Hamtramck Assembly Plant to organize a movement which could resist racism and oppression both on the part of the union and the company. We wanted to be a revolutionary organization which would not be coopted by the moneyed forces.
>
> Briefly, the history of DRUM began with a series of wildcat strikes which we held around the issues of productivity, production standards and overt racism. The first strike was held when Chrysler Corporation speeded up the production line six cars an hour, during the UAW Convention last May.
>
> After this strike in which both black and white workers participated, the company imposed disciplinary action on those who they considered to be leaders of the strike action. This disciplinary action was taken primarily upon black workers. A number of black workers were fired, and quite a few received suspensions from anywhere from three to 30 days. In response to the racist attack which the company laid upon black workers after the first strike, DRUM organized a number of other strikes at that particular plant. (J. Watson 1969)

FIGHTING THE COMPANY AND THE UNION—
UAW MEANS "YOU AIN'T WHITE"

Both the company and the union refused to listen to the grievances of Black workers. Gen continued,

> Out of this history, we had to fight the company and the union. The union was so bad, we developed a slogan—the UAW means "you ain't white." We had picket lines around Solidarity House (UAW headquarters). We tried to talk to them about discrimination. We couldn't even get a conversation with the UAW leadership. They said, "The only discrimination that existed in the union is what you started." (G. Baker 2016)

TACTICS OF THE STRUGGLE

In their struggle against the union and the company, two key tactics became central for Black workers. The first was the necessity of developing an organizational form that was not a union-sanctioned caucus, because a caucus within the union would have to follow union rules. The second was the wildcat strike—a powerful tactic. Strikes called by the union required ninety days' notice to the corporation, allowing it to stockpile needed parts and prepare. Wildcat strikes, on the other hand, were called by the workers without union agreement or negotiation with the company. In the environment of their struggle against the union and the company, Black workers found wildcats to be the only effective tool in their confrontation with capital and the UAW, which was collaborating with the company. DRUM was born out of a wildcat.

Gen, who was fired for leading the wildcat at Dodge Main, explained,

> We were in lockdown battle. We developed organizations in the factories to fight back. I got fired for leading the wildcat strike at Dodge Main, and we used my discharge as a calling card to build DRUM. We said, "You have declared war on us. We're gonna fight you everywhere." That freed us from the constraints of their rules.
>
> We followed labor reps home. The UAW hired a couple of Black labor reps and they'd come in the plant and start firing people and drive home to the Black community. Me and Alonzo locked and loaded and drove up to the house of one of them, parked in the driveway, and waited for his ass to come home. You ain't gonna come in here and fire somebody, and come back in the Black community and live damn it. He called his wife and had his wife come out and beg, "Please leave." She was scared he wouldn't come home. . . .
>
> The Urban League was giving Len Townsend, a UAW vice president, and the CEO of Chrysler an award. We went in with picket signs, kicked over the damn tables. "You ain't gonna give him no damn award with the hell we've been through."
>
> We decided where the battleground was gonna be, not them. We weren't messing with grievance procedures or sitting around waiting on the UAW to do a WWP [withdraw grievance without prejudice] after it gets a year and a half old. We're doing whatever we got to do. (G. Baker 2016)

John Williams brought his perspective to the Dodge Main wildcat:

> Shortly after Gen entered Dodge Main, the situation jumped off the map. They had the wildcat strike and DRUM was formed in 1968. Seven years before we were involved in our study dealing with the Black vanguard. When DRUM happened, we thought the heavens had opened. We weren't looking at where technology was because it hadn't begun to affect the workers at the point of production. The struggle was a real fight for reform. We were in it. (John Williams 2017)

BUILDING OUR BASE—NEWSLETTERS AND FLYERS

Organizing in a plant with ten thousand workers presented the leadership with communication challenges, especially at a time before social media. In those days the printed word, in flyers and newsletters, was the tool we used. When the company retaliated against the workers for leafleting, the workers turned to an emerging partner—mainly high school students—who stepped up as the leafleters.

Gen discussed their methods:

> We began to build our base by putting out flyers and newsletters. Dodge Main was so big, ten thousand people, that people on one end of the plant didn't know what was going on at the other end. We needed a newsletter. We did one and put it out once a week.
>
> The first day we passed out newsletters, the security guards took pictures of the workers and used them for discipline. The high school kids like Darryl said, "We'll pass out leaflets for you. They can't fire me because it'll be another ten years before I'm old enough to have a damn job!" The kids became the troops, passing out flyers and newsletters.
>
> After about nine weeks of putting out leaflets, workers said, "Y'all talking shit about what you're gonna do. It's time to do something." We didn't wanna strike right away. We had a series of things we were gonna do called "testing the strength." (G. Baker 2016)

Darryl shared how he became involved with DRUM and joined the LRBW journey:

> In Detroit and the factory system—everyone was connected through a network of working and living. My dad was an electrician at the famous Ford Rouge local 600. Gen knew my parents and my dad's brother, Leroy Mitchell, who ran on the Michigan Freedom Now party ballot. Our paths crossed in 1968 when I went over to League headquarters at 179 Courtland and the rest is history.
>
> We studied Marxism and the science of society in a way no other generation or section of the revolutionary movement had. It was in more places than Detroit, but it happened in a concentrated way in Detroit.
>
> In the late 1960s the plants needed huge amounts of labor, so they hired young men. I started at Chevrolet Gear and Axle local 235 at sixteen. I ended up at Chrysler Mound Road Engine at nineteen. Thirty years later in October 2001, at forty-nine, I retired. My time and my cause during those years was the League. (D. Mitchell 2017)

Mike spoke to the critical period of the formation of DRUM leading into the LRBW. Ron March, who worked with Gen, joined the ancestors on October 16, 2023.

> Gen and Ron March, an auto worker at Dodge Main and founding member of DRUM, were having discussions. I joined 'em, and we began publishing stuff Ron gave us. Gen and Ron got a group of people together. We got stories from all of them. We started the DRUM newsletter to address things in the plant. We distributed them at the plant gates and the police and guards didn't mess with us. Seldom would a Black worker turn down a leaflet or a DRUM newsletter. Students and people who worked at other places, like I did, did the distributions. Folks who could not be hurt on the job. So we had a degree of security. (Hamlin 2017)

Mike also talked about the importance of radical newspapers in organizing workers and students in the mid-sixties, the period of the rebellion, DRUM, and the LRBW.

> We started the *Inner-City Voice* before the 1967 rebellion. We published radical articles and wrote our own stories. John Watson and I did the paper. I did the first front page article about the farm workers in Monroe County, Michigan, living in near slavery conditions. We were laying the groundwork and John was learning how to do a newspaper. I was gathering money and getting a plan together. (Hamlin 2017)

Mike explained the importance of the *Inner-City Voice* (1970) and the political struggle to find publishers for it.

> The *Inner-City Voice* drew in high school students at Northern High, college students and others. People came to us because they saw strength. We were angry, we were daring, we were reasonable, and we were developing power. College kids came from University of Detroit and elsewhere. John Watson assumed if we got this launched it would take off. He said we'd get Gen and John Williams and Luke would come from Montreal.
>
> The *Inner-City Voice* was based on Lenin's *What Is to Be Done*. John Williams came up with the idea. When you start a newspaper, you draw people to you. And we did. We put out some really powerful stuff. Every time we published an edition, we'd have to find a new publisher because somebody—probably the FBI—would tell them not to do that anymore.
>
> The police came right up to me and Gen on the street and said we wanna talk to you guys. Gen taught me how to handle the police or the FBI if they came up

to you. And that happened several times on our way to work or the office. After the Eldon wildcat strike, which was after the Dodge Main wildcat, Ken Cockrel, a lawyer by then, advised Gen to leave town and he did. (Hamlin 2017)

THE WILDCAT STRIKE AT DODGE MAIN—CONGA DRUMS FOR THE WORKERS AND RIFLES FOR THE POLICE

Conditions and organizing opportunities varied across time and place. Gen described some of the specifics of plant life, paychecks, and bars and delis in close proximity to Dodge Main that informed our organizing:

> At Dodge Main, when you came out of the back of the plant, there were three bars, two delicatessens, and a motel. They set it up so you could lose every dime you made before you got a block away. They used to bring a Brink's truck out to the plant that had check cashing windows in it. On Thursdays on the afternoon shift when the young workers would come out for lunch, they'd have wives and girlfriends pulling up there trying to get the check before you got home with it. They'd give you some food to eat so you'd pass the check on and go back to work.
>
> We had about a hundred people that used to go behind the plant to the bars in the alley. They'd work eight hours and drink eight hours. That was good for us 'cause we had an automatic base. A hundred folks in that alley all the time that we could count on for whatever we wanted to do. Those were our troops. When we got ready to have rallies and meetings at the union local, we'd get our troops out of the alley. We'd march down to the local hall and put forth resolutions and things like that. (G. Baker 2016)

Leadership and organizing had to be agile and responsive to the demands of the base. They also had to use whatever tools were available culturally and practically. Gen explained the particular circumstances of the wildcat at Dodge Main, the creative use of existing forces and resources and of conga drums to call the workers to the plant gate.

> We weren't going to strike right away. But one of the guys got excited and, damnit, called for a strike the next morning. All the guys stormed out and we're sitting there saying, "Everybody's gone, we're gonna have to strike."
>
> We had a coffee shop we ran at night—the Ghetto Coffee Shop. Guys would be playing conga drums and drinking coffee all night. We got those guys, we had all the people around the *Inner-City Voice*. We drove out to the plant that morning. The main thing was we took the conga drum players with us to the plant.

> They set up at the plant gate and we started passing out flyers. With the drums kicking and everything, in a half hour we had about five thousand Black workers lined up on the streets. They refused to go into the plant.
>
> The company and the government had state troopers with high-powered rifles on top of the plant. The Hamtramck police and the Detroit police had us in a pincer movement, coming at us with double-edged axe handles. All our people were breaking off beer bottles and other bottles, trying to figure out a way to fight. We were able to quickly get our people in cars and take them down to Solidarity House, UAW headquarters. We had a picket there and one at Chrysler Headquarters.
>
> We were able to defuse that battle where we were gonna get slaughtered. But, at the same time, the Chrysler Corporation didn't know what to do with this strike. They declared it to be an "extralegal" strike instead of "illegal." They were scared. (G. Baker 2016)

Abdul Donald Roberts, who worked at Chrysler Detroit Forge, was called to the LRBW journey by the drumming of Iban, an LRBW cultural worker. Iban also worked at Frito-Lay.

> I was riding the bus and went right past Dodge Main. I was reading C. L. R. James's *Black Jacobins* and got to the part where they were drumming in the hills. As we pass Dodge Main, Aaron "Iban" Pitts is on the drums. I'm fucked up. "Wait a minute. I'm reading and then I hear drums. Hell no." I jumped off the bus and asked, "What's this about?" Iban said, "The wildcat strike and we're holding a meeting tomorrow. Come to the meeting." And I went. (Roberts in Chandler et al. 2017)

Gen and Chuck met at Dodge Main. Gracie talked about Chuck getting fired because of his participation in the Dodge Main wildcat.

> There are a bunch of different stories about why Charlie got fired. They claimed he struck a supervisor. He said somebody else actually did it. But we didn't have children. People thought it was him. So he said it was him and he got fired. (G. Wooten 2017)

Jerome commented, "So nobody else would get fired with kids, right?" (in G. Wooten 2017). Gracie continued,

> Right. I was at the wildcat—the conga drums in the background, everybody partying and a lot of festivity. Iban did a painting that was on the cover of *Black Scholar*, I think. The female standing next to Charlie was me, I'm famous. (G. Wooten 2017)

Workers' Struggles Breaking Out—In Come the Revolutionary Union Movements (RUMs)

The rapid spread of the struggle brought about new challenges for us. It stretched our capacity and resources. Gen spoke to developing RUMs across many plants:

> The workers started coming from everywhere after they heard about DRUM—from Eldon, from Ford Rouge. Everybody wanted a RUM in their plant. We told them, "We have paper and we have ink. We have type setting equipment and we got a mimeograph machine. We have some young kids that'll help you distribute. You write your own flyer, we'll help you print it and we'll let the kids help you pass it out." We could not handle all of these different organizations coming at us. (G. Baker 2016)

Jerome worked at Chrysler Detroit Forge and shared how he ended up with the LRBW. In retrospect, it began with his aha moment while serving in the military in Vietnam. He explained,

> I have to start with being in the military. I joined when I was seventeen and convinced my mother to sign for me. I said, "I feel like I'm getting dragged into something that I don't really wanna be into." She said, "Where are the papers?" and she signed them.
>
> I had no knowledge of Vietnam. The military was my way of escaping. I found out there was a war going on and then I get orders to go to Vietnam. I'm going, "Lord have mercy. What is Vietnam?" I talked to my fellow soldiers. "What the hell is going on in Vietnam?" "Hey, man, there's a war going on and your ass ain't coming back." That was basically the sentiment.
>
> Going to Vietnam was the turning point. The incident that turned my life around happened when I was on a detail going to the river to get water for the site. We found leaflets on the ground that said, "Black soldier, why is it that in Vietnam you march at the head of the line, and at home you're at the end of the line?"
>
> That leaflet touched me. I remembered my fellow soldiers said, "You're not coming back from Vietnam. Your ass is gonna die." I began to think, "Why am I here? How did I get here? Am I gonna get back?" That set me on the course that made me end up with the League. Once I got out of Vietnam in one piece and back to Detroit, I worked in the auto plant at Chrysler.
>
> One of the first things I did was say, "I've been in places and didn't know where I was or why I was there. I wanna know what my responsibilities are. Tell me what I'm supposed to do, and how I'm supposed to function." Basically, I asked for

the contract. I didn't know it was a contract, so I didn't ask in those words. The supervisor I was talking to was flabbergasted. He was like, "What? Who do you think you are?" Finally, he directed me to the union. I went to the union steward and got a copy of the contract. Word got around the plant that some young guy just got hired, and first thing he does is ask the supervisor for a contract. That was just unheard of. That set me up for my stay at Chrysler with workers around me and with management.

I went into the Detroit Forge plant in 1967. Dodge Main was already a hotbed. We heard about Dodge Main workers being organized and General Baker as one of the major players. In 1968, after the wildcat and after DRUM was established, we went to meet with Gen and figure out how to connect up.

Ronald Troutman worked for the food service company at the Detroit Forge plant that delivered food to the cafeterias in many plants. We talked and said, "How do we raise the money to support workers organizing in the auto industry?" We had this brilliant idea of taking over the cafeterias and having Blacks cater them. We went to Gen and other folks at Dodge Main. Abdul, Alonzo, and James Edwards were there. We told them this idea. They said, "Are you crazy?"

We said, "Don't you want to have financing for this process?" They said, "Yeah, but the same company runs the cafeteria in every shop. You can't just take over the cafeteria in Dodge Main or Detroit Forge." James Edwards was really critical. He said, "Jerome, what's gonna be y'alls first product?" I said, "Maybe sandwiches." And he said, "Were you thinking about making some black, red, and green sandwiches?"

We thought, from the outside, that DRUM was a nationalist organization. So pitching them a Black sort of franchise and whatever Blackness we could wrap the franchise in was a good idea. They didn't think about it like that. They said it wasn't a feasible idea. Yes, we need to finance it. But what we really think you should be doing is organizing in your plant. That was their instruction to us. We said, okay. That's how I hooked up with DRUM and then the League. (Scott 2017)

A Movement and an Organization

Class-conscious actors, such as Gen, made a careful assessment of objective forces and the subjective understanding of the base to analyze the difference between the spontaneous movement and the development of organizations that reflected the changing conditions. Gen explained,

There's a difference between a movement and an organization. A movement breaks out spontaneously, and that's what happened. Movements broke out at all the factories and other workplaces like the *Detroit News*, a major Detroit newspaper.

Organizations are always running, trying to catch the movement and the motion. It's an important lesson that movements are spontaneous, they break out. Be prepared so when you see them, you can take advantage of them. That's the way history poses itself for us. (G. Baker 2016)

CHAPTER 6

The League Days, 1968 to 1971

> After the correct political line has been laid down, organizational work decides everything, including the fate of the political line itself, its success or failure.
> —Joseph Stalin, *Problems of Organizational Leadership* (1934)

The conditions that gave rise to the 1967 Detroit Rebellion set the basis for workers to start forming DRUM and RUMs in 1968 throughout auto and related industries. The LRBW itself was formed in 1969 out of this motion. In this chapter we consider the critical tactic of wildcat strikes and movement lawyers, the essential task of resourcing the movement and LRBW propaganda, and the political question raised by the Panthers coming to town.

We begin with Gen's words:

> The League of Revolutionary Black Workers originally came out of the consolidation of organizations such as DRUM and ELRUM (Eldon Avenue Gear and Axle Revolutionary Union Movement), both at Chrysler Corporation, FRUM (Ford Revolutionary Union Movement) that comes out of the Ford Rouge Complex, and UPRUM (United Parcel Revolutionary Union Movement). DRUM was the beginning of the League. (G. Baker 2016)

John Williams summed up the early years, the transition into the LRBW, and the relations among the Executive Board in the making:

> There was Luke Tripp, me, Gen, and Ken Cockrel when we started. Ken was a student at Wayne [at the time]. He was attracted to what we were doing, but didn't get involved until later. Mike and Ken worked at the *Detroit News*. John Watson was there too. When Ken came in he brought Mike and Watson. I may have been

the only one who had worked in the plants—at Jefferson. Mike had worked in the warehouse. Watson had done a lot with the *Vanguard* newspaper. Ken, [later] as a lawyer, was assisting Black workers. All these things were important.

We became the Executive Board because the workers saw us through Gen and Chuck Wooten. They respected us, but it was contingent on Gen's respect for us. It also had to do with the workers seeing us supporting, picketing, getting people out, getting the students to distribute stuff, and getting buses and resources. I worked with the International Black Appeal and set up schools. Ken didn't do any picketing. Watson did limited stuff. But the rest of us were out there. Workers saw that, but they saw us differently.

From an educational standpoint, we were not smarter, but we were exposed to a different type of thinking. We were beyond the workers at that point in terms of understanding the vanguard. I don't care how high your education, you always remember where you came from.

So, when it was proposed that we become the Executive Board, the workers approved it. It wasn't an election. If Gen had not supported it, it would not have gone that way. Gen was the key to why we ended up on the Executive Board. (John Williams 2017)

This was the solidification of LRBW leadership. John, Gen, Luke, Ken, Mike, Chuck, and John Watson had been in long-standing relationships and working together in various struggles for six to seven years, culminating in serving on the LRBW Executive Board. The workers knew firsthand and suffered racial discrimination in the plants, in the UAW, and in the larger society. They recognized that they were in a protracted fight against the historic reality of white supremacy and class exploitation in America. In taking the civil rights and Black liberation struggle to the point of production, the workers who formed the LRBW were intentional in their struggle for both racial justice and economic equality.

Wildcat Strikes—a Critical Tactic

The story of the LRBW opened with wildcat strikes and was continuously energized by wildcats. The Dodge Main wildcat in 1968 gave rise to DRUM and to other RUMs and was consolidated into the LRBW. The LRBW understood the point of production as the strategic center of working-class struggle during the period of large-scale industrial labor—they sought to disrupt capitalist production, circulation, and accumulation. During that period and thereafter, the wildcat strike was the primary tactic used by the workers because of their unpredictability and illegality under the contract. Legal defense for the wildcatters was thus necessary for the ongoing struggle.

Mitch, who worked at several plants over the years, reflected on the LRBW struggle:

> The League was built on the backs of the workers at Dodge Main and Eldon Avenue Assembly. Many of them carried the banner of the League, of the liberation struggle to the point of production. And many lost their jobs. These are the heroes, these are the great people in my eyes. (W. Mitchell 2017)

Mitch spoke to his experience inside the Dodge Main wildcat strike:

> The League hadn't come about yet. DRUM transitioned into the League. Gen had gotten fired in a wildcat strike. I think seven people who were involved in the strike were disciplined—five whites and two Blacks. The five whites got their jobs back, the two Blacks didn't—Gen and me. We started to publish a weekly newsletter under the title *DRUM*. We printed it, and eventually our organization was built around that newsletter. It was a tremendous success. Workers from other plants saw the literature and came by the office and wanted to be involved. Eventually that grew into the League. (W. Mitchell 2017)

Mitch shared his experience in another wildcat and the feeling of working-class unity and power:

> One night I was involved in another wildcat strike. The shop steward was off. Our relief man took over as an alternate steward. They tried to speed up operations while the real steward wasn't there. Jim, the alternate, wasn't going for it, so they carried him off to the office. Me and a few other guys huddled. We said, "If they suspend Jim, we're walking out." I said, "Sounds good to me, because I've been waiting for this." An hour and a half or so later, Jim comes walking down the aisle with the security guard. He had been suspended. I had the job of setting the frame on the pedal. I cut the line off, took my apron off, and bam, "Let's go." Me and about seven or eight other guys headed toward the door. When we got to the door and looked back, ain't nobody behind us. This is the death knell. If you wildcat and don't stop at nothing, you're through. You just walked off your job. We got outside and it was just us. We stayed out there about twenty or thirty minutes, and the whole plant came out. It was one of the greatest feelings I ever had. The people who were afraid to walk out just backed away from their jobs and wouldn't work. We were successful to that degree.
>
> What a wildcat does in most cases is shift the struggle to whoever the company disciplines—getting their jobs back, if they're getting time off, whatever. I got time off. One person got fired. In his fear, trying to protect himself, he went and punched the clock like it was gonna make a difference. He got fired and they couldn't do nothing about it because he had punched out. (W. Mitchell 2017)

Jerome, who was part of FORUM (Forge Revolutionary Union Movement), was fired from the Chrysler Detroit Forge plant as a result of the 1973 wildcat. He reflected on wildcats, union collaboration, and lessons learned during the LRBW days for later wildcats and the struggle for working-class power:

> The 1973 strike was after the League split. But there was a wildcat strike at Detroit Forge in 1970 that we were involved in, just before the split. In that wildcat, it was all Black workers who walked out. None of the white workers or skilled trades workers joined in. The strike lasted a couple of hours, several people got fired, and nothing came of it. The 1970 wildcat influenced our thinking. If we were to wildcat again, we had to figure out a better way. We began to do serious work in the shops, trying to build relationships with white workers and skilled trades people. We needed a broader base to have a successful action.
>
> When the 1973 wildcat strike came, we shut down the entire plant and the entire corporation. Leading up to that strike we had shift meetings after each shift with all the employees that came. The night before the strike started, everybody said, "We want to strike." I tried to get them not to strike. "I've been through a wildcat before, it's not a pleasant thing. And we don't wanna do this unless we're really gonna do it. Otherwise, it's just gonna get some people fired and everything will go on like it is."
>
> People said, "We're ready." We were supposed to start the wildcat on the midnight shift. We set up the picket line at ten P.M. and the strike was on. No one went into the plant that midnight shift, not the skilled trades people, not any of the other rank-and-file people. (Scott 2017)

HEALTH AND SAFETY ISSUES

Below, Jerome and Russell Jackson, who also worked at Chrysler Detroit Forge, describe the horrific health and safety conditions that were part of the cause of the strike. Jerome described the dangerous health and safety conditions all workers experienced and how they fed into the workers' support for the wildcat strike.

> The wildcat was based on health and safety issues in the plant. This is critical because health and safety issues affected everybody whether you were a skilled tradesman, worked on the line, or worked in the hammer shop. Health and safety issues were centered mainly on cranes above our heads that carried material—the load—from one part of the floor to another. The buildings were old and had dead spots in the tracks for the cranes. If the crane hit a dead spot "just right," the load would drop. Nobody had control over it, not even the crane operator.
>
> This didn't happen a lot. But it happened a few days before the wildcat. The guy who was guiding the crane with the load—his fingers got caught in the load

when it dropped and yanked his fingers off from his hands. That was the buildup. If you were a white worker or a Black worker, you were subject to the same conditions. That was the reason the 1973 wildcat strike was so successful in getting people across the plant to participate. (Scott 2017)

Russell described the horrendous safety conditions that moved white workers to support the wildcat:

> So many people hurt and the conditions were so horrendous, oil on the floor. You had to see it to believe it. We went to the union meetings, and Jerome tried to convince 'em that we ain't gotta take this. Jerome never made statements like "Mother fucker, blah, blah." He was always diplomatic, intelligent. They didn't know he was my mentor, they saw me as independent. I got up there and said the exact same thing. They'd say we know this is a good kid, the work he does. Even the white Klansman said he's one of us. We were convincing them we gotta strike. Some people said no wildcat. We said we gotta do it.
>
> We took that strike vote, and they said shut it down. Chrysler only had two forging plants in the world. We shut the mother down. From there, it was a political battle. I hate we were young and inexperienced—I was twenty-three—because we could've done a lot more.
>
> We were strong. This wasn't a Black strike, wasn't a white strike, it was a strike of the workers. To see the whites, especially some of the white Klansmen, I'm in arms with. We were talking and the truck with scabs, strikebreakers, was coming through. We said "don't." The scabs turned the truck around and didn't come through. The solidarity was unbelievable. They sent the police in, but they couldn't break the strike. And Doug Fraser, president of the UAW, got on television and said the striking workers are heroes.
>
> These dirty bastards. At the forging plant there were so many workers crippled and hurt. When we did the wildcat, we had to go to court. We had two and a half rows of people with fingers cut off, broken bones in slings. We were white, Black, Mexican, everybody. The judge said I know what the law is. She was not recognizing any of these injuries as reflecting the conditions of the factory. I wanted to tell her if I never wanted to be a revolutionary in my life, you just did it! That did more to make me a revolutionary than a lot of other stuff. (Jackson in Chandler et al. 2017)

Jerome added,

> We shut the Chrysler Corporation down for a week. There was only one other plant in the world that made the internal engine parts that we made—the crankshafts, the caps and pistons, all the internal engine parts. That was a forging plant

in South Africa, and they couldn't keep up. We ended up shutting down the production lines throughout the Chrysler Corporation for a week. (Scott 2017)

THE INTERNATIONAL UNION ATTACKED THE WORKERS AND BROKE THE STRIKE

Jerome explained the class collaboration of the UAW in breaking the wildcat.

> The strike got broken because the international union broke it. There used to be the flying squadron—a group of union organizers who went from strike to strike to support the striking workers and drum up community support. This time the union called in the flying squadron to break our strike. The president of the UAW, Douglas Fraser, came to the picket line to lead the charge. He told the flying squadron to break down the picket line and break the strike—that's how the strike got broken.
>
> Fifteen of us got fired as a result of the wildcat. Seven were white and eight were Black; and five of the seven white workers were from Appalachia. Eight were skilled trades people and seven were production line workers. We were reflective of the workforce at that time in terms of race and skills. The wildcat terrified the UAW and Chrysler. Chrysler identified who they thought was the leadership of the strike and fired us. The UAW and Chrysler decided early on the three people they did not want to go back to work. It was me, a comrade named Carl Williams, and Tom Stapansky, a white guy who was a skilled trade worker. "These are the three people we do not want back in that plant."
>
> But one of the guys who got fired with us—Earl—was in the process of buying a bar across the street from our plant, at the corner of Van Dyke and Lynch Road. Six plants were in that block. Everybody from all six plants came to that bar for lunch, or for drinks after work, or before work. Earl hired the three of us who were fired permanently as bartenders. I swear, that was the best job I ever had in my life as far as organizing is concerned. All I had to do was go to work. All the people I knew or people who had heard about the strike and wanted to sit down and talk came to the bar. It was the perfect organizing spot. Unfortunately, we lost that organizing spot because Earl, the owner, got killed in a bar robbery and the bar shut down. But it was a great job while it lasted.
>
> We found out that in 1968, '69, and '70 there were no Black folks in the UAW hierarchy and hardly any Black committeemen or stewards on the shop floor. The majority of the workforce, particularly at Chrysler, was Black because the plants were in the inner city. You've got majority-Black plants and the union representatives—the stewards and committeemen you have to bring your grievances to—were all white.

> We did know that every chance the union got to block the work we were doing as part of the RUMs in any of the plants, they always sided with the company.
>
> We did research to find out the union's motivations and the company's connections with the UAW. We learned that the union and the company were codependent and totally intertwined. The UAW owned stock in the companies, and sometime in the 1970s the money the union took in from dues was outflanked by the money they took in from their investments in the company.
>
> We determined early on that our battle was not just with the company, but more so with the UAW because the union was supposed to represent us and all the workers.
>
> The UAW put out the notion that the League represented dual unionism. It is a "sin" to have more than one union in a workplace because this means the company can split the workers by playing one union against the other. The League never proclaimed, or even moved in the direction of trying to be a union. We were what our name said—a revolutionary union movement. We wanted the union to be more responsive to the workers. But they labeled us, from the UAW perspective, as dual unionism and did everything they could to stop the process. (Scott 2017)

As the auto industry restructured in relation to automation and globalization—from the 1970s through the 1990s—UAW leadership increasingly collaborated with the corporations, and the wildcat strike began to diminish as an effective tactic for working-class struggle. The LRBW as an organizational form was short-lived and represented a very particular moment in the history of class struggle—of class, race, labor, unions, and capital—in U.S. auto and related industries. LRBW comrades embodied class consciousness and embraced study and struggle to stay the course into the current moment.

Movement Lawyers in Defense of the Working Class

Ron Glotta, a movement labor lawyer, moved to Detroit in 1968, just after the Dodge Main wildcat. He cofounded a labor law firm that handled 90 percent of the workers' comp cases and many of the wildcat strike cases. He described his political journey and being a radical movement lawyer defending workers in and around the LRBW:

> I went to work in Muskegon, Michigan, for a labor law firm, mostly workers' comp lawyers. Ben Marcus looked like an old labor organizer and educated me on the labor movement and what you need to do. Later Harry Filo came up to Muskegon from Detroit. (Glotta 2017)

Ron continued by describing his Detroit days—becoming politicized, being a lawyer for the wildcat strikers, and meeting Gen:

> I got to Detroit in 1968 and got connected with the League. It was almost immediate with Ken Cockrel, because people came into the law office and I was doing the worker's comp. When Harry moved to Detroit we set up the law firm of Filo, Mackie, Moore, Pitts, Glotta, Cockrel and Robb. Mike Edelman came in and he and I did the labor work and started representing all the wildcat strikers. Mike and I went out on our own after Dodge Main in April of 1968.
>
> I'm educating myself in the process. In the first Eldon strike, I think, Mike and I went down to the court. We got a call and the judge wanted to know who we represented. We said, "We represent John Doe and Richard Roe." The UAW was willing to have an injunction against the Eldon strike. We didn't want an injunction so we demanded the right for a hearing and all the things you do in wildcat strikes.
>
> That's how I met Gen and the League, and became involved with the legal aspect of the League on a fairly continuous basis. We started representing all of the wildcatters because we couldn't represent any union locals. I remember when Jordan Sims became UAW president of the Eldon local. George Morales [a representative of the international UAW] went to him and to every local in his district and said, "If you send one case to the Glotta firm we'll put you under trusteeship [international UAW takes control of UAW local]." (Glotta 2017)

Ron and John Williams commented on the events around Ken's advice to Gen and Gen's leaving town after the Dodge Main wildcat. Ron shared,

> One of the mistakes was when Ken told Gen he should leave town, which wasn't necessary. He could very well have fought all that. Once Mike Edelman and I got involved, we were able to neutralize some of that crazy stuff. (Glotta 2017)

John spoke to Ken's role as a lawyer, his advice to Gen to leave town, and the call to "off Gen":

> Ken was there with legal support. I remember when they were gonna try to "off Gen." Gen never wanted to talk about it. But he got a call. It was somebody in the union higher up. The police would've been in on it, but the union initiated it. That was the point. Ken told Gen to leave town. Gen left and went to Cleveland for a long time. (John Williams 2017)

Ron shared other labor issues he and Mike Edelman handled for the LRBW and the different views on the role of lawyers in labor organizing and wildcats:

We went down to Birmingham, Alabama, to help organize RUMs and to explain how you protect yourself legally as well as how you organize.

That was a big debate in the legal community between two factions. One said you're a lawyer, not a revolutionary. You couldn't be a good lawyer and be a revolutionary, so be a lawyer. My firm didn't agree and we were in debates about that. So, we did a lot of the wildcat work. (Glotta 2017)

One of the historic cases that Ron won was the worker's comp case for James Johnson. Mitch set up the situation and recited from memory the poem "James Johnson Needed a Thompson."

James Johnson was a worker at the Eldon Avenue Gear and Axle plant. He shot three people. Killed them. Detroit was split on how they felt about it—whether these guys deserved to die or not. It was real controversial.

Gen had an old friend, George Jones, who was good at poetry. Gen asked George to write a poem and this is what George came up with. It was scary for some of us because it made no excuses, no pardons, no forgive me. It was, "James Johnson Needed a Thompson." He just ran out of bullets.

This was a different kind of radical approach. A lot of people said, "He should've done it but killed more." Gen, in his genius, took the poem, and we went to the courthouse during the trial to pass out leaflets every day. "James Johnson needed a Thompson, he didn't kill them for nothing, yo." That was Gen. I just wanted to lay that out before I start, but this is the poem from my memory.

> It was the second shift on that hot July, moods would drift and tension was high. You could almost feel the clang of steel, you had to choke on factory smoke. James Johnson came to work. Never duty, known to shirk. He came undaunted to do his job, and was confronted by a jive-ass slob. He came to do for what he was hired, and for being Black this man was fired. He was thrown from the plant like a human ant, he was tired, abused, and hurt. For three long years, he had been Chrysler used and treated worse than dirt. So he walked away that summer day, his fury was great indeed. For his home was near, his duty clear, at home he went with speed. He got his carbine, this man so lean, and returned to get his due. For these are the times that freedom chimes, and days of slavery through. He entered the gate, tall and straight, and nary an eye did turn. For the clock of fate was ticking late, for three he had to burn.
>
> Foreman Jones was forty-four, and the first to die on Eldon's floor. Gary Hinz was thirty-two, he had to die for Chrysler too. Joe Kowalski is in his grave, 'cause Jim Rhoades was a well-paid slave. All three men are in the ground 'cause coward Rolls could not be found. And just like snakes

> always sliding, the union long had left for hiding. The air was filled with deathly odors as men transformed to human motors. Through with slavery and breaking his back, he walked into the security shack. The squad car wail said County Jail, and that's where he was rolled. And there isn't a trace of human grace in his den of savage and bold. Brother James exposed his shames for all the sin in here. For the true are strong, would fight a wrong, and only the false should fear. There are those at hand throughout this land, who work and sweat and cry, while the races band against commands, they smirk unwet and dry. But there's a coming tide of Johnson pride, and this is very plain. Men rise to bravery in times of slavery, and damned to woe and pain. Men give their breath and challenge death, to see their people gain. Brother James has given his soul. He even fights from a prison hole. And though it may seem that his breed are few, many will do what they have to do. Forever workers are under attack, there will be millions of Johnsons, back to back. James Johnson needed a Thompson. (W. Mitchell 2017)

Chuck Wooten, a founding member of the LRBW and an Executive Board member, affirmed the horrific working conditions at Eldon where James Johnson worked.

> Working conditions are like being in a cesspool. Workers work in grease and oil which are very hazardous. Some slip, fall, and break their arms. Some brothers work in poor ventilation and suffer from silicosis. On several occasions management would not address these conditions. The union walks through the poor safety conditions, through the water, the polluted air and they do not deal with it. Workers cannot understand why the union does not address these problems. It seems this even led up to the James Johnson thing. The brother got very disturbed with the working conditions. I saw that the union and management was working against the brother, along with all the outside realities he had to face and couldn't deal with. (C. Wooten n.d.)

Then, Ron got James Johnson worker's comp. Ron addressed the complexity of political positions and polarization up and down the line, from the shop floor to the union and even among politicians:

> An important lesson I learned is that revolution is a process where every institution turns on itself. I learned that when we were organizing at the plant level. We always believed our workers were on our side. We found very quickly that there were people in the high parts of the UAW on our side. There were people in the political system who were on our side. There were guys in the plant who were just assholes and absolutely opposed to us.

Revolution is not simply a process of people coming up against the system. That's not how it works. Historically there was a split within the United Mine Workers. Same is true of the AFL-CIO. Splits occur all the way up and down the line. We have to take that lesson into account. And hopefully give it to the younger generation, if they wanna hear. (Glotta 2017)

Legal work defending workers—workers' comp, wildcat strikers—was a critical component of organizing in the LRBW. Like wildcats, other strikes and many protests are considered "illegal." Then and now, the legal defense of all forms of working-class struggle is essential for the revolutionary process to move forward.

Resourcing the Movement—a Political Task

Fundraising to support organizing at the point of production, cultural work and publication of various newspapers, and Black Star Publishing began early on and continued through the LRBW years. During this period five different newspapers were founded (the *Crusader*, the *Razor* for students, the *Vanguard* for workers, and the *Inner-City Voice* as a community paper) or taken over (*The South End* on Wayne's campus). We had to have vehicles that we control to report our news. It was essential to get out to the community and the world the independent voice of Black workers in Detroit.

John Williams, Mike Hamlin, Gen Baker, Ken Cockrel, John Watson, and the emerging collective were busy appropriating financial and other resources for the growing movement—the Wayne State student paper, vans from the archdiocese school system, and reparations from faith institutions using the *Black Manifesto*.

John Williams explained how he, Ken, Gen, and Mike commandeered resources for Black workers' struggle in the plants:

> We had a community agency called North Woodward Interfaith—me, Don Bagley, and Ken. We worked with youth and young people in the plants. Glanton Dowdell, the artist who painted the Detroit Shrine of the Black Madonna and was forced into exile because of his leadership in the Kercheval incident, came by. He had a retreat up North and we sent youth up there. We also had vans we used to take workers to work.
>
> We were trying to raise resources for the *Vanguard* newspaper. So, I got a job running a school in the archdiocese. Gen and Mike drove the bus, and Luke was

a teacher. We used the school for meetings and we used the two buses to pick up the workers when we had demonstrations at the plant.

We met quarterly with Archbishop Dearden and he asked, "Why are our buses out at the plant?" The corporation who owned the plant called the school and they forced us to stop using the buses. Gen said, "Don't worry about it. Take the buses." I said, "No, we don't want you to lose your job." We decided we wouldn't take the buses anymore. When I got a job teaching at Wayne State, we brought the students over to our office on Linwood to meet up with us.

But the point was we wanted to use the resources for the struggle. That's why we set up the International Black Appeal, in opposition to the United Way, to raise funds to help workers. (John Williams 2017)

Mike elaborated on initiatives to raise funds from faith institutions:

James Forman, from SNCC, had come through a conference of the Interfaith Organization for Black Development. It was a Black pastors' organization, mainly from Protestant denominations. I took a contingent to the conference. There was an analysis that denounced the role of the Christian churches and Jewish synagogues in the exploitation and oppression of slaves and their profits reaped from slave labor.

The *Black Manifesto* demanded reparations and church men were backing it. The idea was to disrupt church services across the country in 1969 and 1970. This was interesting because it was the first motion toward reparations. (Hamlin 2017)

The *Black Manifesto* (1969) and the National Black Economic Development Conference, in the first call for compensation for centuries of slavery and Jim Crow rule, demanded $500 million in reparations. The *Black Manifesto* begins this way:

We the black people assembled in Detroit, Michigan for the National Black Economic Development Conference are fully aware that we have been forced to come together because racist white America has exploited our resources, our minds, our bodies, our labor. For centuries we have been forced to live as colonized people inside the United States, victimized by the most vicious, racist system in the world. We have helped to build the most industrial country in the world.

We are therefore demanding of the white Christian churches and Jewish synagogues which are part and parcel of the system of capitalism, that they begin to pay reparations to black people in this country. We are demanding $500,000,000 from the Christian white churches and the Jewish synagogues. This total comes to 15 dollars per nigger. This is a low estimate for we main-

> tain there are probably more than 30,000,000 black people in this country. $15 a nigger is not a large sum of money and we know that the churches and synagogues have a tremendous wealth and its membership, white America, has profited and still exploits black people. We are also not unaware that the exploitation of colored peoples around the world is aided and abetted by the white Christian churches and synagogues. This demand for $500,000,000 is not an idle resolution or empty words. Fifteen dollars for every black brother and sister in the United States is only a beginning of the reparations due us as people who have been exploited and degraded, brutalized, killed and persecuted. Underneath all of this exploitation, the racism of this country has produced a psychological effect upon us that we are beginning to shake off. We are no longer afraid to demand our full rights as a people in this decadent society. (Black National Economic Conference 1969)

Mike continued,

> The National Black Economic Development Conference couldn't be held together. Too many egos, agents, and all kind of things, but it was a legitimate concept. We had a convention in Cincinnati, presented the organizational concept, and people joined. Forman went to New York and occupied Riverside Church.
>
> We did it here. John Williams and I disrupted services at Christ Church Cranbrook, a Presbyterian Church in Detroit, and took it over. I had to quit my job at the *Detroit News* before getting fired because I sat in at the Episcopal Bishop's office on a sick day, and the television camera took a picture of me there through the glass door. A friend called me and said, "Mike, you better get in here tomorrow morning and resign before they fire you 'cause they got you." I called in and resigned. That was the end of my job. We did get $250,000 from the Episcopal Church, but that was all.
>
> With the *Black Manifesto*, we eventually got printing presses and started Black Star Publishing. We attracted a lot of women. Helen Jones ran our printing operation. We grew rapidly. (Hamlin 2017)

Edna Watson summed it up this way:

> The League grew out of the funding that came from the National Black Economic Development Conference. It was a national coming together of leftists interested in using economic development to raise money for their endeavors and to legitimize the left. The left had been decimated in the media and everywhere under the McCarran Act, the McClellan Committee, and McCarthy and the House Un-American Activities Committee (HUAC).

> In the *Black Manifesto* we demanded maybe $500 million. The money started trickling in. Vince Harding from Interreligious Foundation for Community Organization (founded in 1967) in New York gave us one check. We got a check for a hundred grand. You're looking at it and wow! It wasn't easy to get the money that had been gained over a lot of blood, sweat and tears. We demanded funding for a Black publishing house, a Black productions house, and several other things. Black Star Publishing was the culmination. We didn't have to go to Chicago to print the *Inner-City Voice*. Prior to that, we used *The South End* as our own political organizing tool.
>
> When they shot up the New Bethel Church, John Watson and others got Judge Crockett out of bed so he could free those people. We used a sixteen-page daily tabloid insert in *The South End* to do community leafleting. We were actually publishing radical rags at public expense. We had people on the committee and people on the paper who were getting salaries. Nick McBecky, Mike Hamlin, a few others were like full salary and John Watson had a salary. They had tuition reimbursement from Wayne State. That was not just a good hustle, it was a good strategic move. (E. Watson 2017)

Gracie Wooten was an important part of the cultural work and publishing. She explained,

> After Charlie got fired from Dodge Main, I did typing—the role of women at the time. I typed for *The South End* and the *Inner-City Voice*.
>
> We published the *Inner-City Voice*. Gen's sister did most of the type setting, layout and copy work. I helped with the layout and they taught me how to make negatives and work in the dark room. Charlie and Gen, or maybe Mitch, took the paper to Chicago to be printed by the National of Islam.
>
> I worked at Black Star when it opened and was paid a salary. We printed James Forman's book, *The Making of a Black Revolutionary*. We tried to have a separate printing business. Carl Smith ran the day-to-day operations and built relationships, including with the *Michigan Chronicle*, a large Black publication in Detroit still in production. A lot of businesses and printing shops gave us work. (G. Wooten 2017)

Gracie continued,

> [We] were thinking about DRUM and how to print and get the independent voice of the worker into the community. The *Inner-City Voice* was widely distributed and read—a real alternative. People in Detroit read it and people around the world read it—it was international.
>
> Being self-sufficient in terms of the literature and running the whole oper-

ation. We did day-to-day things to generate money—flyers, leaflets, business cards for the community—trying to make money for the business and become self-supporting. All towards the greater goal of having our own printing operation and having our voice. (G. Wooten 2017)

Charles Simmons reflected on the cultural work of the LRBW, its many facets, and his role as a "cultural ambassador." He lifted up the importance of cultural expression in protests and the labor movement—drumming, spoken word, and theater—and his work with Watson to get *Finally Got the News* out to audiences. *Finally Got the News* was a film about Black workers and capitalism and, in particular, about the LRBW and the realities of work in the auto and steel plants and coal mines. Charles explained,

> I was fortunate to be an international correspondent for *Muhammad Speaks*, probably the major Black progressive voice in the community with an international presence. We were a force in the country. We had the *Inner-City Voice*, *The South End*, and people in the League and friends were involved in the Black Arts Movement. Young people played drums during protests. There was spoken word and theater around the rising labor movement.
>
> I was not a member of the Executive Board, though we were close. I came to Detroit for meetings and got stories for publication. When *Finally Got the News* came out, I helped John Watson navigate New York City to circulate the movie and get it viewed. That was quite an experience.
>
> As an employee of *Muhammad Speaks* [the newspaper of the Nation of Islam], I represented the League when traveling abroad. I went on assignments and met with groups. A group in Paris, organized by the brother of Frantz Fanon, was fighting for the rights of people from the West Indies and the Caribbean. I brought greetings and messages to freedom fighters in Algeria and met the wife of Frantz Fanon, the great author and one of the leaders of the Algerian revolution. I did an extended tour of Africa during that period, around 1970, and I did a Middle Eastern tour. I traveled with the Palestine Liberation Organization (PLO) and represented the League. I went on to Algeria and met with leaders of African liberation movements. They got to know something about what we were doing in Detroit. (Simmons 2017)

The power and voice of Black workers at the point of production reverberated throughout Detroit and the world through leaflets, newspapers, film, and LRBW comrades traveling abroad. Internationalism and making connections with workers and anticolonial struggles across the globe became very important.

LRBW Executive Board members, General "Gen" Baker and Mike Hamlin, at a protest in Detroit during League days. Courtesy League Collective.

The Panthers Come to Town—a Difference of Leadership in the Working-Class Struggle

Even before the Black Panther Party (Panthers) showed up in Detroit, LRBW members discussed the best way to deal with our different organizational positions on which section of the working class would lead—workers at the point of production or the lumpenproletariat. The LRBW's approach to that struggle was to join the Panthers rather than confrontation.

John Williams explained and shared stories about LRBW conversations with the Panthers.

> The Panthers were not in Detroit yet, but we knew they were coming. How could we turn the Panthers toward what we thought was the vanguard—the workers? Many of us—myself, Marian, Cass Smith, and Luke—got involved.
>
> We set up an office. DRUM and the Panthers didn't share the office, but DRUM came there and we brought the Panthers in to do the work we wanted them to do. They were involved in protests and passed out leaflets. That got back to Panthers' headquarters and to Fred Hampton. The Panthers wanted to know, "Why aren't you out in the streets with your berets and all that?" We said, "We're addressing the workers, as we explained."
>
> Almost simultaneously, Luke (Tripp 1969) put out the article, "D.R.U.M.— Vanguard of the Black Revolution." Huey Newton and the Panthers sent Fred Hampton and Mark Clark to Detroit to find out what was going on. We took

the bulk of the Panthers into DRUM and then the League. They couldn't really get into DRUM, an organization of auto workers, but they came into the League. That really upset things for a moment. The problem exhibited itself when we met with leaders like Eldridge and Kathleen Cleaver. They focused on the police and all they were gonna do was with police departments. Our thing was beyond that. (John Williams 2017)

John offered this account of the meeting in Ann Arbor and the deep contradiction in the politics of the Panthers and the LRBW. Participants in the meeting included both Panthers and members of the Weather Underground, an offshoot of Students for a Democratic Society (SDS).

> We went to Ann Arbor where Eldridge Cleaver was speaking. I was in the car with Kathleen Cleaver. Her position was, "All we have to do is off the pigs." This was ridiculous and nonsensical.
>
> We went into our meeting, and they were talking about putting bombs in wastepaper baskets in banks. I said, "How are people gonna see that connected to the world? What does that mean?" A woman sitting there said, "Who in the hell are these people?" It was Bernardine Dohrn. She's muttering this nonsense. And, tragic as it was, I knew Diana Oughton, a good woman, very informed. Two weeks later, Diana and two others were blown up in a townhouse explosion where they were building a nail bomb.
>
> The difference was in our perspectives. We were looking at workers as a vanguard, the Panthers' leadership was not. That's how it split and went down. It wasn't too cool for them because they had a guy here, George Sams. Sams had all kinds of tie-ups with the police department and was an informant. We scoped him out. He went up to Connecticut for the government and got two people killed there. You can see what happens when folks talk about "off the pigs" with no real base to do it.
>
> If you don't understand the level of the struggle, where it is, you do things that end up like what happened to them. They tried to move past the level where the struggle was. You can't take people beyond where their consciousness allows them to go. That's the essence of the thing with the Panthers. (John Williams in *Wayne State* 2017)

An excerpt from Luke's article in *The South End* exposed DRUM's sharp difference with the Panthers in terms of the vanguard of the Black revolution and revolution more generally.

> DRUM is the hope of the black worker and it loudly proclaims and realizes that only a struggle led by black workers can triumph over racism and exploitation....

> Why is it that DRUM has become famous all over the country? Because of all of the antiracist organizations, it is the most revolutionary, the most progressive, and the best fighter for liberation and social emancipation of black people. DRUM is revolutionary and progressive because both its membership and leadership and its program are revolutionary and progressive. Without this character it could never lead the black workers and win the praise of revolutionary people in this country as well as abroad. Both the UAW and Chrysler Corporation have attacked DRUM; they are racist and do not want to see black workers united. (Tripp 1969)

Luke added this lesson about the Panthers, organizations, and leadership:

> If you're building an organization, build from strength. If you get shaky people, you'll have a shaky organization. If you organize like the Panthers—building on the most backward elements—you're gonna have problems. People involved in criminal behavior, drugs, domestic affairs, chronic problems. They will consume all your energy. You won't be able to address the problems of the people and you'll become weaker. (Tripp 2017)

Mike spoke to the loose security and danger of infiltration in the Panthers and many organizations at the time:

> The Panthers' documentary film shows how loose the Panthers were in terms of infiltration. It was massive. We knew it was happening to us, but we couldn't identify who it was.
>
> Our organizations were thoroughly infiltrated. The Panthers showed one of the government's main ploys. They'd go to somebody in prison and say, "If you go and join this group and keep us up on what's happening, we'll cut you lose."
>
> The question becomes, "How do you keep your security and integrity?" Years later there've been a few people who have been talking out of school. We, in the League, had secrets, we had lots of secrets. (Hamlin 2017)

Darryl offered this analysis of the LRBW and the Panthers:

> League history is just starting to come out. There is a powerful tendency to glorify non-working-class groups like the Panthers. I always found the Panthers' movement amusing and interesting—their love affair with the gun. The Panthers didn't start out like that, they got diverted. It was obvious to us that the Panthers were under attack by political forces. Their politics changed. The League didn't reject guns but we didn't have a love affair with things. We were dealing with a social movement and we knew that our role at one level or an-

other was as propagandists on the side of the proletariat. We always understood that. (D. Mitchell 2017)

Jerome described the LRBW and Panthers political differences within the historical context of Detroit and working-class power:

> About the Panthers, John Williams already told that story. It was really funny. The struggle between the League and the Panthers stemmed from the different theoretical views that the two organizations took. The Panthers took the view that the lumpenproletariat was the vanguard of the revolutionary process and was the section of society that should be concentrated on. The League, of course, took the position that workers were the most important point of concentration in the revolutionary process and the struggle was about that.
>
> The Panthers came to Detroit to meet with the League—partly in response to Luke's article, "D.R.U.M.—Vanguard of the Black Revolution" as opposed to "Panthers: Lumpenproletariat Vanguard of the Black Revolution." What the article really said was "the lumpenproletariat, there's no vanguard here." Luke did an analysis of the lumpenproletariat versus the workers. The Panthers came to Detroit to talk to us about this "slander." After that meeting we decided that our best defense against the Panthers was to start a Panther chapter in Detroit and be a part of the chapter so we could influence what they were doing.
>
> That's what happened and it worked. A Panther chapter got started and people from the League who were part of starting the chapter ended up being part of the leadership. The chapter and the League never had any beef once that took place. (Scott 2017)

For the Panthers, the strategic path was direct confrontation with the police and mobilization of the lumpenproletariat. At this time working-class forces were not powerful enough to directly confront state power.

For the LRBW, the strategic path was organizing workers at the point of production. This was a lesson learned during the Detroit Rebellion when the National Guard escorted auto workers to the factories through the police lines during curfew to ensure that production was not interrupted. The tactical success of wildcat strikes in the DRUM and LRBW days also reflected this reality. The industrial proletariat was still a source of huge profits for capitalists, and Detroit was an essential site of capitalist accumulation.

In the period of the LRBW journey from 1968 to 1971, the LRBW was becoming a comprehensive organization. This encompassed leadership and organizational forms at the point of production, in the community, and among high school students. It included political tactics and strategy and legal support, and resources for the struggle and for publications and propaganda to share the voice of Black workers nationally and internationally. This period also solidified our understanding that the workers at the point of production have to lead.

In the next chapter we explore more deeply the question of sexism in the LRBW and hear from LRBW women and students in the BSUF about their experience during LRBW days and after.

CHAPTER 7

League Women and Students—the Woman Question, the 1960s to 1971

> Before the League, the men used to say, "Make the dashiki, make the flags, cook the grits, and shut the fuck up." They'd say it in a joking way but it was serious.
>
> —Gracie Wooten (2017)

> When I went into the plant, it was a nightmare. League organizing prepared me. We got together as women and organized to get the respect we deserved.
>
> —Cassandra Ford (2017)

Sexism and gender oppression were pervasive in society and movement organizations of the sixties and seventies—and continue today. The LRBW was no exception. In interviewing former LRBW members and friends, we specifically asked about the role of women and how they were treated by the men of the LRBW. We have gathered the responses in this chapter. In terms of a timeline, the times and places we discuss span the early years before DRUM through the LRBW years and up to the present today.

The women of the LRBW stepped up to fight gender oppression in the plants, schools, and larger society as well as within the movement and the LRBW. They reflected on LRBW life and family life and the huge amount of work they did—especially in the production and distribution of LRBW materials—and yet their lack of leadership roles. They spoke to the sexism they experienced and how the sexual revolution of the times played out in the relations between LRBW women and men. They formed the Black Women's Committee for solidarity and support and multitasked their way through these complex realities. The young women and men of the LRBW came into the LRBW family as students in the BSUF. They carried their LRBW experience with them into the plants and throughout their lives. The LRBW men acknowledged the significant work women did and the sexism within the organization and society and offered their takeaways.

The Voice of League Women—Reflections on LRBW and Family Life

We share the stories, struggles, and victories of the LRBW women—wives and mothers, daughters, sisters, and workers. We begin with Ilene Baker and Ilene and Gen's daughters, Yvette and Kadesha. We hear from Valerie Baker, Gen's youngest sister, from Gracie Wooten, who was married to Chuck, and from Judy Williams, who was married for a while to John Williams. Then we offer reflections from the LRBW women on the incredible amount of LRBW work they did, especially running Black Star Publications and being part of the larger working-class struggle. Marian Kramer, Edna Watson, Maureen Taylor—who joined the LRBW journey after the split—and Leah Rogers add their recollections of women, work, and sexism in the LRBW. Marsha Music and Cass Bell Ford, who entered the LRBW family as students in the BSUF, also weigh in on women's work and sexism.

Ilene met Gen in 1967 after he went to Cuba. They were together at the time of the rebellion and the Dodge Main wildcat. Ilene recalled those early years, the danger and fear during the rebellion, Gen's arrest, and the intense activity in their home during the wildcat:

> I met Gen after he went to Cuba. Yvette was a baby and we stayed in an apartment building on Gladstone. Gen lived in the basement with John Watson. I went down to his apartment and listened to Malcolm X records, and that grew into a relationship. Things got more political when Gen, John Watson and Mike Hamlin started the *Inner-City Voice*. I helped print the paper on the old mimeograph machine at their office on Hamilton.
>
> When the rebellion happened, we were living down the street from where it began. We left, thinking it would be safer staying with my mother. I was pregnant with Kadesha. It was a scary moment because Gen was arrested. They put him on a bus with a gun to his head, drove him off, and I didn't see him for weeks. I wanted Gen back, but I understood things were going to happen.
>
> Snipers [police] were on the roof at the corner of Linwood—on top of my grandmother's building. She called to check on me and said we can't talk now, we're hiding under the table. It was a real occupying force. (I. Baker, K. Baker, and Y. Baker 2017)

Ilene described what it was like in their home during the wildcat at Dodge Main and her role in LRBW life:

> It was always busy. I cooked for people who came by and Gen was gone a lot. I can't remember whether Gen had lost his job or was about to lose his job, but we were always supportive. I was quiet and helping—in the background. We talked, and I understood and was comfortable with what was going on. (I. Baker, K. Baker, and Y. Baker 2017)

Gen was fired for his leadership role in the Dodge Main wildcat. After a time he assumed another name and got hired at Ford Rouge in Dearborn.

Ilene picked up:

> Gen had to change his name in order to work. He went back to work under an alias, Alexander Ware. (I. Baker, K. Baker, and Y. Baker 2017)

Their daughters Kadesha and Yvette added to the story:

> I remember mail came to the house for Alexander Ware. Many moons later I found out who he was. I didn't know then it was my dad. I used to think, Alexander Ware, guess he'll come and get his mail eventually. (I. Baker, K. Baker, and Y. Baker 2017)

Ilene continued,

> Gen got busted for taking a new name several years later. He made a legal case out of it. (I. Baker, K. Baker, and Y. Baker 2017)

Jerome explained,

> Under the rules of the contract, if you work for two years no matter how you got in there, too bad. Gen had worked over two years, they couldn't fire him and he won the case. Gen was able to give up his assumed identity as Alexander Ware and take back his real identity as General Baker. (I. Baker, K. Baker, and Y. Baker 2017)

Kadesha and Yvette shared life as younger children in the LRBW family—going to meetings and protests and living in a pivotal moment in history.

> During meetings the kids who were teenagers looked out for us. They were cool. What was happening was normal to us and was never hard on us. What were protests to the adults, were fun parades we were in. We got to hold signs, to chant, and to march—nothing like the parades other people went to. We lived normal kids' lives and enjoyed ourselves. We just happened to be enjoying ourselves as kids in a pivotal moment.

> My best friend Lisa lived across the street when we lived at 179 Courtland. I went over to her house all the time, but she never came to my house. I didn't know why. When we were older she said, "My mom said I can't come over because you have panthers in your garage." I'm like, there's no panthers in our garage. Later on I realized she thought we were part of the Black Panther Party. We were affected in childhood that way, but it was just way over our heads at the time. (I. Baker, K. Baker, and Y. Baker 2017)

In conversation with Jerome, Ilene shared memories of Jerome's and Theresa's daughter Yolanda when they all first met.

> When we lived on West Grand Boulevard I met your daughter, Yolanda. I thought she was the prettiest little girl I had ever seen until she started running around. That was when I met and got to know you, Jerome, and Theresa and a lot of folks. (I. Baker, K. Baker, and Y. Baker 2017)

Valerie Baker, Gen's youngest sister, shared her recollections of Gen and LRBW life growing up—the meetings, the FBI, and Gen's love for learning:

> I wasn't involved with the League, my interaction was through Gen. One of the League headquarters was at his house and when we visited there were always meetings. My older sister Jeanette, who passed away, was close to Gen and was the family intermediary. Gen stayed away from us because what he was involved in brought attention to our family.
>
> The FBI visited our house frequently. I didn't know they were the FBI, I just knew these white men in black suits were talking to my mom. One day Carolyn, our oldest sister, came home from school when they were there. There was a conversation and the FBI never came to the house again. But they interviewed our neighbors.
>
> I walked to school and had my own escort. I laughed about it later. The FBI would be at each end of the block because sometimes Gen would take me to school or pick me up. Our phones were tapped and we weren't sure what else was. So we didn't talk much about Gen on the phone or in the house.
>
> Gen studied and loved learning, even before the League. When he got fired and didn't have a job, he went to the Christian Science Reading Room to get a global view. The communist thing was touchy, and I only heard bits and pieces. Gen gravitated toward learning about what he was involved in and how to change things. When I was little I asked Gen, "You stay away so much, why are you doing what you're doing? Can't you come home?" Gen said, "You might not understand now, but what I'm doing will help change life for you and others." I was like, "Okay."

> I don't know what my life would have been if Gen wasn't my brother. I was exposed to what was going on in DRUM and the League. It was on the news and I got negative comments from some of my friends—like your brother is that crazy guy. I was, "No, he's not" and defended him. I'm proud of what Gen did. Everybody has a price. Gen's price was success in his struggle to correct things he saw that were wrong. (V. Baker 2017)

Gracie added to her family story with Chuck and their children. She spoke to the committed women of the LRBW who worked so their husbands could do the political work that had to be done.

> I have two children now, James and Melissa. My son, Charles, and my husband are deceased. We raised our family in Highland Park where I live. I worked as a math teacher in middle school and high school to help Chuck stay politically active. A lot of League women worked to allow our husbands to have freedom. Theresa, your spouse Jerome, worked so you had the freedom to do activism. (G. Wooten 2017)

Judy Williams, who was married to John Williams early on and is an educator, shared her LRBW experience:

> I was married to John Williams, one of the founding League members. Marian always teased that I was the first white member of the League. I was involved and supportive. John and others asked me to help produce League materials, and I type well so I did a lot of that.
>
> John and I had a daughter in common. We separated, but I still knew what was going on. I came back at the start of the next period, the transition to the Communist League. (Judy Williams 2017)

WOMEN'S STRUGGLE FOR EQUALITY AND REPRESENTATION—
DOING THE WORK AND FIGHTING SEXISM

Marian, a community organizer and force within the LRBW, spoke to the role of women in the LRBW and the Black Women's Committee.

> Women played a hell of a role in the League. Ilene and Gen were married at the time and Ilene was active. When the first strike happened at Dodge Main, one of the things was what was happening in the workers' homes. Gen asked if the women in the League, particularly Ilene, Gracie, and others, could form a Black Women's Committee to educate the wives of the men who were in the wildcats about why the men were so needed in the strike. The men would get jumped on

at home, rightfully so, because their wives didn't know why they weren't working. (Kramer 2017)

Marian also described the sexual abuse in the day and how the LRBW women organized to stop it:

> A lot of men at that time in the movement felt it was their privilege to hit on women. We got hit on a lot, and that still exists. And there was the brutality to women that still exists. We fought back, and the men became conscious too. If we found that someone was beating their mate, we tried to expose it and talk to the person to get them to stop. That couldn't be tolerated. We told the League Executive Board, "You better do something about this." It was a slow process. We finally got to the point where women did begin to emerge as leaders in the League. (Kramer 2017)

Ilene reflected more generally on the women in the LRBW:

> When I first got involved, women were seen as help mates, as secondary. There weren't a lot of strong women or many women in the plants. I never met Betty, but I heard about her. But it changed a lot. As the League grew, they started recognizing women. Many strong women did come forth in leadership roles, like Marian and Sandra. It was good. (I. Baker, K. Baker, and Y. Baker 2017)

Edna added her observations about LRBW women and her own situation during the LRBW years:

> The only women really active were the Moses sisters, Marian, the one who married Robert Higgins, a woman named Shirley Campbell, myself and Helen Jones. Helen Jones never was co-opted onto the Executive Board, but she had a lot of power in the movement as a woman with respect and with labor credits.
>
> I had children with John Watson, but we were doomed to not be together. (E. Watson 2017)

Maureen Taylor, a community organizer who connected with LRBW comrades after the split, spoke to gender oppression, especially of working-class Black women, and their place within the LRBW:

> Women organizing in the 1960s and 1970s often brought up the rear. They were typists, ran the copies off, and counted how many copies go in the box. Women didn't write and weren't the brain trust. We were the support staff.
>
> There were women who were leaders in the League—Marian and others—some of the most serious revolutionaries I knew. These women said, "We're not gonna be in the back anymore. There're things we need to say and we can write and have thoughts too."

Over the last thirty or forty years, the role of women in revolutionary organizations has increased and more women are in leadership roles. (Taylor 2017)

Judy offered her take on the women, the times, and gender relations:

I knew several women during the whole struggle—Marian, Maureen, and Theresa. Regardless of the male supremacy that exists in any organization—that's part of this culture, part of a long history—they stood up and took a leadership role. They were gonna be heard and do what had to be done. They were strong, they demanded that. I respect them because they are real leaders and good models for women. They were part of the fight and understood the role of women. We're half of the population and we better be doing something. (Judy Williams 2017)

Marsha shared her perspective on LRBW women as a student in the BSUF at the time and from her vantage point today:

There were important women in the League, and they were constantly railing with the male leadership about their lack of proper respect and recognition. As young people, we weren't always privy to the struggles going on with the adults. I knew the League had a printing company, Black Star. Helen Jones, a venerable woman, ran it. Gen's sister Jeanette was a typesetter. I'm only now realizing that we were involved in the most advanced and revolutionary forms of printing and communications at the time.

The women did important work, but were also relegated to bringing food and providing child care for meetings. These tensions probably plagued all organizations during that time. Underneath the struggle for workers' rights and everything taking place externally, the women were trying to assert themselves and be respected as leaders within the organization.

The woman question is also the issue of protecting and caring for the young people around the organization. I love these people who became my surrogate family. But today I question why they didn't make me go to school. I dropped out of high school and didn't go to college. I tried for a minute, but was bored. My life and home situation were so chaotic that I probably would not have been able to bring myself to go back even if they had demanded it of me. Others in the organization possessed a family and family structure that supported them. They went to school and college and many are professionals today because of the education they got. (Music 2017)

Leah appreciated the LRBW's awareness of the need for women's equality and leadership, and the reality:

> The line and theory was that women were on an equal footing with men, and there was a big effort to make that happen in the organization. It happened at a certain level. When a man would have been put in leadership—instead women would be put in the leadership position with support brought in to make it work. That conscious effort made an impact on me.
>
> One example was child care. Instead of child care falling to women, if there was a room full of babies the League made an effort for a man to be in there with them and do babysitting duty. That was revolutionary. It didn't happen in the real world or outside of the League. Yet the Executive Board members were all men for the whole time the League existed. Were there ever any discussions about that question of why there weren't any women on the leadership body? (L. Rogers 2017)

BLACK STAR PUBLISHING AND WOMEN'S LEADERSHIP

Women performed a huge amount of the day-to-day work of the LRBW that was outside of plant organizing. When the LRBW acquired Black Star Publishing, women stepped up to basically run the technical and printing work.

Marian explained,

> We acquired Black Star to get information out to our base. It was the written voice of the League and was very professional. We also opened it up to the public to do printing.
>
> Black Star was run by the women. Helen was over the whole printing operation. A few women were sent to school to learn how to run the IBM word processors—Jeanette Baker, Cassandra Smith-Cook, and Diane Bernard. I had some training, but had so many meetings and so much work in the community, I couldn't be full-time. (Kramer 2017)

Marian described a scene of the women working on the paper at Black Star from *Finally Got the News*, the best-known film about the LRBW. She shared the tensions about Newsreel filming the LRBW:

> Some of the women had jobs during the day, so we had a standard time at night for getting the paper together. If you look at *Finally Got the News* you'll see us in operation. We boycotted the filming at the beginning. We told Gen, "Why should Newsreel be filming us?" We thought filming the League should be an internal thing. We finally gave in, and in the beginning of the film you see and hear us operating the press. That's about the only time you see the women in the film. (Kramer 2017)

LRBW WOMEN AND INTERNATIONALISM

Marian also spoke about the internationalism of the LRBW women and their connection with the women of Vietnam, Laos, and Cambodia:

> The North Vietnamese government invited a few of the League women to North Vietnam after an international conference in Toronto. During the conference we helped stop a crisis that developed between workers who were gay and some of the unions. We were able to bridge that divide and the conference was successful.
>
> After that, the North Vietnamese asked us if we would come to Vietnam and other places. We said, "No one has ever asked us, but maybe we would." The letter of invitation came to James Farmer and I got it from him. This was our invitation to Laos, Cambodia, and North Vietnam so we could get a better understanding of their situation. And they really wanted to talk to the League.
>
> In relation to Africa, I think John Watson went with League women on some of the trips. This was happening at the time the League was beginning to split, but the split was later. I worked in welfare rights, and later we had an opportunity to travel. We were invited to Uganda for the Pan-African Congress—and it was paid for. This was right before the escalation of the war in some of the countries around Uganda. In all of the countries we got invited to we saw how they began to check into the people in the League. (Kramer 2017)

Despite all the work and visibility of the LRBW women, no women served on the LRBW Executive Board, the highest decision-making body of the LRBW. Marian spoke directly to this reality and the error of the LRBW leadership at that time:

> Women were not on the Executive Board, but they had to come to us for a lot of things. It was the women who said, "We will go on strike and not deal with any of this mess." We told Gen and all of them, "We need an apparatus for all the organization. We need to have a meeting."
>
> We had a meeting and it was packed. We had the women in the Black Women's Committee and the young women in the student movement, BSUF. We all knew what needed to be done within the League.
>
> Many of us played a part. My base of operation was the community, I was always there. And I got leaflets out in the factories and was in the meetings to put the leaflets together. The Black Women's Committee did a lot internally, but did not get the respect that was needed. Someone should have been on the Executive Board. Ilene headed up the Black Women's Committee and she should have been on the Executive Board. But that didn't enter into their heads at the time and we didn't fight for it then. (Kramer 2017)

The Black Student United Front (BSUF)

Students were an essential aspect of LRBW life. They distributed LRBW literature at the plants, were part of the LRBW family, and carried the study and struggle lessons of the LRBW. Cass Bell Ford, Marsha Music, and Darryl Mitchell were the three members of the BSUF, among many, we interviewed. They all began their LRBW life in the BSUF and worked at factories, Cass and Darryl in auto plants, Marsha at Frito-Lay. They shared that part of their LRBW family story, how those early years informed who they have become and how they carried the struggle to the point of production and beyond.

Marsha described the turbulent sixties and the era's impact on youth, the racism in the North as well as the South, and how she connected with the LRBW:

> I remember the tumult of the 1960s—how overwhelming it was to be a young person. We're watching the Vietnam War as it intensifies on television, a war people were questioning. Newsreel films of body bags coming home and people protesting. We personally knew young men who were drafted, some from the neighborhood. The antiwar movement was heating up. We saw the civil rights movement on television. Dogs sicced on children, children blown up by terrorists in the South, the memories of the funeral and Emmett Till's body displayed for mourners.
>
> Our parents didn't talk about these things. But we absorbed this reality from our environment. I recall the neighbors calling us the N-word across the fence. And while I received an exemplary public education in Highland Park schools, they had racial issues. On career day everyone said what they want to be when they grow up. It was my turn and I said, "I wanna be a lawyer." The teacher said, "You know your people can't do that." This was in front of the class, and it made me feel small. The teachers had us sing slavery songs in front of the class. They didn't really know what else to do with these Black kids that were now in the schools.
>
> A lot was going on in Detroit—there was virulent racism and police actions against people. All these social movements are heating up, including the women's movement. In 1967, some of the social anxiety and oppression boiled over.
>
> I began hanging out, and that's how I ran into the League. I was on a date and we went to the Masonic Temple to see a concert. Some guys were passing out leaflets giving voice to what we're going through. It's just after the rebellion and things have gotten worse. I decided, "Let's check out these people." Their office, the League office, was in Highland Park five blocks from where I lived. (Music 2017)

The social motion of the times and meeting up with the LRBW converged in Marsha's life. Marsha went from the BSUF and LRBW life as a student to a job at Frito-Lay, informed by her LRBW experience. She began with her first encounter at the LRBW office:

> I was studious and had a love of learning as a child that was transferred when I came around the guys in the League. We were young people, about fourteen, attracted to League life. Fourteen-year-olds now—they're kids. It was a different time for us. We were serious and wanted to figure out how to fight injustice in society.
>
> We went into the Courtland office and they're printing leaflets. I learned how to operate the Gestetner machine and the offset presses. They had a voluminous library with significant works—from the movement to Shakespeare and the classics. It was a wonderful library because people donated their books, and I spent a lot of time there. I studied about society with the League with intense intellectual rigor. (Music 2017)

Marsha continued, discussing school protests, strikes, suspensions, Freedom Schools, and the importance of LRBW education. She also mentioned the philandering of some LRBW guys.

> We were involved in student struggles and shut down the high schools as part of protests and strikes. In a few strikes they wouldn't let us back into school. We were suspended—either temporary or permanent. Freedom Schools were set up as alternative schools to keep us in the education loop. The Freedom Schools we went to were the second generation.
>
> The League did a good job of educating us and trying to keep us from doing extreme acts that would have gotten us killed. A lot more of us could have gotten in serious lifelong or mortal trouble. We were around a group of people at the Courtland office who were working guys. These proletarian guys had a discipline and rigor of life, a proletarian practicality about life.
>
> They said, "No, don't do this." The acts people in the left were doing—blowing things up, stuff like that—were totally verboten. That wasn't in the framework of what we talked about. They were disciplined about taking on struggles within a framework of not doing anything crazy.
>
> But you had this other side, not central, but an aspect of life around the brothers and sisters in the League. There was a certain amount of philandering among the adults, a craziness that was going on. It wasn't primary, but it did affect people's lives. (Music 2017)

Marsha shared her personal reality after dropping out of high school—having a baby, not going to college, and working at Frito-Lay, where she was a union leader:

> Most of my peers were primed, they were going to college. But here I am. I have a baby, I'm in the movement, and I want to be in service to the workers and people of Detroit. I got a job at Frito-Lay. It was like potato chip hell. It was the same level of industrialization you would find in an auto plant, except you're making snack food. It's highly industrialized, the work is intense, fast, hard, and hot.
>
> Iban Pitts got me the job. He was a union steward there. I didn't have a car so he drove me to work for months. Iban encouraged me to run for election. I ran for shop steward and won. This plant was overwhelmingly white, in Allen Park. We could almost count the Blacks on our hands.
>
> We were really fighting against Frito-Lay, which had a strong corporate center. They were antiunion. They had to have the plant in this market in Michigan, but they didn't like having to deal with the union, unlike in their southern plants. I was a leader for some time and was elected as president of the union. I represented not only workers at Frito-Lay, but also workers at Hostess Cake, Tasty Bread, and Wonder Bread—the big industrial bakers. A lot of it was based on the things I had learned being around DRUM and around organizations of workers. (Music 2017)

Cass described growing up in Highland Park, connecting with other student activists around protests in the neighborhood, and becoming part of the LRBW struggle and the BSUF:

> I grew up in Highland Park and got involved in the League through some school friends—Linda and Terry Wheeler. We went to Highland Park High School, which was next to the Community College. Folks at the college were demonstrating. Terry and Linda said we should support the students and I joined the protest. After the demonstration we went to the League office on Courtland and I met one of the protest organizers. That was my first introduction to the League and all the activity.
>
> Then something happened—somebody was killed or there was a stress unit trying to catch somebody. The community was outraged, and we went to the Courtland office to organize and spread literature. It snowballed and we began meeting and talking. We were in high school and didn't have education on Black history and what was going on. We started questioning a lot of things.
>
> Our solution was to do something. The League worked with students. They were organizing RUMs in the plants and got us to pass out leaflets there. We decided to do the same thing in the schools and that's what we did. It was successful. And there was so much social upheaval going on. (C. Ford 2017)

Cass had to transfer to Cooley High School in tenth grade and confronted racism in a way she never had before. Her mother didn't believe her at first, and the LRBW and the BSUF became even more important socially, intellectually, and politically:

> In tenth grade I transferred to Cooley High School because the Highland Park school system was on strike. Cooley was different—my first real experience with racism, white flight, and people in turmoil. I had to stand up and fight, things I didn't have to do in Highland Park.
>
> One teacher asked us, "What do you want to become?" People tried to answer. She said the most you guys can do is eat watermelon and shine shoes. My mouth fell open. I didn't know how to respond, but I knew that was wrong. I went to science class and opened the textbook. The teacher pointed to a picture of a dark-skinned person who they called Mongolians or something. I was overwhelmed and couldn't believe this was happening—incident after incident.
>
> I told my mother, and she said, "This is not happening." I said, "Believe me, this is what's going on."
>
> We organized so we wouldn't be isolated, and formed the BSUF. We spoke out and wrote in the *Black Student Voice*. We talked about incidents at our school and others, and got kids together. Sticking together helped us. Doing all this was a good experience and taught me things.
>
> We had some wins. We got Black studies, Black literature, and more minority teachers. But it didn't solve the problem. I was sixteen—and we didn't understand it all. We did these things and I'm thinking we've arrived. By the eleventh and twelfth grade people started using drugs and our whole thing fell apart, I didn't graduate. I got pregnant with my daughter, got married, and left school. (C. Ford 2017)

Cass summed up her BSUF and LRBW experience:

> Being in the BSUF was a very good experience in terms of understanding what was going on. We were the student unit of the League and that's how we were connected. We were trying to uplift Black students. When we sat around, we talked politics and what we were doing. We were always reading and I'd go to the library to get books. At Linda and Terry's house, we'd bring our books and talk. It's funny—now that I think about it. What teenagers are doing now, and what we did then.
>
> The BSUF and the League was an historic experience for me. I appreciate that time and that history because it gave me a family to hold onto, something I didn't have. I tell people all the time, if you get involved in something that's right in front of you that you can do, you never know where it's gonna lead you. (C. Ford 2017)

Cass carried her LRBW experience of organizing and study to her work struggles in the plants and the union. In the 1970s sexual harassment and sexism were rampant, and she helped organize the women at the Cadillac plant to address their oppression as women.

> In 1974 I got hired at the Cadillac plant because a law was passed that they had to hire women. When I got into the plant I saw the way women were treated. It was a nightmare. I was never treated like that in the BSUF or among the people in the League. So, I organized the women to get the respect we deserved and not be treated like we were cattle.
>
> The supervisor told me, "If you had married a man, you wouldn't have to work here, you wouldn't need a job." I was shocked. But League organizing prepared me. We got together as women and organized. We said, "We do not have to be talked down to. The union has to respect us and represent us." We had all the same fights that the League had with the union and the company.
>
> My mother didn't allow me to cuss, so I had to learn how to cuss to survive in that environment. I had to learn how to tell people on the job, "Get away from me, I'm not interested in that." If somebody drove you to the bus stop or drove you home, the next thing you know is you went to bed with them. Women were not thought of as being able to work and to be respected. Think about it. In 1974 they had to pass a law for women to be able to work. Women didn't have that right. They were property, pretty much. This was a whole other social movement that was going on, and I ended up doing that too. I worked through that in the union. It's all good. (C. Ford 2017)

Darryl explained how his first encounter at the LRBW office on Courtland shaped his life as a student looking for Black history, educating and getting educated, and preparing for life in the working-class struggle. The LRBW was family.

> Gen dated my first cousin Rita, so General Baker was going to be in my life and future one way or another. Our paths crossed in 1968 and the rest is history. I went to League headquarters at 179 Courtland and have been involved ever since. I was still in high school and hadn't gotten a job at Chrysler yet.
>
> We became the BSUF. Before that we had a newsletter called the *Black Student Voice*. Everything was organized around newspapers and newsletters back then. We built a propaganda organization. Our activity was geared toward the production and distribution of literature. The literature of that time talked about the issues of the mass movement.
>
> In those days you didn't have Black history. You could study history through-

out your school years and never see a Black face other than Carter G. Woodson for Negro history week and George Washington Carver for peanuts and farming. Not to belittle him, he was a genius. And there's Booker T. Washington in debate with Du Bois.

At the time you don't know how all these threads of history will be woven together forty-five years later. Things look a lot different now. But I grew up inside the League as my extended family. (D. Mitchell 2017)

The LRBW women and students organized against class exploitation, racial oppression, and male supremacy in all aspects of their lives.

LRBW Men Step Up on the Question of Sexism and Inequality

The men of the LRBW fessed up. In the spirit of self-criticism and self-reflection, they acknowledged their complicity in the patriarchal relations between the women and men back in the day and the need to change those relations moving forward into new organizations. In this section we hear from John Williams, Allen Ray Bernard, Jerome Scott, Mike Hamlin, Abdul Roberts, Darryl Mitchell, Alonzo Chandler, Russell Jackson, and Wylie Rogers.

John expressed it this way:

> The women provided a service and they were very dedicated. But no women were in the leadership. When the League was going on, there was this ideology that Black men should lead—and this relegated women to the role of service. That ideology was in the League. It wasn't stated, but it was there. Some of the women kind of supported it. Was it correct that women were not in the leadership? No, as we look back in retrospect.
>
> This question came up because some of the women saw themselves—and they were right—as basically servants asked to do this and told to do that. The roles they played in terms of printing, writing, getting stuff out—they were a vanguard within the organization. But it wasn't until we hit the Communist League (after the League split) that some of this stuff got dealt with. That's where it was. That doesn't mean there wasn't friction, but women's leadership never came up where we had to discuss it. (John Williams 2017)

Allen Ray headed up LRBW security and had another take on the LRBW family and gender relations:

> The League didn't just embrace the worker, we embraced the whole family. You can get a guy who's working in the plant or a woman who's working in the plant, but if you don't educate the family, there'll be hostility as to why the workers believe in the League, why they're doing work, and classes, and education. We took on the personal problems, the marital problems of League members. It was beautiful. We had child care. Nobody wanted to babysit, but everybody without exception pulled babysitting duties. We had the youth program, a lot going on.
>
> When the League formed we had the minds of capitalist society. Women played a "back" role in everything. But the men soon found out that wasn't going to be the case. We got criticized for male chauvinism. I was in charge of security, and we took the women to the range. They could shoot better than we could—no question.
>
> Women played a very leading role. Once the women got a taste of that knowledge and power, it was over for male dominance. That carried us through our whole lives. We had to look at the woman question differently. When I went to New Orleans and worked in the unions, I found myself immediately speaking up when I saw exploitation or oppression of women. (Bernard 2017)

Jerome summed it up this way:

> The leadership of the League was all men. And there were only two plant workers on the seven person leadership body. There was always a struggle around how much of the political work women were gonna do. The women in the League did a lot of work all the time. They helped with leaflets, distributions, everything. Every step in the process, the women were deeply involved in except for the decision making process. From that perspective, if women are not part of the decision making process, they're gonna be relegated to a second-class status.
>
> That's what happened in the League. It was manifested politically by them not having leadership roles, although they influenced the leadership tremendously. It was the 1960s and the sexual revolution, so it manifested itself sexually within the organization. The League was a pretty good reflection of the role that women had in society as a whole at the time. And we didn't do anything to correct that. We rolled with it. (Scott 2017)

Mike spoke about the strong LRBW women through his reflections on his mother and acknowledging the times and context:

> I'm a mamma's boy, and it's important we treat women correctly. Folks have to be conscious of the need to check their libido when dealing, especially, with young girls. I considered myself a feminist, though I had my slips. But if I had a sixteen-

Conversation at Darryl Mitchell's house with Russell Jackson, Darryl Mitchell, Alonzo Chandler, Abdul Roberts, and Jerome Scott. Photo by Can Tuzcu, courtesy General Baker Institute.

> year-old daughter, I wouldn't want folks exploiting her in the name of an ideology. We had some guys who said sexist, outrageous things. We kind of checked 'em. But it was the times.
>
> Women and their roles in the operation of the organization were essential. Women did a lot of work—most of the typing and some of the leafleting. We had international contacts the women were in relation to. Women were loyal and supported the organization. But the guys weren't ready. The abuse of young women brought us low. (Hamlin 2017)

Darryl, Abdul, Alonzo and Russell, in a group conversation with Jerome, offered their take on the role of women and sexism within the LRBW.

Darryl began. He acknowledged the amazing work women did and put forth the position that the LRBW was no worse than other left organizations of the day:

> Women were the backbone of the League, a lot of them were important organizers. The League was not particularly bad—it wasn't worse than other leftist-type organizations in their treatment of women. Most of the women, the younger women I was associated with, went on to become the next generation of leaders in every endeavor.
>
> The only criticism I had was that some of the older fellows should have left the younger women alone. When you're fourteen, fifteen, sixteen, you need a chance to grow up. I didn't know much about who did what until I was older. (D. Mitchell in Chandler et al. 2017)

Abdul added his perspective:

> The Black movement was strictly male chauvinist and our shit was no different. Who did the work is what counted. Those young sisters who were around the Black student movement got high honors. They were beautiful, they had brains, they had courage, they had determination, and above all, they had this hellified willingness to learn from men. This or that could've been better. But on the whole they received respect. It might not have been respect in the classical revolutionary sense, because we really didn't understand it. (Roberts in Chandler et al. 2017)

Darryl further explained his thinking:

> The student part of the League was set up different. The majority of active people were women. It wasn't a question of inclusion. The League, as a whole, was a federation of organizations. The women were concentrated in organizations that dealt with neighborhoods and community issues and welfare. But, when you look at the old DRUM posters, there's one woman, Betty Boo. There're objective reasons for this—the degree to which women were in the workforce and their positions within the workforce. But I don't wanna say it was unconscious, because that isn't true. (D. Mitchell in Chandler et al. 2017)

Alonzo offered his perspective:

> Darryl made a correct analysis. The BSUF was set up one way. The League was set up another way because the composition of the factory was male. I worked on lines where there were no women.
>
> It wasn't a formal thing of women in leadership positions, but we had to go to women to get things done. We had to interact in a respectful way, we were trying to accomplish the same thing. Women had an impact and they still do.
>
> The young people from the BSUF were in the struggle and trying to study. Study was always a component and some of the earliest study groups had women leading, though not formally. These women grew. Marsha grew to be president of a local. Cass Bell and other women grew to hold positions in their unions. (Chandler in Chandler et al. 2017)

Finally, Russell shared his take on women and sexism:

> I came in after the split in 1971—into a stabilized group and everybody was a soldier. The men had the leadership, but every woman was a soldier. It was male supremacist dominated, and I don't remember it changing until we made a conscious effort to start elevating the women. (Jackson in Chandler et al. 2017)

Wylie reflected on what he called the "spontaneous leadership" of women in the LRBW, including the young women:

> In the League proper, not earlier or later formations, it was a spontaneous thing. People jumped in and did stuff, many were women. We had an organic appreciation of the role of women in the League. It was not what came later, where there was a conscious effort to bring about that equality. There were no women on the Executive Board. That's why I describe it as spontaneous and make the distinction. My sense is that women forced their way in.
>
> With the youth, Marsha stands out—how forceful she was. And Cass Bell. They were my militant models. It was strange to see such outspoken and fighting girls in high school. It was amazing. I'm not saying there was anything organizationally or policy wise. But you could see the assertion of these women leaders in the League at that time. (W. Rogers 2017)

The LRBW family was truly multigenerational. We embraced the participation and power of youth in struggle. At the same time, we failed to formally recognize women's leadership during the LRBW days, even though women of all generations fought for that. LRBW men did acknowledge this error—some more bluntly and honestly than others. As the LRBW transitioned, women did assume formal leadership roles in new political organizations, movement organizations, and unions going forward.

Despite the sexism that the women of the LRBW endured, they emerged as strong leaders and carried the struggle to end male domination, white supremacy, and capitalism into the organizations and spaces of their lives. Beginning in the study period after the LRBW split, conversations developed about the role of women in the movement, women's leadership, and dealing with male supremacy organizationally and in society as a whole. That conversation and the struggle to change our practice continue.

CHAPTER 8

Class, Race, and Revolution— Understanding the Real World

The relations of class and race at the point of production was the context of the daily struggle and developing study of the LRBW. LRBW members and our communities were living the legacy of chattel slavery in the twentieth century that Marx ([1867] 1887) had written about a century earlier, that Du Bois lifted up in *Black Reconstruction* ([1935] 1962), and that scholars such as Bush (1999, 2009), C. Robinson ([1983] 2000), Roediger and Esch (2014), Roediger (2017), and others continued to address.

Class Exploitation and Racial Oppression in LRBW Struggle and Beyond

Informed by Marxist analysis of the color question and labor in the United States, LRBW comrades were powerful voices within the multiracial, multinational, and multigendered working-class struggle. We analyzed the class content of capitalist exploitation and racial oppression and infused class consciousness within the reform movement to end racial discrimination. Darryl Mitchell, Jerome Scott, Marian Kramer, and John Williams spoke to the complex interrelations between class and race during the LRBW days and to shifting realities leading up to the LRBW split in 1971.

Darryl, part of the LRBW student movement and later a production worker, reflected on conditions that made the LRBW possible at the time it was founded:

> The League was not designed to get Blacks into the labor force because they had already gotten in. Its task was to shatter and destroy the segregated structures. Simply because you changed a law doesn't mean the structures built up over decades are gonna cave in and disappear. They literally have to be shattered. In that

sense, the League played a unique role in history. It was able to play that role because it was a point in American history where you have what I would call "benevolent neutrality."

A huge section of the white workforce did not fight the League and did not resist. This was for specific reasons. As the industrial system went through its last period of expansion and Blacks came into the system, everybody was able to rise. You can accept integration when the system is expanding and everyone is rising, because competition for jobs doesn't exist. It was because of this dynamic that a moment of "benevolent neutrality" opened up. Yes, there were ideological diehards, but you weren't arguing over the same physical space. That created a unique situation and the League was able to play this role. (D. Mitchell 2017)

Jerome spoke to this process of class and race in LRBW thinking and practice:

When we talked to the Black workers in the plants, they were focused on how workers in the plants were being treated. There was a lot of racial discrimination and they recognized that. But that wasn't the motivating force. It was a mixture—they treat us like dogs, but not just because we're Black. They're treating these white folks like dogs, too. They put us in the worst jobs, so we understand the racial overtone. But the real content is that they're making a ton of money off of us. And that exploitation is true for us and it's true for everybody else that works in the plant. (Scott 2017)

Marian shared her work in the Black struggle but stressed the reality of the multiracial working class in the United States and the ruling-class strategy of divide, control, and rule.

It's good that I participated in the struggle of the Black movement. But reality steps in. We have to see how we have been pitted against one another for the benefit of those who rule this country, for the benefit of the corporations. We've all been used. We're part of the whole working class, but Blacks have been used as the whipping board. The stick to whip the rest of the class into shape. (Kramer 2017)

John emphasized that race cannot be the basis of class unity:

The bourgeois have been great at developing the issue of race. It's very prominent out there. But race is not the basis of unity. It's not now, it has not been, and will not be. Unity will come around economic factors that will bring people together.

I stress that because in some of the sessions I'm in, people say it's the race question. I don't mean to shun Black lives matter. But when you say, "Black lives matter," you pose a race situation and not class. As opposed to saying, "Black lives matter within our class, the working class," but we don't say that. You leave it off. (John Williams 2017)

Jerome expanded on the interrelations of class exploitation and racial oppression:

> The moment you say to someone you have to understand the way this world functions—you're saying you have to understand why exploitation and oppression are part of the same coin, of the monster that is standing on our chest. You can't eliminate one without the other. You can't eliminate exploitation and not eliminate oppression. You certainly can't eliminate white supremacy without eliminating exploitation, because that's the basis of white supremacy. Once people begin to look at concepts like that, they begin to understand it takes more than just working and practice to get a grasp on how we develop a plan and what we gotta do. (Scott 2017)

We carried this understanding and the concrete struggle for human emancipation—the end of class exploitation, white supremacy, and gender oppression—on our journey beyond LRBW days. It informs our ongoing work as working-class revolutionaries in this volatile and chaotic twenty-first-century moment.

Setting the Basis for Moving Forward— Developing Working-Class Intellectuals

LRBW comrades reflected on the LRBW experience and the revolutionary process moving forward. We were united around the necessity of developing working-class intellectuals as key to staying the revolutionary course. Luke Tripp, Wylie Rogers, and General Baker spoke to the dialectic of theory, study, and struggle.

Luke offered this analysis about changing conditions, the need for education, and the struggle today.

> The League, as we conceived it and organized it, didn't have a future given the larger changes taking place. There was no way to stop the flight of plants. The ruling class had already made the decision about the most efficient and cheapest way to operate. It didn't include the masses of Black workers we had organized. League strategy was correct at the time, at the level of development in Detroit. It would be foolhardy to try to reproduce the League today. Not gonna happen. That's why you need constant education and strategy, because of the dynamism. Everything is in motion and if you get behind, you're gonna become irrelevant. (Tripp 2017)

Wylie affirmed the lifelong impact of study and analysis during the LRBW years and after:

> One of the significant contributions the League made was to implant the idea of analysis and study within the working class, in certain sections of it. For the first time in my life, I knew what I wanted to do.
>
> I hate to admit this. John Williams and I were talking about struggle and say-

ing, "We got to do something!" That's me—"We gotta do something." I was so backward then, politically lacking in knowledge. I actually thought there had to be some kind of formula that could figure this shit out. John looked at me incredulously, and said, "No, man. You gotta study." I said, "Study what?" He said, "Marxism." I said, "What in the hell is that?" He shared with me some of the study circles they had in Detroit, at Wayne State and other places. It was an utterly eye-opening experience. (W. Rogers 2017)

Gen, whose life, analysis, and struggle were central to the formation of the LRBW, summed up the shifts in history and what the times today require of revolutionaries:

We gotta make thinkers into fighters and fighters into thinkers. . . . Today is not like the 1960s. The 1960s left us with people who fought and refused to think, and people who thought and refused to fight. It took us twenty years to try to make thinkers into fighters and fighters into thinkers. We're in a long, difficult battle. We gotta have a protracted outlook. (G. Baker 2016)

As part of the LRBW we began our lifelong process of study. We developed a method that worked well for point-of-production workers and for students. Many had not gone to college or studied Marxism, or any theory, before. Collective reading, discussion, and study were at the center of the process. We read the materials together, so educational level was not a limitation. We learned how to pull out the key concepts presented in the readings, which was critical for grappling with their application in our political work. We discussed the material until everyone understood and grasped the concepts and the analysis of the revolutionary process. We all became learners and teachers.

For the comrades of the LRBW, the dialectics of theory and practice, of study and struggle marked the beginning. We all joined the LRBW journey through our personal paths to becoming politicized. Some of us were at the founding of the LRBW and some connected along the way. A thread that runs through the LRBW story comes from our southern roots—living and knowing the state violence of white supremacy, gender oppression, and class exploitation. Another thread comes through our study and our political practice. From the early years, the 1960s rebellion and wildcat strikes, to DRUM and the LRBW, Marxism provided theoretical grounding among the leadership and the Executive Board. Most of the rank-and-file workers came to Marxism in the period of the split in the LRBW and the monthslong political study.

Part Three

The Split and Coming to Revolutionary Consciousness

CHAPTER 9

The Split and the Struggle for Education, 1971

> Without revolutionary theory there can be no revolutionary movement.
>
> —Vladimir Lenin, *What Is to Be Done* ([1902] 1961)
>
> Marxism—Marxism-Leninism—was the theory that related most closely to our lives. We were production workers and Marxism was written for workers.
>
> —Jerome Scott (2017)

Our Journey Continues

Tensions and contradictions had been developing within LRBW. They finally came to a head. The LRBW split in 1971, three years after its formation in 1969. The organization had accomplished what it was designed to do—its purpose when it was formed out of DRUM and the RUMs. Black workers were increasingly integrated into the job structure within the plants and into the union leadership. The robotic digital revolution and globalization were transforming the auto industry domestically and globally. These forces created new objective conditions that made the LRBW "history." It was less relevant to what was developing within working-class struggles and the revolutionary process.

But it was the struggle over whose priorities would guide the organization that resulted in the split. The leadership of both sides argued for socialism and the abolition of capitalism and imperialism globally. Strategically we were united, but tactically we embraced very different paths to power.

One section of the leadership focused on organizing the BWC as a national formation modeled around the LRBW, but throughout the country. Critically, the decision to go national was not collectivized within the LRBW.

The other section of LRBW comrades embarked on an educational retreat. Meeting and developing a relationship with the California Communist League (CCL) and Nelson Peery—a revolutionary intellectual who was a Black worker, a bricklayer to be precise—was essential to our next steps. We were transforming ourselves intellectually and in relation to new revolutionary formations—the Communist League (CL), the Communist Labor Party (CLP), and eventually the League of Revolutionaries for a New America (LRNA). Comrades from the Motor City Labor League (MCLL, a grouping of primarily white workers in Detroit who knew and worked with the LRBW), from the Capital Collective (a grouping of white auto workers in Detroit who were studying *Capital*), and forces from SDS, the Marxist-Leninist Workers Association, and the Colectiva were part of the journey going forward.

The Split around Who's Going to Run the Organization

Former LRBW members—point-of-production workers, community organizers, and students—detailed our perspectives on the split and our political and intellectual journeys. We shared the story of our study retreat and becoming working-class intellectuals. Jerome remembered it as lasting eighteen months, while Marian recalled it being a year. Regardless, it was an intense and transformative experience.

We came to Marxism not as ideology but as living theory and practice that explained our experiences, our victories, and our ongoing struggles. We lived the realities of capitalism, class, race, and gender. We embraced the dialectics of theory and practice to better grasp the unfolding revolutionary process in Detroit, the United States, and the world.

John Williams, who was in the process leading up to the LRBW and was on the Executive Board from the beginning, summed up the split this way. He pointed toward the next steps in the LRBW journey—the study retreat, connecting with Nelson, and the CL:

> We put up such a struggle and we were so widely known, that things began to change. There were Black foremen, Blacks in the skilled trades, and Blacks on the executive board of the unions. It was sort of a dilemma. Where was the LRBW gonna go from there?
>
> In 1970 Ken Cockrel came up with the idea of the Black Workers Congress (BWC) under the guise that we needed to spread out nationally and internationally. But the birth of the BWC was also the basis of the split. There were differ-

ences in terms of who they saw leading the BWC as opposed to where we were in the workers struggle. The bulk of the BWC's base was gonna be the workers, but the orientation of Watson, Mike, and Ken was away from the workforce.

So when the split came, that left the rest of us—the bulk of the League—still with the question, "Where do we go now? We've accomplished some of our needs, now what?"

That's actually an introduction to the Communist League (CL). Chuck went out west and brought Bob Williams back. Bob was effective leading political and theoretical education for a while. But he wore out his welcome. Nelson Peery came in periodically for political discussions and helped clarify the times and what was needed.

The LRBW was not ready for a racially integrated group. To go through the transition from where we were to the CL, required an analysis to show where we needed to go. Nelson did that and that's how we entered into the CL. (John Williams 2017)

Marian offered her perspective on the split and the need for education:

It was coming to a head before we went through the split, but the split ushered in something bigger. It was a Saturday when Iban came to the house and said, "Did you hear what happened? Gen walked off the Executive Board."

I said, "What in the hell is going down now?" I called Gen. He said, "Who are we gonna let rule this organization?" It was two different concepts. The LRBW should be based at the point of production and workers in the factories and the hospitals, or the intellectuals should run the organization. I said, "If you're gonna walk, why in the hell didn't you call us so we can walk with you?"

I asked who's still with you. Gen said, "John, Luke, myself, and Chuck. But Ken, Mike and Watson all went." The workers didn't care because we got what we wanted. We saw the contradictions forming around who was in the leadership.

I told Gen, "We need a meeting." He said, "I'll get back to you." I didn't hear from Gen, but John called and told me how the split went down. We had another meeting and started reorganizing.

At one of the first meetings, a gang of us sat around the table and said we need to get education and make sure that everybody gets this education. We had had some education before, but it didn't move as fast as we wanted. (Kramer 2017)

Luke shared his take on the split, the changing objective conditions, and the lifespan of organizations.

To understand the split, you have to understand the contradictions and problems that emerged with the expansion of the LRBW. The question of resources and the type of leadership needed. Before the LRBW, when it was only DRUM, all the Executive Board members were involved in leadership questions and strategic questions. For instance Ken, with a legal background, played an important role in how we dealt with the police.

As the LRBW expanded, it was a question of who had the experience to help other units organize. Workers from other plants looked to the LRBW for services, direction, and leadership. Who's gonna do that? We were dealing with a mass movement, a growing organization, and people's immediate needs. We used resources to build the organization and we were doing welfare. This situation, in terms of limited resources, was directly related to the split.

Ken, Mike, Watson, and especially James Forman were looking at the broader terrain. They wanted to go national, to spread the LRBW model. How were we going to send folks to other cities to organize when we couldn't organize the plants here? The workers understood their local situation and their problems, including family problems. But, many workers didn't have an understanding of the national plan.

Leading up to the split, we hadn't tightened up operations in Detroit and we had a resource question. We didn't have paid staff, it was all volunteer. Gen, John Williams, and I and some others—since we were here to deal with day-to-day concrete stuff—weren't enthusiastic about expanding quickly without taking care of the administrative things necessary for a viable organization.

But, we had no control over the question of the demise of the LRBW. The impact of technology was in the bigger picture. It was global and it was shifting. The LRBW as we envisioned it—organizing Black workers in the plants—had to change if the plants moved out of the country. Who you gonna organize? It would be foolhearted to try to reproduce the LRBW today, not gonna happen. (Tripp 2017)

Luke explained why he did not opt to continue the LRBW journey into the CL:

Some LRBW members went to the CL. My view was that it was too orthodox, too rigid, and too doctrinaire. It became like a club. This is the volume 1, volume 2, and volume 3 of Marx. If we just understand that, we have the solution. The solution is not found there. Very brilliant ideas and you can use some of those concepts, so it's worthwhile to study. It's not finding all the answers. It's like somebody saying all the answers are in the Bible, kind of true believer.

After the split I connected with people who had been around the LRBW in Ann Arbor at the School of Social Work. Bill Jones was involved in a community skills project and I went to Ann Arbor to work in the project. (Tripp 2017)

Darryl added his analysis of the transition in society, the labor movement, and the split in the LRBW. He explained that the LRBW appeared as the trajectory of history was from reforms and concessions toward shifts in class relations within the revolutionary process:

> Reform, from the standpoint of the science of society, is the ability to change relationships within and between classes without changing the material conditions of production, without changing fundamental class relations. Destroying segregation changed the relationship within and between classes without changing class relations. The industrial form of unionism changed relationships within and between classes without changing class relations. These are reforms. A concession is simply winning something from a specific opponent, an employer or corporation. If you win a fifty-cent raise, that's a concession. It does not change relationships within and between classes.
>
> The LRBW emerged when the system could still be reformed. Today the system can't be reformed and people have not grasped that. We can win concessions because they're based on the balance of forces, on who deploys what forces in a fight. But we can't win reforms because relations within the system can no longer be altered. The system is in the process of changing from one quality to the next. There's nothing left to be reformed. (D. Mitchell 2017)
>
> When the LRBW appeared, its role was to assist Black labor entering into the general house of labor, to shatter the walls of segregation. It carried out what it was formed to do. From that perspective, it had to disintegrate. It began splitting. I initially thought it was these different class forces that couldn't comingle together. But I think the process was bigger, the general transition in society and the labor movement. None of those organizations were gonna persist beyond carrying out their job in terms of fighting against segregation. (D. Mitchell in Chandler et al. 2017)

For Marsha, the LRBW split both was personal and signaled a new direction toward a Marxist understanding of society and work in the plants.

> The LRBW split was tumultuous. The rift affected me personally because this was my surrogate family and they're splitting apart. I remained close to Gen and his first wife Ilene, who opened their house to me when I left home. I lived with them for a few years with my baby.
>
> The LRBW began to fracture and they were seeking a way to continue struggling. They gravitated toward a Marxist view of society, of work in the plants, and everything they were grappling with. They brought in some outsiders. I was one

of the few who openly challenged one of these outsiders—they were exerting so much influence. (Music 2017)

Cass offered her perspective on the split, as a member of the BSUF and a tenth grader.

> When the LRBW split in 1971, I was in tenth grade and was in the BSUF. Everybody's got different stories about the split. This is what I remembered. We had a big meeting. Mitch presented a paper and when they got through presenting the paper everybody walked out. After the walk out, we started meeting at the LRBW office on Courtland. Trying to figure out where do we go from here? What do we do? (C. Ford 2017)

Jerome shared his view of the split as the LRBW was going through it and from the vantage point of the current moment.

> When we were going through the split, it was one thing. Looking back, it's another. As workers in the shop, we had to do a flyer every week—and get to the mimeograph machine and the printing press. When that went smoothly, we were fine. Then, it became difficult because resources were being used for other projects.
>
> Meanwhile, I went to Atlanta with Mike, James Forman, and Chuck to talk to Black workers about developing a LRBW-like organization around the country. At first I thought that's cool. But when we got back, we talked about what it would mean to develop a national organization energized by the LRBW in Detroit. How are we gonna resource ourselves and this other thing, the Black Workers Congress (BWC)?
>
> James Forman was the main connection. He came out of SNCC and had connections around the South. He was attracted to the LRBW because the organizing we were doing in Detroit was beyond anything he saw anywhere. What if we could do this on a national level?
>
> But, the more people tried to create new organizations around the country, the less we were able to do our work in Detroit. The split seemed to be between keeping a strong local apparatus that could maintain itself versus having a national organization.
>
> Looking back, if I was thinking like I think now, I'd say going national is the thing. But at the time, we said we can't do this because we don't have enough resources. We had not consolidated the work in the twenty or so plants we were in in auto, steel, and rubber. We couldn't expand nationally and consolidate locally. We had to slow the expansion process.
>
> Some people thought that was reactionary. For us, the workers at the point

of production, it was a practical question. It was presented back to us as a political question. The workers were backward and didn't understand the importance of doing what needs to be done. That became the context for the split.

But I really think that the content of the split was the question of "Who's going to lead?" Is the leadership from that section of society that has no choice but to win, the workers at the point of production? Or is it going to be from that section that has choices—the workers who became lawyers and professors? We didn't think about it like that then. The other important thing was that the decision to go national was never discussed and collectivized throughout the organization.

Now, I think if we had been more politically developed, and they had been more practically involved, we might not have split. The question was not if, but when we would expand nationally. But we never got to that point. The split ended up going along the lines of the workers, the students, and community people on one side. The lawyers, some other community workers, and some of the people who started off as students like John Watson who were doing international work on the other side. There was no way to avoid it. The split was gonna happen and it did. And that's the way it went down.

After the split the workers began to think about the work we did in the plants and the benefits we got in the period from 1969 to 1971. The UAW was terrified that the workers were organizing in the plants and looking at the UAW as part of the problem. We made inroads into the unions. We got Black stewards and committeemen elected and some local presidents elected at local shops.

We reflected on what section of society leads. Usually it's college educated people, who say it's an insult to workers to tell them to read a book or even a paper. It boils down to them calling the workers backward if we disagreed. When the split happened they told the point-of-production workers that we were backward and hadn't read anything. But, they are the ones who said we didn't need to read. This view is a reflection of what section of society feels they are the people who should lead. And if they're the people who should lead, why do these other people—the workers—need political education? They never say it that way, but that's the essence of what they mean. (Scott 2017)

Mitch offered this analysis of the split as a worker at the point of production.

We were always surrounded by intellectuals who considered themselves to be Marxists, and a lot of us were not. We knew we had to study and they were pushing Marxism. We studied Che Guevara, Kwame Nkrumah, Rap Brown, Malcolm X, Robert Williams, and others.

As we were studying we had a little split. Ideological and political unity never actually existed in the LRBW. That was a great part of leading to the split that occurred. We were on two different wave lengths.

Gen was important in our study. He said, "I didn't understand this thing until the 1967 rebellion." They had a curfew and Black people had to be in the house from seven P.M. till four A.M. But during the two-week siege, the curfew was lifted for people with a badge for Chrysler, Ford, or General Motors. You could go to work. The National Guard and, if necessary, the army would take you. The workers were gonna build those cars. That said to me if we got any kind of power as Black people it's at the point of production. That's why we went in that direction.

The LRBW had grown and we had seven Executive Board members. Two industrial proletarians were on the Board, Gen and Chuck. The others were lawyers, doctors, intellectuals. As time grew and the LRBW started branching out, the LRBW lost its commitment to our industrial base.

One night we were studying *Labor's Untold Story* [Boyer and Morais 1955]. There was an Executive Board meeting the next morning and we decided to say something. I did most of the printing of LRBW literature for years. Now it was hard to get to a printing press, because Black Star was printing obituaries, newspaper advertisements, and sale papers. The LRBW was losing its commitment to serve us, the workers. We were gonna raise that and a few other issues because there was a lot of tension.

We didn't know that the petty "bougie" element of the Executive Board had caucused and decided to present Chuck with their demands. One demand was expelling me for messing with a young woman comrade and some other demands. Their demand about me was a messed up analysis. They said I was a "lumpenproletarian" since I was not working, but I was a working-class kid. Because I wasn't working at the time did not make me a nonworker. I guess when they presented Gen and Chuck with their demand to expel me, they were not having it. Gen and Chuck resigned immediately.

That crew of the petty "bougie" element—some people consider them great. I consider them "kinda revolutionaries," but really traitors. It almost brings tears to my eyes.

The LRBW was built on the backs of the workers who carried the liberation struggle to the point of production. Many lost their jobs. These are the heroes, the great people. One of them is here, Alonzo. He lost his job. Gen lost his job. I was lucky I didn't lose mine.

A lot of people lay claim to their own significance. I don't see it because I was tutored and mentored by Gen. He instilled in me—you don't look at the person as "dapper dan," running their mouth about something. It was the workers on the picket line, risking their jobs and their livelihoods. They are equally important. I don't wanna disrespect anybody. (W. Mitchell 2017)

Mike, a founding member of the Executive Board who went with the BWC during the split, offered his top three causes for the split in the LRBW. They included infiltration and the Internal Revenue Service fine, the push for ultra-democracy, and the BWC expanding too fast.

> Our inability to deal with the infiltration was the major factor. Ken, John Watson, and I had our names on all the organization's papers because we didn't wanna put other people at risk and they didn't want to take that risk. We got a notice from the IRS. Ken asked this Black lawyer who had been an IRS agent to tell us what to do. We met, he checked into it, and said, "You gotta give them somebody." Ken said, "It's not gonna be me." John said, "It's not gonna be me." I said, "I'll do it." The lawyer was able to work out that we'd pay a ten-thousand-dollar fine, which somebody raised for me. We got by that one. But things like that faced us because of how things were—just full speed ahead.
>
> There was the push for ultra-democracy. People wanna be part of the organization. They want democracy and leadership roles. How do you balance that with the secrets? Some things we were not prepared to share.
>
> The third reason the BWC split from the LRBW was that we grew too fast. We didn't take time to sum up. We had a pretty good analysis of what was going on in the community and in the workforce. But in terms of organizational development, we didn't do that. We did not have a plan. People were coming and we were just plugging them in. You have to have a vision and a plan that's ongoing—that you adapt and adjust. We weren't thinking like that. Only a handful of us gave our all. (Hamlin 2017)

Ken, Mike, and John Watson issued a formal statement about the split, *The Split in the League of Revolutionary Black Workers: Three Lines and Three Headquarters* (1971). This is how it began:

> The League of Revolutionary Black Workers was irreparably split by the resignation of three members of its seven-person Executive Board which occurred on June 12, 1971. These three members, Ken Cockrel, Mike Hamlin and John Watson, declared that as of that date we would work exclusively under the direction of the Black Worker's Congress.
>
> Although many who supported the LRBW and its activity were shocked by the materialization of the LRBW's internal contradictions in what appeared to them a precipitous split the facts are that the split in the leadership and the cadre base had been the source of intensive struggle throughout the organiza-

tion's history from its inception three years ago until the resignation of June 12, 1971.

The decision to resign was neither easy, nor lightly arrived at, for indeed we were totally dedicated to building an organization that would carry us to the development of a party that would consummate in the building of socialism in the United States and participate in the defeat of imperialism in the world.

It was not easy to sever relationships of years' duration which had been forged through years of intensive struggle.

Nonetheless, the point had been reached at which the class and ideological contradictions within the organization had produced a state of virtual paralysis and thus it was necessary to have a decisive and far-reaching action to bring about a *qualitative* transformation of the movement of revolutionary Black Workers, and to quicken the pace of the inevitably successful revolutionary struggle. (Cockrel, Hamlin, and Watson 1971)

The League of Revolutionary Black Workers' life was brief, from 1969 to 1971. Yet the LRBW was a comprehensive organization, embodying the dialectic of theory and practice, and revolutionary leadership. The LRBW brought together Black workers at the point of production, students, women in family and work, community organizations, lawyers, a funding plan, and a propaganda arm—several newspapers and eventually Black Star Publishing.

The LRBW won reforms within the UAW, and within auto and related industries. But our lives at the workplace had not changed, and we wanted to understand why. These realities and realizations set the stage for the LRBW comrades who joined the study retreat after the split and who became part of new revolutionary formations.

CHAPTER 10

Becoming Working-Class Intellectuals and Lifelong Revolutionaries, 1971 and Beyond

> Everybody who had any idea of what political power meant saw the League of Revolutionary Black Workers and DRUM, anything saying revolutionary and union in the same breath, as a step forward. Put Black workers in there, you had the summation of all the social upheaval going on.
>
> —Jim Fite (2017)

> The Communist League did not have a real proletarian base. The significance of meeting and uniting with the League of Revolutionary Black Workers was that this gave us the third leg on that stool. That allowed us to form a stable working-class party.
>
> —Nelson Peery (2017)

From the Communist League to the League of Revolutionaries for a New America, 1971 to the Present

Formally the League of Revolutionary Black Workers ceased to exist on June 21, 1971. But the comradeship and collectivity of the industrial workers, community workers, and students continued and deepened as we journeyed together through study and struggle. We met with Nelson and the California Communist League (CCL). That set in motion the political journey to join in forming the Communist League (CL). LRBW comrades were the critical working-class base for the CL. The next step was the formation of the Communist Labor Party (CLP) in 1974. Many of us participated in the transformation from the CLP to the League of Revolutionaries for a New America (LRNA) in 1995 and are still raising revolutionary hell.

Comrades who joined the journey from the League split to our journey to the Communist League, the Communist Labor Party, and the League of Revolutionaries for a New America today. Courtesy General Baker Institute.

Our Study and New Political and Organizational Homes

This leg of our personal and political journey began with our study retreat. We went from scattered political education when we could or wanted to do it to organization wide political education daily—preparing for the long-haul revolutionary process. We studied many works—Marx, Engels, Lenin, Stalin, of course, and Ho Chi Minh, Mao Zedong, Kwame Nkrumah, Frantz Fanon, C. L. R. James, and Walter Rodney. What really hooked us was Nelson's analysis in *The Negro National Colonial Question* (1973), prepared by the CL in 1972. It connected our reality with the international anticolonial movements. We understood we were exploited and oppressed not just because we were Black but because of our colonial status within the U.S. context and history. We joined with revolutionaries from Detroit, Chicago, California, and across the county in the preparty activity culminating in the formation of the CLP.

Marian reflected on the split, our study, and our political journey. She presented a wide-ranging view of this next stage in LRBW life and spoke to the need for education, but not in the same old way. What type of workers' organization were we going to become? She insisted that women be included in the leadership. She explained how Bob Williams got to Detroit to "lead" the study, the drama around his style, and how he got booted out. Bob was part of the Muni (municipal transportation) workers in the Bay Area around the CCL. Marian remembered connecting with the CCL and Nelson and being part of the transition to and formation of the CLP.

> We needed education and couldn't let time fly by. We had the base of the organization with us and had to go forward together. Chuck knew Bob Williams in California who could get us started. We got the money together and Chuck went there to get him.
>
> We had a big meeting and brought up the question, "What kind of organization are we gonna have?" I raised having women on the Executive Board. From that day, I was on it. We were learning how to work collectively, making sure people got education, and seeing where we're going as an organization.
>
> We set up the educationals when Bob got here. He was a bit harsh, but people were determined. Some fell away, and we had about a hundred people in the process. Because of the way Bob taught, we reached the point that we needed somebody else. Bob told us about the CCL and we brought them here. We told the CCL to get Bob out because he would destroy the organization.
>
> We learned how to educate. We read and discussed, and we exercised. We went to a community gym to run and walk in the morning. I got in good shape. Some people acted like they had a heart problem. It was funny.

> At the Courtland house office we were all on different committees—the team to clean it for the week, to cook, to babysit the kids when we were in class. The men learned what they hadn't learned in the past. Nobody refused to do our tasks because the education was taking us to a different level of discipline. Eventually, we said we got to go back out. (Kramer 2017)

Marian offered her perspective on our journey from the split through the transition into the CL, the CLP, and the LRNA. This thirty-five-year period saw major shifts in the U.S. and global economy and political landscape, especially in the late eighties and early nineties when LRNA was formed.

> We retreated for a year, studying and learning. Our work in the field was reflected in the classes. We recruited new people. We talked to Nelson about the CCL and said we're interested. We took about a hundred people into the CL at that point. It was good for all of us to be together. Judy was the first white woman in Detroit to join the CL during that period—our favorite first. After that, it became integrated.
>
> It was a long journey into the CL. Then we had our first congress for the founding of the Communist Labor Party (CLP) in 1974. I learned from my many committee assignments. I was on the committee working with other leftist organizations to talk about setting up a party. To prepare, we all studied all of our positions on certain things. People write so much. But it equipped us to know what they were talking about and what their opposition was to our analysis.
>
> It was amazing to see all the people who gathered at the congress. We joined together to build . . . the CLP. Many Latino people joined. Over the years the CLP changed. (Kramer 2017)

Marian fast-forwarded to the formation of the LRNA in 1995 within the context of our understanding of a rapidly changing world:

> Now we are the League of Revolutionaries for a New America (LRNA). We're on a different plateau.
>
> Looking back, the split was good because it made us understand we needed education to go to the next level. We'd won about every reform in the factory to be won, and in the school system, in health care, a lot of things. The split had to happen because we needed a new direction. I hate that a lot of folks felt they had to take credit for what they didn't do. People always ask, "Why can't we have another League of Revolutionary Black Workers?" Because those days are over.
>
> Today we're talking about a party for the working class as a whole, the unemployed or never worked. It's got to be based on the rising class, what's happening, the question of technology, and that we need a new society. It's not whether or

not it's electoral politics. That's just a tactic we use to gauge where the working class is at a particular time. We didn't expose a lot of that. But when we talk about democracy, we're talking about two democracies—from the community up and from the government down.

I had a taste of it when we went to Cuba. It was when everything was being reevaluated, including Committees for the Protection of the Revolution. We learned a lot. The Cubans were evaluating the representatives they sent to the region and from the region to the national, whether or not they represented their interest. If they didn't, they didn't go back. Cubans were informed about what was happening in the government. They took a role in their five year plan or whatever plan they might have. That does not happen here. People are not taught to be part of the whole.

The split was good for us and we were step-by-step reaching out. I'm glad we went on. Sometimes you gotta make drastic moves and you gotta deal with it too. (Kramer 2017)

Deepening Our Relations with Nelson and the California Communist League Comrades

Connecting with Nelson Peery and the California comrades was the essential next step in our journey. Nelson was a working-class Marxist theoretician and philosopher who grasped and applied revolutionary theory and philosophy to the objective conditions of the economy and society and to the subjective realities of consciousness and revolutionary struggle. His analysis in *Entering an Epoch of Social Revolution* (1993) of the antagonism and rupture in society around new electronic and robotic technology in the production process informed all of us on our intellectual and political journey.

We interviewed Nelson shortly before he joined the ancestors on September 6, 2015, and asked him to address the LRBW and its significance to the formation of the CL and CLP at that historical juncture. Nelson explained,

> The development of the CLP had a couple of strands. One was from the old Communist Party to maybe 10 years before the CLP. The other was the recruitment of young people primarily out of SDS, and some floating radicals looking for a place to express their revolutionary activism. That meant that the CL, as the founding group of the CLP, was somewhat unstable. It did not have a real proletarian base. The significance of meeting and uniting with the LRBW was that this gave us the third leg on that stool. That allowed us to form a stable working-class party....

> We were consolidating the CL's national base when the explosion at Dodge Main happened. The information we got was that this was a Black nationalist movement, which didn't appeal to me. But I began to read more about them and realized—you look like you're Black nationalist, but you're in a plant that's all Black. We got this.
>
> Chuck and Gen were looking for somebody to teach Marxism. They were in San Francisco and met with our people. I got this phone call. People from Detroit were coming down to Los Angeles—I lived in Watts—and they wanna talk to us.
>
> We had a productive meeting and were on the road to unite. There were things that disturbed me about the LRBW. They were in army uniforms and everybody was saying the same words the same way. But they were ready to become communists, to become revolutionaries.
>
> I talked with Gen before he left. I said all of us are gonna develop differently, but our goal has to be the same. That our next door neighbor is gonna tell us I'm happy my daughter is in your organization. But nobody's gonna join your organization that gets up at five A.M. and runs five miles. It was a rocky road. But after the unity meeting, we had the basis, not the form, for a national Communist League.
>
> We didn't choose these terms out of nowhere. The Communist League was the first communist organization after *The Communist Manifesto* was written and was the foundation of the Communist Party. That's why we chose that name. (N. Peery 2017)

Nelson further explained the significance of uniting with the LRBW and the basis for the CL's move from California to Chicago:

> The development with the LRBW did a lot of things. One, we had a cadre base we couldn't imagine before. Two, the financial contribution from the LRBW was unbelievable. They threw in enough money for us to shift the headquarters to Chicago. Nobody's gonna organize a revolutionary movement unless they're in Chicago. We began cadre schools where we brought comrades in for six weeks. They had to be fed and taken care of. That was done primarily with the contribution of the comrades from Detroit.
>
> And there was an exchange, a contribution on both sides. By allowing us to get a building where we could hold cadre schools, it allowed them to get trained. It allowed us to consolidate.
>
> The LRBW, like any organization, as it grows it splits. That's part of a law. I do know that when this fight was over, we had the cream of the LRBW. (N. Peery 2017)

Nelson laid out the contradictions and practical problems on the path to unity and merging with the LRBW:

> The path of uniting with the LRBW was not easy. They had rambled around, looking for something. We had rambled around, looking for something. We had discussions to make clear who we were and who they were. We were looking for the same thing, but it wasn't that there were no hostile discussions. We had some problems with some of the leadership that quit as we merged. But by and large, it was a really conscious effort on both sides to find common ground for this unity.
>
> After that unity developed, there was a practical problem. On one side, the development was primarily theoretical; on the other side, the development was primarily practical. We were able to merge because practical experience is a deceptive thing.
>
> You can go through something, but that doesn't mean you understand it. That comes years later. The LRBW rolled out of the practical fight for some kind of democracy in the workplace and allowing the production workers, who were primarily Black at Dodge Main, to develop. On the other hand, we had this problem of trying to substitute theory for the practical experience the LRBW had. It was a trade-off and there were obstacles along the way. But the sincerity on both sides carried the day and allowed us to complete that transition. (N. Peery 2017)

California Comrades Reflect on Meeting the League of Revolutionary Black Workers and Our Collective Political Path

In addition to Nelson, we interviewed several other California comrades who were part of the journey into the CCL, the CL, the CLP, and the LRNA—Jim Fite, JoAnn Capalbo, Beth Gonzales, and Nacho Gonzales. Jim joined the ancestors on January 1, 2024.

Jim Fite came into the CCL in Los Angeles (LA) through SDS in the turbulent sixties and has been part of the political journey ever since. He shared his radicalization growing up in Norman, Oklahoma, his SDS days, and meeting up with the CCL and later the LRBW during the transition to the CL:

> I dropped out of school to work full-time for Students for a Democratic Society (SDS), against the war in Vietnam and worked a bit in the civil rights movement with the National Association for the Advancement of Colored People (NAACP) and SNCC. The SDS national office sent me to LA to deal with some

leaders who did crazy stuff and weren't reaching the people who were against the war. SDS was being torn apart and the FBI put millions of dollars into destroying it. But there was so much opposition to the Vietnam War that we continued even though we weren't politically astute.

It wasn't just the war, the world was aflame with revolution. We supported the Vietnamese and other revolutionaries. We looked at the revolution in China and read *Peking Review* that advertised free books on Marx and Lenin. I got so many books I had to borrow a pickup truck—*The Communist Manifesto* and books by Marx and Engels. Revolutionaries around the world were talking about this stuff.

We realized Marx, Engels, and Lenin were talking about workers. But all the workers we knew were beating our asses in demonstrations. We didn't understand that the workers from the building trades were just one section of the working class, the most privileged and highly paid section. We were confused, but not confused enough to turn away from Marxism-Leninism. (Fite 2017)

Jim described meeting Nelson in the Communist Party (CP) bookstore in LA and joining the journey into the CCL, the CL, and beyond:

> One day I was looking for books and this guy came in with newspapers, the first issue of the *People's Tribune*. He said, "We're a grouping of revolutionary workers in Watts and have this newspaper. Would you put it out here? But don't give it to any students." I hadn't been in school for a while and thought I qualified. I said, "Excuse me, sir, could I have one?" He said, "Of course." The newspaper made more sense than anything I had heard.
>
> They were a group of eleven people. They invited me, my wife Sherry, and others to a Saturday afternoon study about revolution and revolutionary ideas at Nelson's house in Watts. Sue Ying, a revolutionary artist and cultural worker who was Nelson's wife, put on a feast. People gave reports about the situation—why the bourgeois were doing stuff and what we could do to counter them. This made sense. We had a small study group called Marxist-Leninist workers or something. We had dropped out of SDS. The Weather Underground was in charge and it had blown apart. We told the study group there were some people who knew what they're doing. Some have been revolutionaries for a long time and they're reading *Capital*. We all joined at once and probably doubled their size till some of us dropped out.
>
> I worked at General Motors when we hooked up with Nelson, moved to Compton, and started working with the CCL. We worked there for a few years until it was clear that Chicago was the basis of manufacturing. If we wanted to be a revolutionary organization, we had to go there. Plus Chicago and Detroit were

an axis of industrial production. We went one by one till we got enough money to bring others, get a building, and establish the center in Chicago. (Fite 2017)

Jim spoke to the early discussions in the CCL about the LRBW:

> The workers in the United States were bubbling, particularly Black workers. The first grouping the CCL visited was the Muni drivers in San Francisco. The union was primarily Black, very militant, and had revolutionaries in it. We tried to get a relationship where we gave to each other. What we had to give was study, thinking. Not that you should do it our way, but a method of thinking about how to solve our problems together.
>
> We heard about the LRBW in Detroit. One day Nelson said, "We're gonna meet with these guys." We were enthusiastic. The LRBW's reputation preceded you. It was not the syndicalism of the Muni drivers, it was much more open revolutionary attitudes. It was a breakthrough. Nelson said to me, "You're gonna speak" and I'm thinking you don't want Okie up there. I think it was Chuck who held me up. Talk about being paralyzed with fear.
>
> I had written my speech and held onto the podium because my legs were liquid. It looked like four hundred Black militants dressed in army fatigues and going, "Yeah, tell us what happened." The speech was based on our line, which was a collective effort to analyze the current situation using Marxism. The crowd was very kind, allowing me to go through this long-winded discussion. We became good friends and all the relationships with the LRBW were top shelf.
>
> Our growth was dependent upon this relationship. We had to figure out the problems and how to solve them. There were problems on both sides. Some people didn't want the growth to happen and police agents in both organizations were against it. We didn't know who they were so we couldn't tell if somebody was being a horse's ass or they were actually undercutting our activity. But Gen came forward, Jerome came forward, people like that. It gave our organization a quality we didn't have before, not in the depth of the working class. LRBW politics dominated large sections of production. They challenged the bourgeoisie about whether production had to take into account the needs of the workers. It was a tremendous breakthrough, we evolved, and we became something different. The LRBW changed and the CCL changed, both became something else. Those who stayed became the solid core of what is now the LRNA. (Fite 2017)

Jim shared more about how the CCL thought about Detroit, the LRBW, the industrial proletariat, Black workers, and the union.

> We were studying Marxism, the philosophy of the workers. We knew huge sections of workers were bought off, not acting in the interest of workers as a class.

But there were these Black workers who had a revolutionary spirit that hadn't been seen before. The Black Panther Party came from a certain section of society, but not from the auto factories. These guys came from the auto factories and had been involved in the Detroit Rebellion. They had confronted the state and confronted industry. They hadn't been beaten and they hadn't won, but they were still in the struggle. They were reaching out for whoever was honest and thinking to join up with them.

We all came from the civil rights movement in one way or the other. Coming from the standpoint of Marxists, we wanted to find revolutionary workers. Nelson said this was a next step. We had to master this step, to interpenetrate and be a part of and learn from, and teach, and be with this grouping of people. They had something that hadn't come along before in our history, maybe in the 1930s, but not even then. This was a particular time in history with a particular grouping of people and particular circumstances.

Everybody who had any idea of what political power meant saw the LRBW and DRUM, anything saying revolutionary and union in the same breath, as a step forward. When you put Black workers in there, you had the summation of all the social upheaval going on in the country. We began wrestling and trying to learn and make a contribution. Soon we weren't us and they weren't them. We evolved into a new thing that began to press on the political nerves of the United States. This was happening as industries in Detroit began to shut down, shipping production to other countries, using robots, taking workers away from their livelihood and their political power. (Fite 2017)

JoAnn Capalbo, part of the LRNA leadership over the years, connected to the process through SDS study circles and the Marxist-Leninist Workers Association (MLWA) in LA. She joined the CCL in 1970 and moved to Chicago in 1971. That's when she first met with LRBW comrades as part of the expansion and formation of the CLP and later the LRNA. JoAnn explained her journey and the importance of study:

> I first came around the movement when I joined a study circle with people who came out of SDS. We studied *The Communist Manifesto*, *Wage Labour and Capital*, *Value, Price and Profit*, and more. We formed the MLWA from the study circles. We read theory and did practice. We wrote leaflets and took them to our neighborhoods and factories. We didn't get anywhere.
>
> We started to study with the CCL—they were pretty small. We didn't think we were gonna be part of the CCL. These were serious communists. But they recruited the leadership of the MLWA. We had the merger conference and everybody joined individually, we didn't merge organizations.

> We divided into clubs and I was a club chairman. I met with Nelson and Johnny, kind of the leadership, and worked with the Education Committee that Comrade Sue Ying headed up. We consolidated the newer members as we expanded. The education work culminated in the *Marxist-Leninist Study Guide*. A lot of that work was going through *Capital* and other works, and putting it in a form that the organization could study.
>
> I moved to Chicago in 1971 with my family and a couple of comrades to expand the organization. We got in touch with the LRBW. They came here, we went there. Having meetings, having classes, setting the foundation for what was gonna happen. We were clear that the LRBW was very serious. Nelson said we had to expand the cadre base in terms of the LRBW to give us the base in the labor movement we didn't have, to allow us to expand rapidly and take the next step to become the CLP.
>
> Everything started with people coming around some form of study circle—in the 1960s and today in the LRNA. It's been a good foundation for organizational continuity and for developing cadre. Everyone has fought to become a cadre, to find their own way in whatever struggle, to carry out the mission and purpose of the organization. That process was there from the beginning. The comrades who came out of the CP didn't want people to follow some leader somewhere. They wanted everybody to begin the process of developing themselves into a cadre that could educate and train and contribute on that basis at the highest level. That process continues.
>
> The MLWA was a very small group. When we joined the CCL, it more than doubled its size and allowed us to consolidate and expand the organization. That's pretty much where I came from and that was forty-eight years ago. Nelson told us when we first came around, "Well, I've been in the movement for forty years." I was like, "Wow, I think I'll be dead before then." But here we are. (Gonzales and Capalbo 2017)

Beth Gonzales, part of the LRNA leadership today, shared her path to the CCL and the formation of the CL, the CLP, and the LRNA. She described growing up in LA in a socially conscious family during the upheavals of the Watts Rebellion, the antiwar movement, and Marxist study circles in the sixties.

> Many of my parents' friends were or had been in the CP. We were socially conscious growing up, then Watts hit in 1965. Watts was burning. This was big, really historical. And there was the Vietnam War protest, including many young people. I got into a study circle for high school kids led by a retired couple who had left the CP.

My brother and I got some friends together and we studied "straight" Marxism, meeting every week for several years. The world made sense now, I knew how change happened. I didn't go to much college because I wanted to be a revolutionary. My brother said there's a meeting in Los Angeles, this is serious and you should come. I went. It was a merger conference. SDS groups came together to merge in preparation for coming into the CCL. Here were people just a few years older who made so much sense. Of course, people like Nelson made all the sense in the world. It was clear how important study and science were. The people in the CCL were serious revolutionaries. They studied revolution and history. They knew how revolution happens, how the world works. They had experience and drew lessons from that. (Gonzales and Capalbo 2017)

Beth also moved to Chicago and was part of connecting with the LRBW and expansion into the CLP. She spoke about the "fantastic experience" of the cadre schools.

We shared months living, eating, and studying together. We were pushed and challenged. It wasn't just for the newer people coming in. It was a moment of consolidating the CLP as a whole. We got a common scientific framework for thinking that has stood over time. We still have to study, but learning that stuff at that point in our lives meant we could understand the changes in the world. The foundation, the beginning of it is something objective to take to the conclusion. The conclusion is something subjective that depends on conscious revolutionaries. It was different from a lot of the education among revolutionaries where they discussed the movement rather than what's happening in society. They stayed on the surface of things. (Gonzales and Capalbo 2017)

Nacho Gonzales grew up in LA in a Mexican neighborhood and got politicized during the 1960s. There was the Watts Rebellion, the antiwar movement, support for Cesar Chavez and the farm workers, and MEChA—an important Chicano/a student organization. He met up with the CCL and helped form the Colectiva, and they joined the CL in 1972. Nacho explained,

In 1968 I was asked to speak at a SDS regional conference in LA. After I spoke we went to have beer and a couple of SDS guys from New York and Chicago and Jim Fite were there. They said, "You guys are really into Marxism here in LA. Where does this come from?"

In LA there was a grouping that got expelled from the CP and they became the provisional organizing committee (POC). I was acquainted with them. The first time I met Nelson, he was still in the POC. I was in the neighborhood where I grew up in Watts and we're out in the street drinking beer. These guys come walking by and it's Nelson, Sue, a couple of others, and they got leaflets. They tried to organize a carwash in Watts that I went to. Their leaflets were sectarian and I cracked up. Some said, "Free the Negro nation." People with the car wash didn't know what it was—it was real theoretical. Some attacked revisionism and workers didn't know what the hell that was. Once in a while they'd have a good leaflet about organizing the carwash, very practical and agitational—"Are you tired of earning thirty-five cents a day working like a dog?" The POC broke up around 1968. They expelled the LA collective and it broke into the CCL and the United Front.

About 1968 I met Deanna Robinson in the Chicano movement. We formed a study group and she brought in the positions of the POC—the national question, party building, and Marxist philosophy. We were close to Masai Hewitt, who was in the Black Panther Party, and was very theoretical. We studied and eventually formed the Colectiva del Pueblo [Colectiva]—ten to twenty of us. The Cal State campus was a different environment where we got a lot of students. It was a commuter campus, we were older, and many had worked in the factories. We'd have three hundred people at a MEChA meeting. But MEChA got infiltrated by the political police. Police informers were on both sides—nationalists and Marxists—and they forced a split between the Marxists and nationalists.

When I first heard of DRUM, I thought it was real important and people I knew did too. DRUM represented something different because it was grounded in the factories. DRUM, the RUMs, and eventually the LRBW helped bring about an alternative to the Black Panther Party and the extreme nationalism dominant in most communities. The Colectiva heard about the LRBW from SDS and others. We came to the realization that we had to have a national organization, a local organization wasn't gonna do it.

We began meeting with many groups, including the CCL. The CCL was the most grounded, the most scientific, and was based in factories and neighborhoods. We started doing joint work—distributions and studying with them. But our collective was going through internal splits because MEChA broke into two wings. One became the Colectiva and the other became the labor committee of La Raza Unida Party. It was a difficult struggle and took six months, maybe nine to merge with the CL. We merged in 1972—about three months after the LRBW joined the CL.

Someone from the Colectiva went to the CL conference and said, "General Baker from the LRBW spoke there and they joined the CL." It was big. Most of us had gone back into the plants by then and weren't on the college campus. The LRBW being part of the CL helped our argument for being part of the CL. (N. Gonzales 2017)

Nacho explained how he came to Marxism as theory in action and the impact of Marxist education in the CL:

> My father was not a Marxist, but was a real anti-imperialist. My brother moved me towards Marxism. I got a theoretical grounding combined with action. There's a lot of people who know a lot of theory, but they got no friends. They can be radical all they want, they can talk a lot of shit. But they can't explain anything to anybody. There's no base. You see a lot of people like that. They know abstract theory but unless you apply it, it doesn't become real.
>
> We studied a lot in the Colectiva so when I came into the CL I had the rudiments of the national question, and philosophy and dialectics. I finished that with the CL and studied economics. Right before it dissolved and became the CLP, they had these six-week schools. We're meeting seven days a week—maybe a few days off. It was heavy-duty theoretical education. When you came out of there, you had a PhD in Marxism. All that helps give you a grounding. (N. Gonzales 2017)

CHAPTER 11

Other Detroiters Join the Journey and the Study

Many Detroiters were close to the LRBW over the years. It wasn't until the study period after the split, the CL and the CLP, that we became a multiracial working-class organization and folks of other races and nationalities joined the ongoing journey. These are the stories of the Detroit comrades who worked with the LRBW, who became part of the study process, the CL and the CLP in the 1970s, and the LRNA in 1995.

Frank Joyce, Ron Glotta, Jim Bish, and Rita Valenti were part of the Motor City Labor League (MCLL), an important organization in relation to the LRBW. Other Detroiters include Linda Wheeler, a student and movement activist; Judy Williams, an educator close to the LRBW from the beginning; Al Gladyck, an auto worker and member of the Capital Collective; Maureen Taylor, a longtime welfare rights activist; Esther Mauricio, an activist in Head Start and the Latino/a community; Pam Randazzo, a garment worker and antiwar activist; Nancy Allinger, a peace activist; and Richard Fahoome, a labor activist.

Motor City Labor League Comrades Join the Journey

Frank Joyce, Ron Glotta, Jim Bish, and Rita Valenti were part of the MCLL, a collective of white folks who were engaged in social struggle, studied Marxism, and worked with the LRBW. We lift up their reflections on their own journeys and on the enduring importance of political education in understanding and acting in the world.

Frank, a leader in the MCLL, explained their relations with the LRBW and the transition process. He grew up in the Detroit suburbs and was a self-described "young rebel." He was part of the Northern Student Movement

(NSM) and People Against Racism (PAR). They organized to protest and resist white supremacy in the North in relation to the struggle against Jim Crow in the South. Frank went to Wayne State, worked briefly in the auto plants, was a "new left" activist, and connected up with LRBW folks in the early days. He explained how these roads converged and the importance of Marxism and political education in the process:

> I was on a picket line at Dodge Main. Two things had put me in this orbit. The NSM raised the question of a different role for whites than for African Americans. Should white people be talking to white people? If the problem is racism, that was in the white community and you should be there. I was involved in that and was a founder of an organization called PAR, which sort of evolved out of the NSM. We were in the early stages of opposition to the Vietnam War, and when DRUM came along, I was a draft resister.
>
> Wayne State became a focal point for movement activity. That's where I met John Watson, Ken, Gen, Mike, and later you—Jerome—and others. A call went out for the picket lines at Dodge Main. I joined the lines and engaged with Chuck and others.
>
> The MCLL reflected our best understanding at the time. There was something distinct about DRUM and ELRUM and the LRBW. It was the question of race, and the question of point-of-production organizing versus more community-based organizing. We came up with the MCLL as another organization that could be supportive of the LRBW.
>
> We were young. There was a cross-section of African Americans and whites who had quite a bit of organizing experience. We had helped create the *Fifth Estate* newspaper, other communications vehicles, and organizations like NSM. For better or worse, we sensed this was a time to create another umbrella organization.
>
> A significant corollary to that was the Control, Conflict & Change book club. We routinely had a thousand people come together at Central Methodist Church to discuss radical topics and books. We broke into small discussion groups, generally the author was there to make a presentation, and maybe somebody would react. All these threads were woven together—the book club, MCLL, the LRBW, PAR, and the incredible role Detroit played in the antiwar movement.
>
> I stress the richness of all of these dialogues among organizations and the MCLL, in particular. But big movements, I now realize, are also a big mess—the antiwar movement, the civil rights movement. The MCLL was a mess and later had a very bitter split that created hostilities that some people probably still feel. (Joyce 2017)

Frank reflected on the value of Marxism and political education.

> Every once in a while I have occasion to say, "You're looking at a guy who read all three volumes of *Capital*." I think events have overtaken Marx, but there is foundational thinking that has stood me in good stead over the years. It's not just reading and trying to absorb and apply that to what is going on today. Political education is not something you should or can do by yourself. Whether you're trying to build a book club or talking about a study group, it's the interaction and the interchange of ideas. Are these ideas relevant or not, were they useful once and now not so much? (Joyce 2017)

Ron worked with the LRBW as a workers' comp lawyer and was a leader in MCLL. He shared his story on becoming a Marxist and the formation of the MCLL:

> We met on the Wayne State campus. We were reading *What Is to Be Done* and *One Step Forward, Two Steps Back* by Lenin. Debating those issues, trying to figure out where we were going and what we were doing. The Communist Party (CP) had been decimated and we were angry. We felt they should be helping us. In retrospect, I understand what the party was going through with agents and all. They gave me books and direction, and were a big part of my education. Though none of them said they were members of the CP.

> Everybody was talking Marxism and revolution. The sad thing about that period was the nationalism. Mike Hamlin doesn't remember this, but I remember. Sharon, my ex-wife, and I were going to a meeting and Mike said, "You know white people can't be at this meeting." So we left and went to the Panther meeting, Panthers allowed us to be there. I took the position that I couldn't be insulted, because it was my revolution just as much as anybody else's. So we organized the MCLL. (Glotta 2017)

Later, Ron and his ex-wife Sharon made the journey from the MCLL and their collective study to the CL and the CLP.

Jim Bish was a union organizer and joined the political journey with LRBW comrades as a member of the MCLL. He lived in Detroit since 1967, except for four years when the CLP assigned him to go up north to Baldwin, Michigan. He met his wife there, and they became friends with Rob Williams—back from exile in Cuba—and Mable Williams. His organizing job transferred Jim back to Detroit in 1982 and he reengaged.

Jim explained how he connected with the LRBW and the journey.

> I was in the MCLL, which was like a companion organization to the LRBW. Back then you had Black organizations and white organizations. The LRBW was very influential. One of the leaders of the MCLL and the person who brought me into it was Sheila Murphy, who was married to Ken Cockrel. So there was a personal relationship there. Another MCLL leader was Frank Joyce, who had come out of the antiwar movement. Some of the people in the MCLL were attorneys for the LRBW, for Gen, and others. I was organizing with the Welfare Employees Union, an independent state social services union. The lawyers were representing us too. It was a passion, we weren't paying them anything.
>
> There was real collaboration in terms of MCLL supporting what the LRBW was trying to do. That was very positive, particularly in the plants. The lawyers encouraged us to get involved. The book club—Control, Conflict & Change—was a huge and very successful collaboration. We were all involved. We met once a month. They would choose a book and bring in a national figure to critique it, then we had table discussions. We all prepared, the table leaders and all of us. A couple of hundred people attended, including a lot of liberal folks out of Oakland County. They weren't part of the MCLL cadre, but they were very close, and they were foot soldiers in all kinds of stuff. The relationship, until the split, was very good. My real connection was through the LRBW. When they split, some went to the Black Workers Congress. Then I went into the CLP. (Bish 2017)

Rita worked at Metropolitan Hospital and was an MCLL member. She shared her political history in the Detroit area and the relations among MCLL members and LRBW comrades. She talked about the depth and importance of our collective political education, including the Control, Conflict & Change book club:

> My friend Michael and I lived in the Moss House collective. We knew PAR and Frank and his wife Valerie. This was around the beginning of the MCLL. We fell in with John and Edna Watson because of their political connections. I worked at Metropolitan Hospital where Edna was a nurse and we talked about health care and organizing hospital workers. John was still editor of the *Inner-City Voice*.
>
> Michael and I became members of the MCLL. Initially there was a coalition that included Justin Ravitz, Sheila Murphy, and Ken Cockrel. Justin was one of the lawyers who handled the James Johnson case—an important political issue in Detroit and in the MCLL. The MCLL developed political education and shop papers for members working in the plants and sites like the hospital. We organized the Metro S & P Commission—service and production—for folks in service or production.
>
> Control, Conflict & Change was a monthly book club in Detroit. It was polit-

> ical—with the LRBW, MCLL, BWC, and PAR. Before the split, Mike, John Watson, and Ken from the LRBW participated, and Sheila, Ken's wife, from MCLL. The book club had about seven hundred members, with two to three hundred people a month. People did presentations—LRBW folks, later the BWC, and book authors including Howard Zinn and others. We had breakout groups and roundtables with political conversation about the books we were studying. (Valenti 2017)

Rita continued, explaining MCLL's connections with the LRBW, their view of Black workers, health and safety issues, and her path into the CL, the CLP, and the LRNA:

> A group of workers' comp lawyers in Detroit were influential within the MCLL and brought us some of the educational stuff going on in the LRBW.
>
> The MCLL saw Black workers as the vanguard of the revolution. Our understanding had a lot to do with how society works. Black workers were at the point of production, and controlling the point of production was critical to the economics of society and to change in society. The LRBW and the Black worker, in particular, was that section of the class necessary to change society and to change power in this country. You guys were everything to us. There was no question about the centrality of the Black worker. We began to study history to understand why that was true, but we knew it from the practice of the work in the plants.
>
> I worked at Metropolitan, the hospital the UAW ran for the auto workers. Because of the wildcat strikes, we saw the issues around health and safety in the plants. We got a lot of patients with the chronic conditions Black workers were experiencing as well as the accidents. We had a collective working at Metropolitan which developed into what we later called the Cadre Organization. Many were in the MCLL and some were not. Some were old CP members and some militant trade unionists.
>
> The MCLL split in 1972, just a few months after the LRBW split. The MCLL sort of came out on the side of what became the BWC, with Mike, John Watson, and Ken. There was also a struggle in MCLL over who was gonna control equipment—the mimeo machine and Gestetner used to produce literature. Some of the equipment had been scurried away to the Moss House. Outside the house a section of the MCLL gathered in opposition, but nobody got shot.
>
> We did our own study and studied different things—*Pedagogy of the Oppressed*, Frantz Fanon, and Lenin on *What Is to Be Done*. We studied a lot of Lenin and stuff around national liberation struggles. We worked all day and we'd meet at night, then we partied.

I didn't know about the study retreat after the split that LRBW folks were part of. As it was ending, relationships had developed with the worker comp lawyers from MCLL and members of the LRBW through Ron and Josh Lerner. Later I met LRBW women—Lolita, a leader in Cadillac, Sandra, and Marsha at Frito-Lay. I met more folks from the LRBW during the Detroit Forge strike in 1973. It was the CL by then.

Today I'm in the LRNA, which is an outgrowth of that entire process. The link in that process is political consciousness, how you get it, what's the relationship between theoretical study and practical activity, and how do you develop that relationship? (Valenti 2017)

More Detroiters Join the Journey

Linda Wheeler connected with the LRBW as a student activist during her high school days in Highland Park and carried that experience throughout her life. She shared her story:

> I got connected with the LRBW in a unique and fortunate way. I'm a Highland Park resident and went to school there. Our high school is on Glendale and the LRBW office was the next block over. I went over at lunch and after school. It was a progression for me, my sister, and some friends. I knew Black was beautiful. My parents instilled that into me and the importance of reading. We had a strike at the high school for Black studies and we eventually got Black studies. It was an outpouring of parents, community people, and, of course, the LRBW.
>
> The LRBW was a continuation of what I received at home. It gave me that organization, the study, the discipline. Gen and Marian were great—they were my adopted parents. The LRBW understood what we wanted. Black youth, the world is yours. Take it. Believe in yourself, don't be afraid or timid. If you want change, you have to be that change. That's what the LRBW gave us, that's how I got with the LRBW.
>
> I retired two years ago from special education in Highland Park. I slipped politics in even with my babies because they needed to know what's going on in the world and how it affects them. You may be absent for a while from attending meetings, but you never leave the LRBW. How could you ever leave something like that? The LRBW gave me a clear outlook and a political outlook. The LRBW is the heart and soul of who you are, like your heartbeat. I never left the LRBW, and I'll always be a revolutionary. (Wheeler 2017)

Linda offered her take on education and speaking in the language of the people:

> Without education you're lost, and the LRBW gave that. But the LRBW said we have to give it in the language of the people. This is key. To relate to my babies, I had to speak their language to take them where I wanted them to go. If we work together, we can learn together. And when we learn together, we can do things together. Education is key. (Wheeler 2017)

Al Gladyck, who joined the ancestors March 17, 2022, was an auto worker at the Sterling Heights plant, Jefferson Assembly, and Dodge Main. He explained how he first heard of the LRBW and shared his experience as a white worker in the context of the LRBW struggle:

> I heard about the LRBW in early 1970. I knew some people who were shooting *Finally Got the News*. Everyone worshipped the LRBW. It was part of the civil rights period—the 1960s when the auto companies started building plants in what became suburbs. I worked at the white plants in Sterling Heights, the old plants in the city were becoming Black plants. The struggle within DRUM, ELRUM, and other RUMs was twofold.
>
> Black workers were held back from doing anything except production jobs. I understood that because the first day I was at Sterling Heights Stamping, I went to the cafeteria, sat down at the table and got told that table wasn't for me. I said, "What are you talking about?" The cafeteria was segregated. Everybody got along putting parts on the car until you had to socialize. So there's a lot of things that brought me to where I am today and I think Gen was one of the people that I admired most. We didn't talk a lot about things that weren't political, but he was one of my heroes. (Gladyck 2017)

Al and others organized the Capital Collective to study Marx's *Capital*. They joined in forming the CLP in 1974.

> I read *Value, Price and Profit*, and *Wage Labour and Capital* by Marx. They were right on. Some friends in the Detroit Organizing Committee organized to talk about the situation we were in. There had to be a political solution. We agreed to do some studying. I said we should study *Capital* since that's Marx's premier book. We were really curious about how capitalism works. We started *Capital*. For four years, 1970 to 1974, about ten of us met every Sunday and we never got through the whole thing. People called us the Capital Collective. I don't think we ever called ourselves that.
>
> The Capital Collective was one of the groups from Detroit that was asked to

help form the CLP. We said sure. We didn't know what the hell that meant. But it was with the LRBW and the MCLL. It was really the first integrated left organization in Detroit. (Gladyck 2017)

Judy Williams, who was married to John Williams for a while, was part of the LRBW study collective, the CL, and the CLP after the split. She described the deep analytical skills that came from our political education:

> Political education was one of the things that struck me immediately about the LRBW and about John. We studied at home. I was reading all this stuff. Everybody was reading everything. We were excited, we were learning. The people in and around the LRBW, for the most part, were and are extremely intelligent. They understood the importance of studying past revolutions and movements. You're opened up to a new world. A lot of us realized we've been miseducated. We needed to read some of the original works. The role of education in the LRBW and later in the CL set the basis for how everyone coming out of that situation looks at the world.
>
> Even the people who left at a certain point—whether it was after the LRBW, especially after the CL, or after the CLP—were equipped to analyze society. Whatever the setting, you were equipped to add knowledge to what it takes to struggle out here. You didn't always know the exact tactics, but you had a way of looking at the world that was totally different from any other group.
>
> The political education was phenomenal, because I still use it and I'm not directly involved. I used it when I taught social studies to middle school and high school kids, when I taught in the College of Education at Wayne State. I used a lot of works and understandings in teaching teachers who were going to teach others. Even now so much is going on in the world and in this country. The political education allows me to patiently educate people, and not to rant and rave like some people in the union do. It's not effective.
>
> It also taught me something that I heard people say today. You don't educate people by jumping leaps and bounds ahead of them. You figure out where they are and how to move ahead. The political education I got alongside the LRBW and later the CL and CLP equipped me for life. (Judy Williams 2017)

Maureen Taylor, a longtime welfare rights activist and president of the Michigan Welfare Rights Union, told her story of connecting with the study just after the LRBW split:

> I began to be involved with political movements when the LRBW was breaking up. I went to several functions about new arguments and whatnot. I didn't understand what it was about. I became interested in the Black Panther Party and went

to some of their meetings. There were issues there that I didn't understand how they fit in. I thought let me try some college courses.

So, I enrolled in Highland Park Community College and was involved with protests because they were all white faculty. The second year of the Association of Black Students, Larry Simmons was elected as president and I was elected as vice president. How do we demand equality for African Americans and get women off the floor? In one of many protests, I was standing on the roof of the college and throwing rocks down. Somebody started screaming, "Maureen, come down here. You don't even know what you're throwing rocks for." It was General Baker—and I threw a rock at him.

I got off the roof and went down. Gen invited me to some political meetings at the Courtland house. He said, "We are in a transition period out of the LRBW, and we're moving in a certain direction. We are not in opposition to the Black Panther Party. But something is missing in our understanding of how the world works and it looks like you might be a person that might wanna know how the world works." I did want to know how the world works because I couldn't understand why there was so much turmoil, so much pain, so much poverty, so much discrimination based on color. What in the world is going on? All the history books say United States of America is the land of gold and plenty. It just didn't seem to be turning out that way. Something is wrong here.

So, Gen offered the opportunity: "Why don't you stop by these classes?" The LRBW was breaking up. The Panthers were starting to move, but the police were against them. And here's this small group of people that started to be a larger group and a larger group meeting to try to figure out how the world works. That was my initial introduction to the LRBW. That's how I found them. They found me on the roof throwing rocks. That's how it happened. (Taylor 2017)

Esther Mauricio, a lifetime Detroiter, was a movement activist in Head Start and the Latino/a community. Her parents came from Mexico before immigrants needed papers and were legal residents all their lives. Esther shared her history and the significance of theoretical and political education for herself and her kids during the LRBW days and later.

> My dad worked at Great Lakes Steel and went out on strike sometimes six months at a time. During strikes in the summer we worked in the fields in Monroe, Michigan—picking tomatoes, carrots, whatever so we had something to eat. We helped other workers on the picket line because whatever my dad had, we shared with his compadres. Nobody was gonna help us.
>
> I met the LRBW when the Head Start moms went to Washington for a conference. The hotel denied us our rooms, so we slept in the lobby. They finally gave us

rooms to keep us quiet. After that, I went to a meeting at the bookstore on Linwood with the Head Start mamas and Wylie. It had newspapers and everything, but the first thing I saw was a bunch of men dressed like Fidel Castro with beards and fatigues. I said, "What did I get myself into?" That was my entrance.

I pulled my husband Dan in and we brought the kids to Courtland for meetings and classes. My knowledge of the LRBW began when I entered that bookstore. I learned about the movement in our classes because we didn't have that knowledge. The political education and study of Marxism affected us. I say us because I mean me and my kids. My kids were always over at Courtland with Jackie, Kashka, Samantha, and Connie, who wrote a poem to Bob about being a proletarian. They became very conscious of what's going on politically though they're not in any group. Growing up around Courtland and learning about Marxism had a big impact on them and me. It opened my eyes—studying the foundations, the woman question. I brought my kids to class and Bob didn't like it. But I had to do what I had to do. If you wanted me, you had to have my kids.

When I listen to all the rhetoric out here on CNN, MSNBC I shake my head. I may not know the correct line, but I'll be damned if I don't go find it out from the *People's Tribune* online or the *Rally, Comrades!* That analysis feels correct. What I've learned over the years, the theory and the analysis, is what keeps me involved. And that theory has been available to me through the CLP and the LRNA. (Mauricio 2017)

Pam Randazzo, another lifelong Detroiter, spoke about her personal and political transformation because of her educational experience:

I lived in Detroit all my life and raised my two sons here. My father came from Italy and my mother was born here, but was from Italy. He worked for Hudson Motor Company that was bought out by American Motors. I worked at a garment manufacturing plant where we organized as Teamsters. I was interested in the antiwar movement and a young worker there, who was in the CP, brought me to several events. My husband and I became more involved and we met people from the LRBW. That started me off.

I got involved toward the end of the LRBW as a separate organization. A young woman at a rally asked me if I was interested in coming to hear a speaker. I said yeah. The speaker was John Williams. He talked about history and I was "jaw drop." What he said made so much sense. He had literature and my ex-husband (now) and I picked up *The Communist Manifesto*. We read it paragraph by paragraph and talked about it. I didn't have any knowledge of the history of the labor movement. It wasn't provided in school.

That was the beginning of my understanding of the struggle before us—that was continuing. If we want to see a better world for humanity, we have to create the world we want to see. My life could not have changed or been any fuller—because of the education I received. Some of what we learned was heartbreaking, hard, and emotion filled. We began to realize there was more to it than you as an individual and your convictions. (Randazzo 2017)

Nancy Allinger, a native Detroiter, first heard about the LRBW when her friend, Pam Randazzo invited her to a CL meeting. She explained her journey from having "no politics" to the CL study.

> My dad came over from Austria when he was four. He was Hungarian and my mom was French and German. He was a tool and die maker for Packard automobile company, and my mom never worked outside the home. I was born and raised in Detroit, the Northeast Side. I graduated from Detroit schools, didn't go on to college until I was fifty-two, after I raised all my kids. I ended up teaching at Detroit Public Schools for almost twenty years. Judy Williams was one of my mentors.
>
> I had no politics whatsoever, except I knew I was a Democrat. I wasn't even against the war in Vietnam. What really started me was the East Side Women for Peace. After the education with them, I was very much against the war. And it was from East Side Women that I met my good friend, Pam Randazzo. She invited me to a meeting of the CL. At first I didn't want to go, I was going through a divorce. She said, "You have to get out, you have to meet people."
>
> After I went to my very first meeting of the CL, I was totally impressed by everybody who spoke and remember how everybody sang. They took popular songs and made them into communist songs. It was so cool. They offered study sessions and I said, "I want to study and find out about this." I started studying with Darryl and Sandra. They made me breakfast and that was the first time I ever ate grits. I was like, "Wow, this is really something." I was learning not only about Marxism, but I was learning about people and different foods and everything. The political education made all the difference in the way that I looked at things. I questioned everything back then, and I still do. (Allinger 2017)

Richard Fahoome, who joined the ancestors on August 16, 2023, was a lifelong Detroiter and labor activist. He entered the journey during the Marxist study days after the LRBW split and summed up what Marxism and intense study meant to him:

> The amazing thing is what we learned. How things develop, they don't come from nothing. My grandparents were active in labor and the socialist movement. Marxist books were around the house. My grandfather came here from Syria in

the early twentieth century and moved to Detroit where he worked at the Ford plant in Highland Park. My mother's family were English and Welsh, immigrated to Winnipeg, Canada, and then came to Detroit. My parents were labor activists. My father was a lithographer and worked on printing presses. I worked with him for a long time, but left to work in the auto factory and got active in the UAW. But factory work was hard and I got hurt. So I went to work for Detroit public schools doing maintenance work.

In the early 1970s we lived at Six Mile and John R, and there was a food co-op. That's when I first met Gen and came in contact with the LRBW and the Marxism around that. So we joined. My aha moment involved Nelson during a meeting at the Belmont Center. The Vietnam War was ending and Nelson gave this analysis that was good. We got more and more involved.

Like everybody, what I remember most is the Marxism and the intensive education. When you listen to the news, it's certainly not a class analysis. Once you're introduced to a method or a way to analyze history, you practice it, read about it, study it and try it. Some things work, some don't. The hardest thing is to keep your feet on the ground and not get too far out front. You develop so you know what to do, what's going on scientifically. (Fahoome 2017)

Marxism, Class Unity, and the Revolutionary Process

The political and educational transformation from the LRBW split to the formation of the CLP was about three years. This motion was deeply rooted in comrades' personal, intellectual, and political journeys—our southern roots, the rebellions and uprisings of the 1960s in Detroit and world over, and the revolutionary communist movement. It was concretely grounded in our struggle against class exploitation, white supremacy, and male dominance in the auto plants, the unions, and our communities. In 1995 the comrades who stayed the course organizationally transitioned from the CLP to the LRNA.

Nelson shared lessons for revolutionaries today confronting new realities in a new moment. He spoke to the critical importance of Marxism and science, the complexities and contradictions of color and class, and political unity in the revolutionary struggle:

When I was in high school they denied there could be a science of society. But, Marxism is a science of society. Like any effort, if you disregard science, you are not going to win. Stop treating Marxism as a gospel, and treat it as any other science. Science is based on observation. If we don't observe the functioning of the real world, how this real world actually operates, we are not gonna be scientists, and we're not gonna be able to resolve our problem.

We gotta look at the entire process. What is happening, and what are the motive forces making this happen. The first thing we have to look at is the economic foundation for what is happening. You can't have political unity unless you have economic unity. Scientifically speaking, we have to look at where this economic unity is developing, why it is developing, and what direction it is going in.

Half of science is continually going back to the real world. If we can't grapple with the contradiction between perceptual knowledge and conceptual knowledge, then we're not scientists and we're not gonna be able to solve any problems whatsoever. (N. Peery 2017)

Mitch captured the revolutionary reality and moment:

We knew after reading and studying some Marxism that we were members of a certain class now. And that all workers, regardless of color or race or whatever, we have the same economic connection. We got to try to unite the class. We've been on that mission to one degree or another ever since. (W. Mitchell 2017)

We embraced our racial, national, and gender diversity. LRBW comrades, particularly the workers at the point of production, captured the transformative potential of political education and especially Marxism as we continued our journey toward becoming working-class intellectuals and revolutionaries for the long haul.

Part Four

Lessons and Possibilities in Revolutionary Times

CHAPTER 12

The Centrality of Education in Revolutionary Struggle

It was in our study retreat after the split in the LRBW that our class consciousness and our enduring commitment to class struggle became grounded in our understanding of Marxism. We connected with our history and our country's history, especially southern history. We became internationalists and connected with struggles around the world. A strategic lesson for developing revolutionaries is that to become a lifelong revolutionary, you have to be engaged with revolutionaries, those who study and stay the course.

In our interviews, we asked about the role of political education in our lives and political work. To a person, we all spoke about the critical importance of political education and Marxism, in particular, in shaping our understanding of the world, of working-class consciousness, and of class struggle.

A conversation between Mike Hamlin, who had been a member of the LRBW Executive Board, and Jerome began with Mike's statement about the LRBW and Marxism:

> Everybody who was a leftist came to Detroit because we were drawing workers to Marxism. (Hamlin 2017)

Mike continued,

> When I showed up, there was hardly anywhere to study Marxism. John Watson and I studied Marx, Lenin, and Trotsky. John Williams and Luke were in charge of education. They did a good job, but I'm not sure people paid attention. I don't know if they internalized a serious Marxist ideology that was reflected in their practice and their daily actions. People were busy, going to high school or college, and some didn't read. I don't know how many people the political education still hangs with, but it's stuck with me. (Hamlin 2017)

Jerome responded,

> It's stuck with a lot of people we've interviewed. In fact, the whole world of political education and theory is probably what most people talked about. That's significant. (in Hamlin 2017)

Mike and Jerome took a deeper dive into who really studied Marxism in the LRBW. Jerome started,

> I'm curious how deep it went. Because the study of Marxism during that period of 1968 to 1970 never touched those of us who were on the front lines in the plants. Someone asked me, "Was the LRBW a Marxist organization?" I said, "Not to my knowledge." Because up to that point, I never experienced study in Marxism. Was it just among the leadership that the study was going on? (in Hamlin 2017)

Mike elaborated,

> No. There was studying amongst some of the groups, but I don't think they were into it. Our approach was to study people who had made revolutions. We studied Che Guevara, Ho Chi Minh, that kind of stuff. Reading Marx and Lenin was different. Lenin is easier to read, but you have to be serious.
>
> But, you asked a good question, so let me back up. We need to understand how thoroughgoing the indoctrination of the people in this country is. People look at somebody talking about revolution like they're crazy. Unless you present it like Bernie Sanders does, and they think he's crazy too. I'm a controversial character. I don't wanna hear any BS about this country, because I know.
>
> Another thing. The civil rights movement, the civil rights establishment, and the capitalist establishment have erased the Black power movement. For them, the only gains made in the struggle were made by the nonviolent civil rights movement. It changed things in the plants and in workplaces across the country. So nonviolence is the only way. (Hamlin 2017)

Jerome, in his interview, shared his take from the perspective of workers in the factories and how they came to Marxism:

> We began to think about, "What kind of programs should we have? What kind of theory is the theory that most relates to what we're doing?" We ended up with Marxism, Marxism-Leninism as the theory that relates most closely to our lives. We were production workers. Marxism was written for workers, so from that perspective it was easy to understand. What's not easy to understand is that this education process for many of us was brand new. For myself, I spent most of my life working off of gut instinct, "I don't like what happened to me. I don't like the foreman talking to me like that." It had nothing to do with any understanding of

what was going on economically, politically, or globally. In our study we began to see connections between the way the plant was run and why it was run that way. Because they had to make maximum profit.

Consider health and safety issues. It costs X amount of dollars to fix a building that's fifty years old and has dead spots in the overhead crane. That would eat into their profit. They might kill one or two people a year, but that's okay, that's cost-effective. Thinking like that you don't get to by just working in the plant. That kind of thinking you have to get by stepping back, looking at the process, and studying the process. (Scott 2017)

Allen Ray explained how he came to the study of Marxism and the impact it had on his life and political work in the plant:

It's like anything else. I'm a mechanic. If I wanna work on a car, I have to find out how it works. In the plant, we're trying to find out how we're exploited, why we're exploited, who's controlling us, to put names to who and what.

We began to analyze and break down everything. You know, dialectical historical materialism. Every problem has four sides. We have to examine all sides to determine where we're going. You can get on a road, but without a roadmap you don't know what's at the end. That's why it became very important, especially for me as a worker, to sit down and read a book. To analyze something was a giant leap, not just "tolling the bell." I remember some of that rote memorizing we did. There was a piece about the foolish old monk that tolled the bell. He went to the tower every morning and tolled the bell. He kept doing it, for years and years. An earthquake came and the tower collapsed. He still went to where the tower was to toll the bell.

With the education we did away with that. That's what helped us so much. We began to study not only where we were at, but we began to study the contractual language in the contracts for the unions. That was supposed to be our protective bible. We studied the constitution for the unions, supposed to be our bylaws and laws of the union. Because Blacks had no recognition in the union, it was important to do all that. The moment you get knowledge, believe me, your voice raises. You begin to ask questions. You begin to demand. It changed everything about us. (Bernard 2017)

Mitch picked up the story of education after the split and studying Marxism as an essential tool for working-class unity. He talked about the revolutionary Ethiopian students who came with Bob and were part of our educationals. They brought an orientation to the national question and the anti-imperialist struggle that lifted up the importance of working-class internationalism. They also connected us to the Ethiopian revolutionary process. When Haile Selassie was finally overthrown in 1974, they invited comrades from the CLP—one of whom was Jerome—to witness and be part of the celebration.

> After the split, the other crew consisted of Watson, Ken, and Mike. There were those that stood in the middle. Some of them eventually came over, I won't mention names because I don't wanna discredit anyone.
>
> But we, the workers' section, were more or less lost. Chuck went to California and heard Bob Williams speak. Chuck met with him, and he was willing to come out and help us learn Marxism. Part of that was a lot of Lenin's and Stalin's work on the national question. The national question is key to uniting whatever element of the proletariat or society that has to be united. You got to deal with the race question some kind of way. That began an intense study of works of Marx, Lenin, and Mao Zedong.
>
> It was important to us because Bob didn't come by himself. He brought three Ethiopian students. I loved them to death, they were great guys. They took time with us, sat down and explained the national question. We were in a certain form of neocolonialism or racism. They were more directly in it, being from another country. Oppression and imperialism had a more profound, open effect on them. That kind of got us studying. (W. Mitchell 2017)

Darryl shared his experience and passion about studying Marxism. He spoke to a new form of Marxism forged in the context of the LRBW in transition and connecting with Nelson and the CL.

> We had an opportunity to study Marxism and the science of society in a way no other generation or section of the revolutionary movements had. It was in more places than Detroit, but it happened in a concentrated way in Detroit. There was this coming together of people represented by Nelson and by Gen. It was something that came out of the industrial proletariat that served as a basis for a different form of Marxism in America. Since the League Education and Media Project began, everyone is aware of these historical threads being tied together in front of us. The past and the present, Gen and Nelson. (D. Mitchell 2017)

During a group interview, Darryl, Russell, Alonzo, and Abdul shared a free-flowing discussion about the importance of education and becoming working-class intellectuals. Russell began,

> We did leaflets, printed, and distributed them. We recruited people, and we worked. The qualitative thing out of everything was the education. That damn education shot the shit through the roof. Prior to that, the social knowledge we had was enough. We wanted be revolutionaries. We're gonna overthrow this

system. Once we started studying Mao Zedong, Stalin, and Lenin, dialectical and historical materialism—oh my god. Especially for those of us who were meant for college. They didn't have to teach us how to read and write, or go to a dictionary. All of a sudden, we became all these intellectuals. We would sit there and quote Stalin's "what is a nation?"—"historically evolved stable community of people formed...."

We were myopic. We'd go places quoting Mao Zedong to people. They looked at us like "Who are these crazy bastards?" My relatives from down South in Florida came to our apartment. I painted it red, black, and green, and all the pictures on the wall—Marx, Lenin, Engels, and Stalin. They'd ask, "What in the hell is wrong with you?" And go on to the next cousin's house.

A light went off due to the study. We were all waiting to meet this guy Nelson. If comrade Bob is this dynamic and whenever he talked about Nelson, he'd get like a little puppy dog. Nelson finally came and between them, they just knew so much. They almost put everything we had learned in school—all the history and everything—in a different perspective. And we believed it. (Jackson in Chandler et al. 2017)

Abdul spoke to gaining clarity and new perspectives through study:

We read to each other and listened to each other, and then made comments. We took it to another level. We did the same thing in smaller groups. That shit made us see things differently. It's like growing up—when you're ten you got a different perspective than when you were five. When you're fifteen, you got a different perspective on the five and the ten looking at the five. By the time you're forty, you changed your childhood learning. You think you understand something, and then you get a different perspective on it when somebody else explains it. (Roberts in Chandler et al. 2017)

Alonzo picked up from Abdul. He explained the importance of grasping the economic foundation of society and what the robotic digital revolution means for jobs and society.

The educational part was ongoing, especially in that period. We didn't fully understand because everything was changing, even to this day. Whether we were studying Lenin, Mao Zedong, or Marx, whether you think these people are correct or incorrect, the basic thing we grasped out of that educational period and began to understand was the deep-rootedness of economics in all this. I don't wanna use the word capitalist economics. I wanna say commodity production economics, economics based on a money system that doesn't use money as just a means of exchange, but uses money to manipulate people, to manipulate commodities, to manipulate revolutions in their favor, to manipulate counterrevolutions in their favor. All of this is basically part of the economic structure.

The flip side is what we didn't understand, and we're beginning to understand more and more. We were in the midst of the industrial revolution. At the same time, we were in the midst of coming out of the industrial revolution and going into the robotics and electronic revolution. This means something different than what the media says. The media says you will be able to produce things faster and better, and everybody will benefit. But they don't tell the side about what this does for jobs. What this does for the educational process of youth. What this does for the municipalities.

The educational part got us to understand why the movement had peaked and was falling off. The movement was based on Black nationalism and on economics in the sense that the white man controls everything and he's manipulating us. He's keeping us out of jobs, out of neighborhoods, out of this and that. But it's a larger picture.

We wound up fighting the last battles of the civil rights era. When that was over most people went back to their lives. Raising families, sending them to college, and not really understanding the deep-rootedness of economics and where things were heading. What we went through set the basis for understanding the difference between the industrial era and the robotics and electronics era. That seed started all of that. (Chandler in Chandler et al. 2017)

Darryl chimed in, talking about the educational and political journey of the LRBW:

It was always a push for education. Gen, John Watson, and John Williams were college students. They were from the first generation of young people to make it into college—the story of America in general. The organization and the network always had an educational component, from jump. When we started studying with Bob, it intensified. Everybody I know enjoyed the collective part of it, and we use that modality to this day.

Most groups and people I was in contact with were messing around. They studied differently—insisting you read your literature and come in prepared to discuss it. Our modality was reading the literature out loud. It told us who we're dealing with, what their educational level was. And in the process of reading out loud, stopping and asking questions, everybody developed a better understanding. Now we go back and forth over what model to use, but the model we developed in the LRBW is the superior.

The Centrality of Education

Before Bob came we had the People Action Committee. The Courtland office was on the corner. We rented one of the offices across the street on Third and had educational classes there. We had educational classes in Courtland to the best of our ability. Gen had gone underground for about eight months to a year, so some stuff didn't hold together. But there was always a serious effort. The old LRBW invested an inordinate amount of time in education. A lot of us spent almost all our extra time locating books. It's not like today where you can locate things. There were no books on Black history to begin with. If we could locate one book, we reprinted it on long sheets of paper and made copies for everybody, using manila folders with metal prongs.

We were organized around the production of literature, the production of educational material, the production of leaflets, flyers. We need to look at what the old League of Revolutionary Black Workers did. It was an organization of propagandists on the move at all times, and that's what we need today. We don't have that today for different reasons. But that was the world of education. It made it where we're together now, with a reasonably common vision. (D. Mitchell in Chandler et al. 2017)

Russell jumped back in on the importance of LRBW study and of working-class intellectuals:

I wanted to add this. I met Ken Cockrel at the University of Detroit before I met Jerome. Ken came there to speak and was a dynamic speaker. When you look at some of the people who were in the LRBW, the Ken Cockrels and John Williamses. A hell of an organization. We were lucky to come into something like that with this quality of revolutionaries and the connections they had. I took for granted Nelson's new perspective on the industrial proletariat. At that time, the emphasis was on the key link in everything. By us being industrial proletarians, those of us that were, a lot of emphasis was put on us.

We would study theory, and practice would show us if the theory was correct or not. The industrial proletarian thing, we would study and the shit became clear as a bell. Just talking doesn't mean a whole lot. But you study and go to a job where you are creating, changing the world. It's extremely enlightening. This made the Marxism-Leninism aspects that much more to the heart for us. Everything we studied, especially dialectical and historical materialism, was a hell of an eye-opener, and a lot of Stalin's stuff. With us coming off Black nationalism, what Stalin was writing particularly on colonialism was real. The fights they had with opportunists, we could see that. Being an industrial proletarian at that time helped a lot. (Jackson in Chandler et al. 2017)

Leah explained the importance of study and education in the social struggle in Flint—as opposed to Detroit:

> We had study groups in Flint with the people around us. It was difficult to do the study in a way that people could grasp it. We grafted the study onto what they were doing. We made analyses of situations, and we stretched to apply that to their experience. It was hard keeping people—they had to be involved in something. Being involved in activities worked better than the study groups, although, we did quite a few. (L. Rogers 2017)

Charles Simmons said that political education is more than an academic exercise. It is a tool of analysis and of struggle.

> In our political education, we had so many questions since nothing was taught in the schools. Nothing about the political system, economic system, about African American history. My grandmother taught Negro history in the church, and my grandparents were activists and talked about racism. But I had no understanding of capitalism, of socialism, of the revolutions going on.
>
> We missed so much, we felt cheated and lied to. Once we discovered that the great leaders of the past were socialists, we had to study them. We knew there was a revolution in China, and the Russian Revolution, all the movements going on, the movement against apartheid. But we didn't know the facts. We figured we had to learn everything immediately.
>
> But the study of social history is a lifetime struggle. We embarked on it and figured we had to learn continuously about what happened in the past, how to apply that to the present, and have a vision to the future. Study was a central part of our lives. But study always had to be connected with practice, with action. That distinguished us from the academic community, where you write a book about it, and that's it. (Simmons 2017)

As workers at the point of production, as working-class students who went to the point of production, as community organizers, educators, lawyers, social workers, and cultural workers—political and theoretical education was central to our lives and struggle. Becoming working-class intellectuals and comrades kept us going.

CHAPTER 13

Riding the Ebbs and Flows of Class Struggle—Longevity and Lessons for Today's Revolutionaries

Dare to fight! Dare to win! Fight, fail. Fight again, fail again. Fight on to final victory!

—LRBW slogan

I love my working class and I hate the capitalists for what they have done to society.

—Marian Kramer (2017)

Till my last breath, I wanna see this system fall. We've lived to the point where we're in the process of revolution right now.

—John Williams (2017)

Our longevity and lessons are intertwined as we journeyed from the LRBW through the split and, for many, as we moved together into the CL, the CLP, and the LRNA. Most important was and is our political education and consistent study with others, and the interrelation of theory and practice within the ebb and flow of the revolutionary process and digital revolution. Our patience, comradeship, collectivity, revolutionary culture, and having fun along the way also stood out. We even developed the Red Label Strugglers, a singing group, as an expression of this.

Other lessons include to engage the fight and stay the course, ask questions and speak up, and take care of one another; ours is a lifelong struggle, a marathon. A vision of the world we want and need, clarity of analysis, and strategy and tactics in relation to conditions, time, and place are essential.

We hope the lessons of the LRBW in the Detroit plants, community, and schools—from the 1960s to the current moment—are useful in navigating today's struggles. We draw these lessons from many perspectives and experiences—of comrades who stayed the course from the LRBW to the LRNA, those who were in the LRBW and left, those who joined along the way, some who journeyed for a while and went their separate ways. For those of us who stayed the course, our ongoing understanding of Marxism and of revolutionary theory and practice and our vision and strategy for realizing a communist society have broadened and deepened over the past fifty years and sustained us over those decades.

Longevity in the Revolutionary Movement

Gen described the dialectic of study and struggle in comrades' political direction and staying the course. He spoke to the critical needs for education, someone to "teach" Marxism to the workers after the split, and fighters who think and thinkers who fight.

> We have to have the theoretical study, but the struggle is the school itself. You got to study, but you got to struggle. Out of the struggle comes the real educational lessons that you apply to things you study. That way it becomes real and live, you really grasp it. We have to do that consciously, we can't do one without the other.
>
> One of the problems we had in the 1960s was we had thirty-five workers at the office, ready to study Marxism as a science, and couldn't find anybody who could teach it. We spent money. We sent for James Forman and everybody else that ran around saying they were Marxist. We brought them here to teach and try to study. We gave them a place to stay, something to eat. They didn't know how to teach and we ended up running them out of town.
>
> The struggle for education was primary for us. We were determined to try to learn, especially after the organization split. The little intellectual section left us, and we're sitting there looking at each other. We gotta figure how we're gonna fight our way out of this. It's indispensable to keep a leadership core, to constantly study and reevaluate the work we're doing so we can keep on struggling and fighting straight. That's important.
>
> I was fortunate to get through those early battles with the police. I went to jail every year from 1963 to 1971. Finally I met someone who told me to sit my big butt down and study.
>
> The 1960s left us with two types of people—those who fought and refused to think, and those who thought and refused to fight. One sitting, thinking, and talking stuff. The other fighting, ain't got sense enough to study. It took us twenty

years to try to make thinkers into fighters and fighters into thinkers. When we get that dialectic, we got something to work with. That was the past we had. That's why you gotta really fight for theory all the time, do your theoretical study and then carry it out. Sum up those practices and keep a steady leadership. We're in for a long, difficult battle and it's gonna take time. We gotta have a protracted outlook. (G. Baker 2016)

Marian, in conversation with Gen, lifted up their fifty years in the struggle and her "love for my class":

People say, "How long have you been in this, Marian?" I was talking to Gen before he died, "We've been in the movement a long time, for fifty years. But you've been in longer than me, you're older." It's amazing, and you never realize that.

I continued organizing welfare rights, with joy from helping people become leaders and from the working class being organized. I'm seventy-one and I'm still here, didn't retire from the work. We got a hell of a job to do. Dealing with emergency managers that never existed before. These suckers don't care if you have water or not because they don't need you anymore. I'm gonna be here until my last breath. I hope this history around welfare rights and so much more will set the tone. People should know and understand the role of welfare rights within the movement. Understand you have to know history to know the future. We have to know the objective situation, how we produce, to know our strategy and tactics for the masses of people, not for the capitalist class.

My longevity in the movement is because education was the key to understanding what was happening, where we have to throw the blow. I love my working class and I hate the capitalists for what they have done to society. We have the ability in this country to have enough food for people around the world, and they shouldn't have to pay for it because we have the technology to grow it everywhere. We don't have to pollute the air. I can barely breathe sometimes. We have to get to the point that we hate to see what they're doing to society. It gets me angry, and I get up every day ready to move. (Kramer 2017)

Jerome added his take on the critical importance of political education for riding the ebbs and flows of the movement and becoming a long-distance runner.

The concentration on political education gave us the ability to survive the ups and downs of the movement from the 1960s to the present, to understand what it means to be a long-distance runner in this movement—not a sprinter. Without theory, it's easy and commonplace to get burned out. You figure you gotta do this now, get this done. You're running like hell and keep running like hell, keep working like hell to get it done. Then it doesn't happen. You think, "I've given it my all." But what we weren't giving it is our thought—our thinking about it, our understanding of it.

Once we stepped back and tried to figure out the world, to get a better handle on what was going on, we were able to see the ebbs and flows of the movement. We realized that if a movement is ebbing, if it's slowing down, that's the time to concentrate on theory, study, and understanding the world. When the movement is flowing, it's time to use that theory to understand the motion as it develops. Without a grasp of this major dynamic, it prevents people from being here for the long haul. From being able to maintain our sanity around the ebb and flow of the movement and the ruling-class attacks on us. It was that process that set up so many of us who are still revolutionaries and fighting in the revolutionary process today. (Scott 2017)

Darryl spoke to learning a new form of Marxism, a unique way of looking at the world:

We learned a new form of Marxism, a new way of looking at the world that's uniquely different in the history of the Marxist movement. There's inequality in the world, but the old world based on the colonial system no longer exists. That means we need a different strategy and a different way of looking at how we go forward. This shit is like Star Trek. We're going where no one has been before, the final frontier. When you don't know where you're going, you have to learn philosophy so you can get an outline of the direction and the course. Theory is not enough because theory is based on what you experience. You're summarizing this data and this experience. It can't carry you into a new thing. That takes philosophy, and that's what we're fighting for. That's different from any communist or Marxist group on earth. We are unique in world history. (D. Mitchell 2017)

John lifted up patience, the great teachers who taught us, and being in the process until his last breath:

The one thing that I know, as revolutionaries, is that we need patience. Deal with the conditions that exist and go from there. Early on, we thought of revolution from a subjective standpoint. We learned that revolutions begin in the economic base of society and we see that now. It's affecting society, not only in the United States, in the whole world. The conditions were coming, they've broadened and now they're here. The question is, what do we do now? All we can do is ensure that this revolution continues in our favor. We've had some good teachers. We lost Gen, we lost Nelson. We lost Marx, Lenin, Stalin, etcetera, but we gotta keep going. Till my last breath, I wanna see this system fall. I may not actually see it, but I'm in the process. We've lived to the point where we're in the process of revolution right now. (John Williams 2017)

Luke spoke to the criminality of the system and his anger in keeping him a revolutionary:

> The system in this country keeps me in a revolutionary orientation. The criminality and the immorality of the system. Billionaires just sucking up all the wealth—super greedy, selfish, and mean spirited. That's what keeps me in a fighting spirit—a lot of outrage and anger. Revolutionaries are fighters. (Tripp 2017)

Mike, in conversation with Jerome, reflected on his work and what Marxism meant to him in relation to longevity in the struggle. Jerome asked, "Were you able to use Marxism in your work with workers around their mental health issues?" (in Hamlin 2017). Mike responded,

> Absolutely. You have to learn how to manage people if you're going to be successful in organizing them, especially involving them in class struggle. You have to understand them, articulate their situation and explain it to them. If you're not of them, immerse yourself in their reality. If you're gonna serve, you have to know the consequences. It may cost you two wives, like it did me.
>
> Organizing is serious. I know people who talk folks into things. They don't know the outcome, the consequences, what to do in the aftermath. Like when we led the workers out on strike at Dodge Main and the question was what to do next. We invited them to our office, held a meeting, and let them know that twenty-five workers had been subpoenaed. Lawyers were on hand to talk and take care of them, but we didn't know what was going to happen. They pushed us for that wildcat strike and we agreed. I don't have regrets, and most of the people were able to emerge from that. They got jobs in different places and some went on to be successful in other things.
>
> But about Marxism. These are my people. I had to have a grasp. Their fight was my fight. My whole life was gathering tools to help my people, because I saw a lot of suffering and pain growing up. A Black man, a Black intellectual—if he understands America—can deal with it through denial, fighting it, or selling out. Most people are in denial. A Marxist, in my view, can manage this country better than anybody. I'm trying to reach out and help people who are suffering. That's what a Marxist is supposed to do, and I used Marxism in every facet of my life. (Hamlin 2017)

Charles described the consciousness of radicals engaged in structural change:

> What we learned in the struggles and in our relationships was buried so deep. This was not an episode or temporary phenomenon that was gonna pass. This was true within the radical wing of the civil rights and Black power movement. On the right wing were the conservatives, the NAACP, the reformists. They saw the movement as a temporary thing. Winning legal desegregation was the solution. We achieved that and they said everything is fine. The middle class expanded and they got jobs. To that group, the struggle was no more.
>
> For more radical people who really embraced a revolution or structural change, you can't really put the blinders back on after you've developed that consciousness. You can be paid off, but it's a conscious decision to sell out. That doesn't happen accidentally. (Simmons 2017)

Gracie said she was not as active now as she should be, but study was essential to her political life.

> I'm not really active now and I feel guilty because I know that's necessary. I still belong to my local, the American Federation of Teachers Detroit (DFT), attend meetings, and go to demonstrations. After the LRBW, I became more active politically when I joined the CL. We studied a lot in the CL, and I worked for Vanguard Printing in Chicago. (G. Wooten 2017)

Leah embraced the Marxist method in her political life:

> Being educated in the Marxist method, Marxist science—even in a small amount—made a difference. It gives an explanation of why things happen the way they do. Nothing else really explains things. I didn't have any life-shattering experiences. It was my gradual involvement with people, day by day, that kept me going. (L. Rogers 2017)

Wylie knew these were the people he wanted to journey with:

> You never know everything. The world's constantly changing and you've gotta change with it. The LRBW years gave me an undying faith in the power of people. We do some stupid things. But in the final analysis, it's people that's gonna change this world. I have to admit, even at this advanced stage I'm still processing it. But I knew where I wanted to go and these were the people I wanted to take the journey with. There's ups and downs. But it was a hell of a transformation for me. (W. Rogers 2017)

Linda experienced the LRBW as family and heart, not just politics:

> There was a lot of love in the LRBW. It was like a family and family is the basis of any society. Having a strong family means having a strong society. It wasn't

just the education and the political, but the LRBW was family and heart. That's why people stayed—because of the heart, the family, the love, the giving. (Wheeler 2017)

Rita explained how deeper analysis helps avoid burnout, and the importance of loving and close comrades.

> If you can only describe what's going on, but not understand the motion, you're gonna get burned out or frustrated. You'll walk away at some point. But if you can understand the inner workings of society, then you begin to get a longer range view of the revolutionary process. Taking the study of history seriously was important. So was taking the study of philosophy as a weapon, not as an ideology, to really understand the world and to maintain an engagement in practice.
>
> The people I learned from, loved the most, and developed the strongest comradeship with were the people that I was engaged with in practical and theoretical struggle over those years. They weren't opportunists, careerists, or narcissists. They are real revolutionaries. That's the kind of person I wanted to be. Struggling to understand that society is knowable—not necessarily predictable, but you can know it. Those relationships gave me the strength to continue. (Valenti 2017)

Frank said we cared for each other, debriefed, and learned from success and failure in the long struggle:

> We took care of each other and nurtured each other, despite bitter divisions and wounds still not healed. We found our way to have fun. Who had better dances, better fundraisers? Remember the cabarets? If building a movement is part of building opportunities for better lives, you better be doing it along the way. Not say this is all gonna pay off in fifty years.
>
> We had a sense of purpose, engagement, and work left to be done, but also a sense of accomplishment. One of the frustrations about working at the UAW when I worked there was that nobody wanted to debrief, to look back, to admit failure we could then learn from. I learned from that. Pay attention to the thinking and the debrief. Learn from failure and from success. It's a cliché—just put one foot in front of the other and everything will turn out okay. No, it won't. (Joyce 2017)

Pam affirmed the worldview of Marxism in our longevity:

> Once you get a worldview that explains things, you can't swallow the propaganda we get on every newscast. TV news isn't where people should get their information. I listen to the radio, watch TV, and read other publications. Once you have

studied Marx and Lenin and Engels, you can't go back, you can't undo the thinking that you have. (Randazzo 2017)

Jim Bish lifted up his materialist philosophy and passion for human rights:

> My philosophy is that I'm a materialist. Human rights was always a passion for me. You can be an armchair radical revolutionary, but that doesn't mean nothing unless you put yourself on the line. I remember thinking that way as a teenager. It's a passion, a belief. The folks I know who stayed in the LRBW and the MCLL shared that. (Bish 2017)

Jim Fite talked about Nelson and study as critical for longevity.

> I was fortunate to meet Nelson when I was young. He was an influential guy, a fundamentally good person, and he made sense. Everything was based in material conditions, in the name of humanity, what you want for your kids and grandkids. And there is study, the science of revolution, continually going back to the real world. Nelson said, "Engels insisted that if it's not happening in nature, it doesn't happen, it's not true." One of the reasons we've been able to hang together is that we don't treat Marxism as an encyclical, but as a scientific guide for how to examine the real world. (Fite 2017)

JoAnn noted the importance of study, self-study, and especially cadre schools in her longevity and in organizational continuity:

> The foundation for all of us was the cadre schools, six to eight weeks long. Theoretical and philosophical study and understanding is the bottom line of what cadre are and how we develop. Change has been our reality. Objective conditions change, it means we have to change. That's been an exciting part of what the organization—LRNA—is.
>
> How do we get back to that? It's gonna take that level of commitment and time to study and learn what we're doing. Something will happen here in Chicago, they will padlock the door and take us away. How do we make sure that we have an organization that can survive and keep growing and reproducing itself? That's what time it is with fascism and the dangers. (Gonzales and Capalbo 2017)

Beth added her voice to the importance of the CL study, understanding the world as it really is, and changing it:

> It's about having a scientific understanding. The system is so brutal and getting worse. If we don't have an understanding of why, we can give up and self-destruct. But when we know it doesn't have to be this way, that there's a science to under-

standing how to transform society, we can push the process forward. So many of our generation got this sense from being in the CL—how the real world works and how change happens. (Gonzales and Capalbo 2017)

Lessons We Learned from Becoming Lifelong Revolutionaries

The lessons from our collective journey are rooted in the ebbs and flows of our struggle over those years and our longevity. One of the reasons we're doing this project is that we want young revolutionaries to look at our historical experience and not repeat our mistakes. Though, even if they learn these lessons, there's no guarantee they won't repeat our missteps.

Marian lifted up our project as a teaching tool—the lessons of education and independent thinking, the importance of collective leadership including women and youth, and the reality of today's multiracial and multinational working class.

> I hope this video project helps people understand you have to learn to think. Don't wait for somebody to tell you, "Take this mountain." Think it out. What's the history, why are we doing this, is there another way? Make sure the leadership is collective, with women and youth in the center.
>
> We don't make the revolution. We bring education for the section of the working class that is rising, people who will never work in this society. How do we understand and play that role of bringing education? It's their education. They have to know how to deal and how to think—and we know the capitalists don't want us to think.
>
> The working class is multinational. It's good I participated in the struggle of the Black movement. But reality steps in. We have to see how we have all been used, pitted against one another for the benefit of those who rule this country, for the corporations. We're part of the whole of the working class, but Blacks have been used as the stick to whip the rest of the class into shape for those who rule the country. (Kramer 2017)

Gen spoke to organizing on fronts of struggle, concentrating and focusing our work, staying in the fight.

> We're figuring out how to organize ourselves on fronts of struggle—the welfare front, the poverty front, old retirees on the single-payer health care front. That's our call. You can't fight on every front.
>
> A person that tries to do everything, does nothing—as the Chinese parable goes. You're like a man with ten fingers trying to solve ten problems and you sit

here paralyzed. One fly under each finger. That ain't the way you kill a fly. Damn it, you let nine go, and kill 'em one at a time. That's the way you gotta carry on these fights. Figure out which front you wanna fight on and throw everything you got on that front till you can make a breakthrough. Don't give up, stay there, learn the lessons.

I always use this quote from Engels: "What childish innocence it is to use one's own impatience as a theoretically convincing argument." You ain't got no right to get tired, you stay in the fight. What happens most of the time is that by the time people rise up, the revolutionaries got tired and went home. Ain't nobody to lead. So you stay in the fight. Those are lessons we learned. (G. Baker 2016)

Gen added this about collectivity and leadership.

I probably haven't made an independent decision in the last 40 years. They're always collective. I don't take individual responsibility for all the things that I do because two heads are better than one. I was fortunate as a youngster to join a little group when I was on the college campus called UHURU, Swahili for freedom. Out of that group we decided to make decisions to take on things. It's so important to have a constant leadership development core that you gotta work on all the time. (G. Baker 2016)

Cass said never give up, get active, you can make a difference.

Never give up. Keep talking to people, do what you can. Even if you don't win the ultimate battle, you win little battles along the way. More people understand what's going on and look at things differently. That's success.

We meet people for a reason, maybe for a season, and it comes together. Do what's in front of you, what you feel passionate about, something that will make a difference. Students can make a difference. They have a voice and a right to say what they feel and think, especially what's going on in their school and in their education. In the BSUF we made a difference. We didn't realize that we could do it until we did it. You can do it too. (C. Ford 2017)

Allen Ray explained the importance of patience and "fight, fail, fight on to victory."

Be patient. A lot of people thought the revolution was tomorrow. Keep striving for change. When you see something wrong, fight to change it. We had a slogan, "Dare to fight! Dare to win! Fight, fail. Fight again, fail again. Fight on to final victory!" When no human being, regardless of color or creed, is exploited, oppressed or in bondage—that's what we believe in. (Bernard 2017)

Gracie described the lessons learned from the LRBW and the movement in general—patience and study.

> I would never take back the experiences because I learned so much. I learned how to deal with people, to accept them for the contributions they could make, and to see that everybody was not the same. That was important as a teacher.
>
> The patience. One of the more patient people I ever met was Gen. He kept coming back looking for Charlie and he wasn't here. Gen came back again and again until he actually moved Charlie to a place of growth. I was very argumentative, like my way or the highway, and had little patience for anything else. Gen used to tell me, "You know, Gracie, you do not have to argue about everything."
>
> There is a real developing struggle now around Black lives. I see ourselves in that because we were so impatient. The revolution is gonna come, we just knew it was gonna happen. That's the impatience of youth. If I was to give advice, it would be patience. Learn how to temper yourself and keep educating yourself. People who really want to see the world change have to become more broadly read, to learn from others, to know the world. (G. Wooten 2017)

Esther talked about the importance of speaking up. You have to start somewhere.

> For immigrants and people who don't speak English as their first language, it's hard to speak up. Maybe it's about something easy to answer, maybe not. Speak up whether it's right or wrong. If you don't ask, if you don't speak up, you won't know. In southwest Detroit, people don't speak up, they're afraid to ask questions. But you have to get involved. You have to start somewhere. (Mauricio 2017)

Alonzo emphasized the importance of education, especially for youth.

> Always be willing to learn, to figure out what the man is doing—however you call the man—and how to counteract him. I'm 67 next month and cannot underscore enough the importance of youth, understanding what they're going through and why.
>
> We learned in elementary school that you can breakdown damn near anything by understanding "why, where, when, who, and how." They have deliberately stopped young people from thinking that way. The way young people dress, talk, the things they do—they don't see how the media, the power structure is controlling all that, and to what end. It's only through education of the youth that change will happen because this generation and the generation behind them are the ones who're gonna do it.
>
> The lesson I learned—the importance of the youth and education for youth. Not just Marxist education, but all education, because these people have de-

stroyed the educational system. That's why the youth go along with whatever the man throws at them.

Another life lessons is understanding that we don't know everything and there's always things to learn and to pass on. It's got to be passed on to all youth, not just Black youth, because they're pretty much in the same boat now. (Chandler in Chandler et al. 2017)

Mitch called for study to understand and transform society.

You need to study to have a clear understanding of society and how to transform it. That's essential. We've fought and brought about changes in the economy. We gotta fight for food, for clothes, for housing, for medical care. We gotta demand it. Revolutions are made by peoples' ideas. (W. Mitchell 2017)

Darryl spoke to being abolitionists on the side of the proletariat, engineers of the human soul.

When we talk about being revolutionaries today, it's not this dry concept. We're talking about being engineers of the human soul, being abolitionists on the side of the proletariat. That's part of our history we have to recapture. When people spoke to the soul. It's easier than we think. We have this idea that revolution comes about from getting people into motion and convincing them that if they are strong and firm enough, we can make change. The change is being made in front of us. We must determine what kind of society we want.

We're talking about a working class that has an opportunity to have a better life. The ruling class is killing you and your children. They don't have a concept that there's another way. We must master our history. The slave master felt that giving up slavery meant the end of civilization and culture as they understood it. This led to the Civil War, the bloodiest war in human history at that time. The South took a horrific beating that it has not recovered from to this day. And it was because the ruling class could not understand and could not leave history gracefully. Today we have come to the end of history where society is based on a ruling class appropriating the surplus labor. (D. Mitchell 2017)

Darryl added how important it is to educate yourself, keep an open mind, and learn to break with the past:

Educate yourself, try to keep an open mind, to treat people fairly. Learn forgiveness for others and yourself. Marx and Engels talked about, "Until the individual is free, the mass cannot be free." We inherited it backwards and I'm not sure we look at things the right way yet. We haven't developed an indigenous form of Marxism that reflects our history and what we're passing through. The point is having the courage to make a break with your past because you wanna become something you can never really be, but you strive for. My life in the movement teaches me that you should never become a victim of the collective. You must learn and become comfortable with your individuality within a collective.

We should avoid name-calling, labeling people, anything that's sectarian. We had some sectarian tendencies in the LRBW because it was an actual organization of propagandists. It was set up to produce and distribute literature and you had to become part of that process. The LRBW was connected with desires amongst a section of people in society and it riveted you to a purpose and a cause. You always had to carry out this function. Things are changing in front of us and we need something very different, but something that I think we have in Detroit. We can make a difference in America and the world if we tap into that thing that made us unique. (D. Mitchell in Chandler et al. 2017)

John Williams reminded us to ground ourselves in conditions, time, and place, to integrate science and practice, to be clear about race and class unity and the abolition of capitalism and private property:

First, you have to deal with the conditions that exist. When I got into the struggle, I was looking at a revolution that wasn't there. The conditions were not there, the timing, and the place. If you don't have these three factors then you're either ahead or behind. Second is education and understanding. I'm talking about study as a science and integrating it with practice.

Race is not the basis of unity. It has not been, and will not be. The only unity will come around economic factors that bring people together.

Years ago we talked about capitalism and the state. We didn't talk about it as the form of private property. When I'm out there today and talk to people about what private property is and how it affects our personal and public property, it comes home. If you can get people to see how private property and control by a few affects every aspect of society, from senior citizens to you—whether it's health care, student loans, working in the shop—they all have a common enemy. (John Williams 2017)

Jerome added his take on understanding the world, today's technology, and the revolutionary process for organizing the working class:

You have to look at the fundamentals of how this country functions, how the world functions, and the role of workers and Black workers in the developing revolutionary process. If you can grasp that and hold onto it, you're able to find what role to play in different moments of the struggle. When to concentrate on political education, put other things on the low burner because they're there anyway.

> When to implement your understanding of the relationship between theory and practice.
>
> We have to step back and look at how we organize—because technology has entered the production process at a level that means two-thirds of the auto workers who used to work in the plants no longer work in auto. That's true for steel, rubber, any other industrial process. Where have those workers gone?
>
> A whole generation of people who are descendants of workers, who were workers themselves are no longer part of the productive process. People who used to work, worked part-time, went in and out of work, whatever the situation. The productive process no longer needs this whole section of society. They're being pushed outside of the productive process and have nothing to lose. They're fighting for a job, just to work. The concentration of our organizing has to shift to this section of society that the ruling class has the least influence over. They're not working, the ruling class doesn't have daily contact with them to constantly make the ideological struggle for their minds.
>
> Concentrating on these forces expelled from the productive process becomes, for us, key for the revolutionary process. Revolution is a process of the whole of society, and that's not the only revolutionary section of society. But if you have limited resources and need to concentrate, concentrate there. Others are working in every section of society in preparing for the revolution. (Scott 2017)

Jerome continued—comparing the different conditions in the 1970s and today, the necessity for ongoing theoretical study in relation to practice, and choosing our own leaders:

> Looking at our work, evaluating our work, having a plan to rectify what was lacking in our work is critical. In the early 1970s we had a program. We fought and won one part of it, and it didn't change anything. To correct that, we tried to get a handle on what the world is so we'd know what kind of program to develop to make a difference in our lives.
>
> We're in a period where the movement is developing. People are getting in motion. More than anything else, we need vision and direction. What is the world we're fighting for and how do we fight to get that world? To do that, we need to study some theory and some history of our country, and to understand the interrelations and interdependence of theory and practice.
>
> I emphasize to young revolutionaries that, first of all, we have to learn. We have to know what this world is, we have to be about helping other people understand this world and furthering our understanding of the world through that process. We need leaders who are developed in the course of struggle—who we've struggled with, learned with, and fought with. We have to know each other.

> Back in the day we used to say—they, the ruling class and corporate media, put this guy on television and claimed, "This is the baddest Black man. He hates the police. He wants to kill people. This is the real leader." They threw that person out there as the leader of the movement with hopes that person would catch fire and become a leader. That's what the ruling class tries to do at every step of the movement, to put people with their interests in charge. We cannot have an atmosphere in which we select people who are not really the leaders that we need to be championing. (Scott 2017)

Luke spoke to the dynamics of thinking and practice in analyzing the world and staying ahead of the curve:

> We saw the world in a certain way. How it could be and should be, what we have to do to get there—a long, hard struggle. Things are constantly changing, so you have to adapt the works of great thinkers and revolutionaries who worked in their time. The lesson is to stay ahead of the curve, study, search for the best ideas and how to use them. (Tripp 2017)

Charles added the importance of youth and of elders offering advice, challenging cultural imperialism, building bridges across historic divides in our communities, and maintaining relations of kindness and humility among revolutionaries.

> As elders we should encourage young people, offer advice when we can. Youth have courage and innocence, and haven't been corrupted. Let them know that youth have been in the forefront of struggles. We were kids when we traveled to Cuba. Cultural imperialism is stronger than ever. Today's youth have many challenges. It's on their shoulders now.
>
> We thought we were going to take state power in two or three years. Whatever the road map is to get there, we need a longer vision than we had. The struggle for justice is a lifetime struggle. We have victories, then another monster appears to struggle against. Don't be discouraged when we lose some battles—they're ongoing.
>
> We need to unite people in the faith community with other folks. We didn't think about that, we thought the preachers weren't doing anything. But the people in the congregation are our family, neighbors, and friends. They're experiencing prison, water shut offs, unemployment, and privatization of everything. We've got to cross these cultural and ethnic borders. To organize these folks in spite of the racism, and the racism is there. Even after a revolution there will be people who are racist and all the other "isms" of negativity. It takes another type of struggle to change people's psychological orientations—despite changing the political and economic system.

> We need to study what's happening now, what happened in the past. And bridge building. We need to gather the environmentalists, labor, welfare rights people, folks dealing with foreclosures and privatization of schools, and gender struggles. All are important. When you work on one cause, it's hard to think other struggles are as important. We're often brutal in our relationships with people on the same team. We've got to overcome that, to be humble and kind in dealing with others. Gen taught us that lesson—of kindness and generosity towards others as human beings, whether we agree with them or not.
>
> Whatever our cause now, there'll be another cause next year. The social justice community is a big family. We don't agree with everybody about everything. But, we have to work together, respect one another. So when we have the opportunity to work together again, we can do it without saying you stabbed me in the back, called me a name. (Simmons 2017)

Frank shared the importance of the lifelong struggle, caring for each other, resolving conflicts, and living the world we want:

> When I talk to young people—which I love doing—I say start a newsletter. When they look at Ferguson, Trayvon Martin or whatever as though this is happening for the first time, I say "not exactly." This is the struggle of a lifetime. Whatever your immediate struggle, there's no magic bullet that's gonna fix it. Pay attention to what you've done, why you're doing it, expand your theoretical understanding and framework. Don't just read people you agree with, don't get in an echo chamber, and don't get stuck in a dogma or a doctrine where you think you have it all figured out.
>
> Take care of one another, take of yourself. If you don't, you won't be able to help. But you can't take care of yourself by yourself. Allow yourself to be helped and taken care of, and do that with others.
>
> Pay attention to how we resolve our conflicts. Conflicts arise—ideological, strategic, and personality conflicts. This is the damage we suffer because of the system we live under. If we don't have a better way to resolve these conflicts, then what do we have to offer to make a better society? (Joyce 2017)

Linda spoke to the imperative of passion and giving back:

> Have passion, the drive to make change. It's your life, have no regrets. Don't say, "I wish I would, wish I could have." Do it, because it's all about giving back, and you will see it turn full circle for you. That's the way the world is, you have to give back as a world citizen. (Wheeler 2017)

Jim Fite said don't give up, study, and struggle for unity even among those we have been told to stay away from:

> The first lesson is don't give up. It might look like you're being beaten, but you never know when something's going to show. We worry about our life problems—how to pay the rent, how to make the study group when I work the night shift. Then something big happens. Like the man said, twenty years go by that don't make a day. Then a day goes by and it makes twenty years. That was like our meeting with the LRBW. Wait for your day, you never know when it's coming.
>
> People say "stay away from each other." But the struggle continually puts us together. You gotta go with the flow and the flow is the struggle. Differences might be good reasons for not being around others. But when that person is slammed by the state and you're slammed by the state, your petty differences mean nothing. Grab their hand, and march on. So, the second lesson is go with the struggle, stay with the struggle, things will come clear.
>
> The third lesson is that you must study. If you don't study the science of social motion, the power structure and revolution, then you don't have the ability to participate. You have to have the tools. Revolutionaries are educators. Our tools are our thinking, our collective study, our sharing of our knowledge with others. Those are our weapons. So study, wait for the good times, go with the struggle, and do more study. (Fite 2017)

Judy urged folks to connect to people where they are:

> You have to find out where people are at and move them from that point. Whatever struggles are out there at the time, get involved. (Judy Williams 2017)

Pam stressed becoming independent thinkers:

> We have to open our minds and be independent thinkers—women and men. We can't be followers, we need to take on leadership roles—where we imagine a different future and people don't have to spend time engaged in surviving. We have to use our talents, our creativity for society, for humanity. To find ways of doing that, of educating young people in a way we haven't done well in the past. We can't reform capitalism. We need to change things, to create the new world that we want. We've got to envision it and create it. (Randazzo 2017)

Rita said to stay rooted where we're planted:

> Stay rooted in the situation you're confronted with. We were rooted in the plants and the factories because that's the situation the class was confronted with. The situation the class is confronted with today is not primarily issues of industrial unionism. It's more issues of survival and poverty. We have to understand two things—what's happening and how we understand what's happening. What are

the tools to understand that? When I was first engaging, most of those tools would get twisted into ideology. We "ought" to do this, this is what "should" happen. Later, I got a better understanding of philosophy and dialectical historical materialism as a way to look at the world the way it really is. How the process moves forward and what it means about the role of a revolutionary today. To me, that's to build a revolutionary political party of the working class. (Valenti 2017)

Jim Bish shared the importance of study for young people:

> It's study. Young people, my kids and grandkids, don't want to hear it. We need a different form they can relate to. Back then, Nelson met folks off the street and articulated materialist philosophy. They understood it and loved it. Our problem now is that technology has changed. Young people don't want to sit and read. Who will they relate to? How do we impart that knowledge and wisdom? That's our struggle today, trying to figure out how in the hell we do that. (Bish 2017)

Maureen spoke to the difference between discrimination around race and gender back in the day and class struggle in the current moment, and new possibilities based on abundance.

> The lessons from the LRBW were valuable and critical. Discrimination based on race and gender were very powerful. Folks like Gen and Marian, like Chuck, Allen Ray, Jerome, and Ed Taylor pushed this question of discrimination in labor to the front. Lessons then were about discrimination—those narrow politics.
>
> Lessons today are about this question of class. We live in a world where there's enough food, enough housing, got cars everywhere and people can't afford them. Why are we living like this? Immigrants in Europe crossing seas, this horrible situation. There is the capacity to build houses and cars, provide medicine and food for everybody. We're on the verge of something new where the world that all of us dream about, we can wake up and see.
>
> We can live as moms and dads and grandparents. We can educate everybody, house everybody, and put everybody in a car. Why does it cost $2,000 to fly to Europe? It should cost about $120. Go and have a good time. We can get to that kind of a world.
>
> Had it not been for Gen and Marian and the people who planted those early roots, this tidal wave of education we got now around all these bad things, we could not have found it without them. (Taylor 2017)

Nacho shared this analysis about the difference between then and now—between reform and system change—and the necessity of institutionalizing revolutionary education:

> The main difference between then and today was then the struggle was for reforms. Reform this, improve that. Today everything is different. They're closing everything down and the fight is to keep the basic necessities of life. The struggle is against the system. The demands are almost impossible to get—the system can't do it. All the money goes to the military, there's no money for education or anything really.
>
> I know people who are revolutionaries, but they wanna form cooperatives. Marx, in *The Manifesto*, said communists have to be involved in every struggle of the proletariat, not just in the ones we, as individuals, think are important. The main thing is to strike blows against the capitalist class, to strike where they are weak and to educate. In that process people are learning and getting radicalized. The important thing is institutionalizing revolutionary education. It can take many forms because everybody's different—from study groups, to organized online classes, to whatever. It's important that a cadre of young people be developed, because the people who came out of the 1960s are gonna be gone in ten or fifteen years. And I don't think the revolution's gonna happen that soon. In historical time, fifty years is nothing.
>
> We're a country of over three hundred million and left groups are small and don't have much influence. We gotta be big to have influence with three hundred million people. (N. Gonzales 2017)

Leah added her voice to the reality of a broad class struggle in this moment:

> It's important to see that this is not a narrow struggle. It's big and it's international. Involvement has to be among people across all kinds of lines—economic, social, and racial. What's going on now is narrow, in the sense we may talk about Black lives matter. Those movements are budding. But they have to go beyond that narrow focus. (L. Rogers 2017)

Wylie recalled the centrality of the Black worker in the history of revolutionary struggle and embraced today's youth stepping up:

> A consistent theme throughout this whole evolution is the centrality of the Black worker, not exclusion. Early on, the LRBW had to march ahead of the rest of the working class and recognize in the system of exploitation that the superexploitation of Blacks and the color question held back the entire working class from the unity it needs to move forward.
>
> To be successful we got to understand our history, and the LRBW is a big part of that history. Revolutionaries today have to understand how people struggled and the forces that give rise to that struggle. As we get older, we should recognize that the most important thing is to call upon our experiences

and use them to see where things are going. Gotta stay active, everything is still good, the struggle is still going. These young folks today are gonna do it. I'm convinced. (W. Rogers 2017)

Mike, in talking with Jerome, emphasized study—especially Marxism—and the world we're dealing with. He took stock of what the LRBW did and the work to be done.

> Understand the power of what you're dealing with, the nature of what you're dealing with. You can move things, you can make a difference, but you have to be prepared. That's the question of studying. You might wanna go immediately into action, but that's not the thing to do. The thing to do is understand. We don't talk about that, about our need for a tool for analysis. Everybody thinks for themselves. That's bullshit. You need to study, to study Marxism as a tool of analysis and understanding.
>
> We are getting away from this. These devices are taking kids' minds. No need for history. I'm constantly talking about genocide of the Native Americans. Don't tell me how horrible these other countries are that committed genocide. Look at slavery, look at genocide. This history is an outrage.
>
> We don't have power because we're not acting, Jerome. I don't know, it's unfortunate what happened to me, to us. Because we did start something, but we ultimately lost that. And I was put in a position of doing the best I could to make myself feel that I accomplished something in my lifetime, but the struggle continues. I applaud you guys for the work you're doing, you know. I'm so happy. (Hamlin 2017)

During the LRBW days and our ongoing journey, we studied together, raised our children together, partied together, and struggled together. Many of us are still doing it. The power of continuous political education—to know the world as it really is and is becoming—was and is the basis of our collectivity, our unity, our vision, our political strategy, and our longevity. Without strategic unity and analysis of the developing objective and subjective conditions, burnout is inevitable. Strategic unity means that our day-to-day tactics reflect our strategy, that we evaluate our individual and organizational practice and tactics in relation to our strategic path, and implement course corrections as necessary. Even when we wander, if we're on the same political path, we reconnect in the heat of the struggle. We were serious and committed, and we still had fun. The LRBW was not a dull revolutionary organization.

CHAPTER 14

Revolutionary Possibilities

> We can (and must) begin to build socialism, not with abstract human material, or with human material specially prepared by us, but with the human material bequeathed to us by capitalism. True, that is no easy matter, but no other approach to this task is serious enough to warrant discussion.
>
> —Vladimir Lenin, *Left Wing Communism* ([1920] 1964)

> Between capitalist and communist society there lies the period of the revolutionary transformation of the one into the other.
>
> —Karl Marx, *Critique of the Gotha Programme* ([1875] 1970)

The AI genie is out of the bottle. AI in the hands of the capitalists, especially the fascists, is indeed a threat to humanity. Working-class forces cannot allow this to happen. We dare not lose this battle.

The multiple and interconnected crises of capitalism—economic, ecological, social, political, and war and militarism—are rapidly escalating. Social protest is intensifying in response.

Today's technological revolution, multiple crises, and rising movement are creating the conditions for the end of capitalism and for revolutionary transformation, for the necessity of ruling-class motion toward fascism, and for working-class motion toward revolution (Amin 2008; W. Robinson 2022; W. Robinson and Fuentes 2023).

Revolutionary Process

The economic revolution, the social revolution, and the political revolution are interrelated and overlapping stages of the revolutionary process.

The economic revolution, rooted in the transition from an industrial base to a digital base, disrupts the functioning of the capitalist system at every level—the economy, society, and politics. The digital revolution of computers, robots, automation, and AI took off in the 1970s and 1980s and became an objective material force in our lives. Digital technology is labor replacing—changing work, jobs, communications, distribution, and surveillance; speeding up jobs; driving down wages; and eliminating jobs completely, particularly in production and distribution—but across all sectors (Dyer-Withered, Kjosen, and Steinhoff 2019; Lee 2018; McAfee and Brynjolfsson 2017; W. Robinson 2022; Srnicek 2017).

The social revolution includes both destruction of social relations and institutions and resistance and rebellion from below in defense of life. The political revolution is the struggle for power between the ruling class and the working class. The class struggle also plays out internally within both classes.

Within the ruling class the struggle is over the question of bourgeois democracy and fascism, about whether bourgeois democracy is sufficient to maintain the capitalist system and control over society, and about the speed of the motion toward fascism. Within the working class the struggle is around how to stop fascism and move toward the socialist reconstruction of society in the interests of people and the planet (Lenin [1917] 1976; Katz-Fishman and Scott 2019; W. Robinson 2022).

Ruling-class motion toward fascism is intensifying as a reaction to the revolutionary motion and, in particular, to defeat working-class unity and motion toward systemic transformation.

The Global Economy in Fundamental Transition

The world is a dramatically different place today than when we started this project in 2015. But one thing has not changed—the transformation of the world from an industrial means of production to a digital means of production. This creates great danger and great opportunity. Revolution has the best chance of happening and being successful in times of qualitative change such as these. That's a key reason we should be revolutionaries in this moment.

In the 1960s many of us believed that revolution was coming soon. Conditions were not favorable to revolution then, but they are favorable today. Then the capitalist system was still expanding globally. Today conditions, both objective and subjective, have changed (N. Peery 1993, 2001; W. Robinson 2014, 2022).

Nelson explained it this way in *Entering an Epoch of Social Revolution*:

> It began with scattered statements during the late 1960s and early 1970s noting the shift from labor saving to labor replacing means of production. By the mid-

dle 1980s, we realized that we were seeing the science of society—Marxism, being vindicated before our eyes. These labor replacing means of production, hostile to the existing productive relations, were creating an epoch of social revolution.

Qualitatively new means of production are in deepening antagonism with private, capitalist ownership of socially necessary means of subsistence. The economy—based on the buying and selling of labor power—is being irreversibly destroyed.

The destruction of the economy will force society to reorganize. This reorganization will change the forms of ownership of socially necessary property from private to public. Only then will the economy conform to the productive capacity of robots and computers. (N. Peery 1993, 2)

The global shift from agriculture to industry took roughly one hundred fifty to two hundred years. That transformation was from one exploitative and competitive society to another.

The transformation we are living through—from an industrial means of production to a digital means—began in the late twentieth century and is in the early stages of its development. This sets the conditions for the transformation from the world's most exploitative and competitive society, through a transition period of socialism, to communism—a cooperative society in which there will be no private property, no exploitation and oppression of workers, and no destruction of nature. A cooperative society embodies the social relations, the knowledge and the tools, and the material means to heal and protect humanity and the earth.

The world today is moving much more rapidly, of course.

Why We Are and Must Be Revolutionaries, Not Reformists

Before the 1970s, the revolutionary motion to overthrow capitalism and reconstruct society was grounded primarily in ideology, consciousness, and political organization. We fought for and won reforms and concessions in the sixties and seventies—the Civil Rights Act, the Voting Rights Act, the War on Poverty, Medicare and Medicaid, *Roe v. Wade*, and more. These legislative and judicial victories expanded basic rights—the vote, greater access to the necessities of life, and control over our bodies. Capitalism was still expanding on a worldwide scale. We thought that revolution was around the corner. We were wrong. Revolution was not on the agenda.

Soon the wins of the sixties and seventies came under attack and were being rolled back. We didn't finish the job. By the 2000s, these rights were being severely limited or eviscerated altogether. The "American dream" became an American nightmare for millions of workers. Well-paying jobs disappeared—replaced by robots and automation—and moved offshore. The housing crisis was the most visible and leading edge of the economic crisis as housing became increasingly out of reach even for the employed, and homelessness soared.

The economic revolution was engulfing the globe. It was driving the social revolution—disrupting capitalist institutions and social life. It was the root cause of ecological devastation, intensifying state violence and repression, war, militarism, and ruling-class motion toward fascism worldwide (Dyer-Withered 2015; M. Ford 2015; Foster 2022; W. Robinson 2022).

Darryl captured the motion we were living through:

> This is deep, and at each stage we didn't realize what was happening. We knew we were going through something different and then we reached the end of this thing called the industrial revolution. It knocked us for a loop. We start waking up to this new reality taking shape in front of us. Twenty years later everybody is starting to talk about what we've been trying to figure out. Everybody says that robotics are changing everything. That's called the destruction of everything we've known. (D. Mitchell in Chandler et al. 2017)

We have to do theoretical study today as part of our developing practice as revolutionaries, to grasp what the revolutionary process is as it unfolds and how we connect with it, to better understand the world as it is and as it is becoming. The revolutionary process is at least half intellectual and half practical. We have to do the work necessary, to think about it, to make correct decisions about the direction and concentrations of our work, to understand that the path to power embraces both long-term and short-term goals and to plan our path, to connect the day-to-day fight for immediate needs with long-haul system change. The intellectual side of our practice has to be a major part of the work of all of us who profess to be revolutionaries.

It is not possible to win and hold reforms under current conditions. We can secure our basic human needs and protect the environment only through revolution. This means the complete dismantling of the capitalist system, the abolition of private property, and the reconstruction of society on a cooperative basis.

Ruling-Class Motion toward Fascism

The world is changing fundamentally, and capitalists have to change with it. They can no longer rely on bourgeois democracy and their political parties—the Democrats and Republicans—as their form of rule. Robinson explained,

> Fascism seeks to rescue capitalism from its organic crisis, that is to violently restore capital accumulation, establish new forms of state legitimacy, and suppress threats from below unencumbered by democratic restraints. . . . The project involves a fusion of repressive and reactionary state power with a fascist mobilization in civil society. (W. Robinson 2022, 137)
>
> Three sectors of transnational capital . . . stand out as the most prone to seek neo-fascist political arrangements to facilitate accumulation: speculative financial capital, the military-industrial-security complex, and the extractive and energy (particularly petroleum) sector (the core of Koch industries is oil). (W. Robinson 2014, 172)

Fascism is the way the ruling class, as a whole, is moving to maintain control over the economy and society during the transition. The interpenetration of corporations and the state means that the state serves corporate interests rather than those of the working class and society as a whole. Fascist rule means suspending the Constitution, the rule of law, and any rights or legal recourse to anyone in the United States. It means embracing state violence, repression, lies, militarism, and war. Invoking the Insurrection Act would allow for the mobilization of the U.S. military as a tool for coercion and control to repress all forms of protest and rebellion (Dutt [1935] 1974; W. Robinson 2022; Whitman 2017).

The ruling class is strategically united in their defense of the capitalist system and their protection of continuing profits, wealth, and private property. They are compelled to roll back the reforms and concessions won over the years, to politically and ideologically divide the working class, to secure and hold their social bases for fascism, and to criminalize the rising working-class motion from below.

Sections of the ruling class differ in their tactical approaches. Divisions within the ruling class around the implementation of fascism are in plain sight. One section seeks to consolidate fascism under any conditions—striving to unite all forms of legal and extralegal violence as tools. Another section seeks to continue laying the legal and judicial basis for consolidating fascism. From the Patriot Act to the Heritage Foundation—the conservative think tank behind the Project 2025 plan for fascism—to the American Legislative Exchange Council (ALEC)—funded by oil and gas interests—as the leading architect of reactionary legislation, to the Federalist Society's recommendations and congressional approval of reactionary judges, to ensuring a fascist-leaning Supreme Court majority willing to reverse decades of legal precedent, all these represent tactical differences.

The intellectual and legal foundation for the motion toward fascist rule is being laid. This encompasses the attack on science and evidence-based knowledge and laws and Supreme Court decisions gutting bourgeois democracy—suppressing electoral participation and representation, establishing Cop Cities, criminalizing aspects of protest, censoring books, language, and education, restricting or eliminating bodily autonomy and reproductive justice, reversing affirmative action, targeting and controlling immigrants and refugees, removing regulations protecting the environment, and supporting and funding war across the globe.

Key to fascist development is the denial of science and promotion of the big lie—in our understanding of reality, of the climate and ecology, of disease, health, and wellness, of history, of class exploitation, of racial, national, and gender oppression within capitalism, and more.

Militarism is intensifying globally and domestically as part of the ruling-class motion toward fascism. The continuing war on the Palestinian people erupted in October 2023 in Gaza with a genocidal slaughter and twenty-first-century Nakba "catastrophe." This is happening with the U.S. ruling class's consistent political support, funding, and military armaments. On December 8, 2023, the United States was the only Security Council member to veto the U.N. resolution calling for an immediate ceasefire in Gaza.

In the United States, Cop Cities are proliferating as police training facilities spread across the country. The militarization of the police and the criminalization of protest are in preparation for urban warfare to control and contain working-class resistance. In addition to the Cop City in Atlanta, similar facilities have been or are being constructed in Chicago, Baltimore, Nashville, and San Pablo, California, with others in process (Black Alliance for Peace 2023; W. Robinson 2020, 2022).

The right to vote and to have our votes counted is under attack. Since 2021, thirty-nine state legislatures have considered 393 voter suppression bills, with eighteen states enacting thirty-four bills restricting ballot access—disproportionately impacting voters of color. Eleven states are moving another thirty-four restrictive bills through their legislatures (Brennan Center for Justice 2022).

Twenty-seven states have proposed 148 election interference bills dealing with election procedures, the vote count, and certification of election results. Six states have approved nine election interference laws, and another five states are moving seventeen such bills through their legislatures (Brennan Center for Justice 2022).

By September 2022, forty-five states have considered 246 bills criminalizing protest. They enacted thirty-nine into law, with thirteen bills pending. Most of these laws criminalize interference with critical infrastructure—including blocking sidewalks, street intersections, interstate highways, and especially the construction of oil and gas pipelines (International Center for Not-for-Profit Law 2022).

Police murders continue, even after the groundswell of protest following the murder of George Floyd in 2020. Mapping Police Violence reports 1,151 police murders in 2020, 1,177 in 2021, 1,250 in 2022, and 1,261 as of November 30, 2023 (Mapping Police Violence 2023).

The Supreme Court, in their June 24, 2022, *Dobbs v. Jackson* decision, overthrew the right to control our bodies and to reproductive health and freedom—a legal right guaranteed for fifty years in the 1973 *Roe v. Wade* decision. Even then, in 1977 Congress passed the Hyde Amendment prohibiting the use of federal funds for abortion, except to save the life of the mother. *Dobbs*, at the federal level, eliminates the constitutional rights *Roe* had established and returns to the states—read states' rights—the legal authority to legislate reproductive autonomy and health.

As of December 2023, fifteen states have passed laws banning reproductive choice—many with no exception for rape or incest. Eighteen states have passed laws with gestational and other limits on terminating a pregnancy. Reproductive choice remains legal and protected in seventeen states and the District of Columbia (Guttmacher Institute 2023).

Othering—the dehumanization and demonization of the "other"—is an essential tool for division in society. The Indigenous peoples were the first "other" to confront ruling-class genocide. The ruling class targets many "others" to divide society and pit us against one another as a necessity for consolidating fascism—using race, gender and sexual orientation, nationality, religion, and more.

Immigrants and refugees are an increasingly significant "other"—forced to migrate because of deepening economic, political, and ecological crises and global war. In the United States thousands are subjected to increasing exclusions, expulsions, violence, and militarization at the border by both legal and extralegal forces. One of the most abusive programs is the 287(g) program of the Immigration and Nationality Act. It authorizes U.S. Immigration and Customs Enforcement (ICE) to partner with and deputize state and municipal law enforcement agencies—many white-supremacist and violent—to enforce immigration law and run detention centers. The program expanded under the Trump administration and remained at 142 partnerships under the Biden administration. In 54 of these partnerships, the American Civil Liberties Union (ACLU) found extensive racial profiling, civil rights violations, anti-immigrant and xenophobic statements, and inhumane policies (ACLU 2022).

Education, especially public education, from elementary through higher education, is under attack. States have passed laws banning books and banning teaching real U.S. history that the "big lie" tries to hide and distort, especially teaching Black history and Indigenous history. Beginning in 2020, forty-five states introduced 283 bills to limit teaching about critical race theory and race, gender, and sexuality, to limit student access to "banned" books in school libraries because of "parental rights," and to limit transgender students' participation on sports teams matching their gender identities. Twenty-five states passed sixty-four of these bills into law (Schwartz 2022; Natanson et al. 2022).

Speech and protest critical of U.S. funding and support for the Israeli war against the Palestinian people and in support of a free Palestine are increasingly under attack, especially on college campuses (O'Rourke and Said 2023).

The U.S. South, the historic location of fascist motion—genocide, the slavocracy, Jim Crow, the Black Codes, and states' rights—is again the location of the vast majority of these reactionary and repressive laws. This is especially the case for massive voter disenfranchisement and suppression and the denial of bodily autonomy.

It is imperative that we defeat fascist rule and move beyond the source of fascism—the capitalist system. We must fight in defense of the interests of workers the world over. To do this, we must unite the sections of the working class who can be united, especially those who are labeled and treated as the "others."

How Do We Take the Offensive?

> It is not enough for revolution that the exploited and oppressed masses should understand the impossibility of living in the old way and demand changes; it is essential for revolution that the exploiters should not be able to live and rule in the old way. Only when the "lower classes" do not want the old way, and when the "upper classes" cannot carry on in the old way—only then can revolution triumph.
>
> —Vladimir Lenin, *Left Wing Communism* ([1920] 1964)

We are living in a time when revolutionary conditions are developing.

What does it mean that all of society is in transition? That all sections of society are in motion? To take the offensive against fascism?

The digital means of production create an abundance of all the things we need and the conditions to end scarcity—including the knowledge and tools to protect and heal ourselves and nature (Amin 2008; Bastani 2019; Katz-Fishman and Scott 2019; N. Peery 2001). The capitalist system of distribution and consumption based on markets and money blocks our access to this abundance and tools. But in the hands of the working class and a cooperative system, we can distribute these necessities and tools based on human need and ecological repair.

The objective conditions are ripe for the abolition of private property and transformation along socialist lines moving toward communism—with working-class leadership and direction. Nelson explained,

> The new era is producing a new movement. Production without work demands distribution without money. The cause of communism is practical. The objective character of the movement demands, more than ever, its subjective, i.e., political, theoretical, ideological expression. (N. Peery 1993, 5)

Capitalism will never die of its own accord. It can be put to death only by human beings organized to bring it down. Working-class forces are on the move. Darryl reflected,

> When you talk about being revolutionaries today, it's not this dry concept at all. We're talking about being abolitionists. The change is being made in front of us. We must determine what kind of society we want. (D. Mitchell in Chandler et al. 2017)

HOW DO WE WIN THE CLASS WAR? MOVING TO THE OFFENSIVE

To paraphrase billionaire Warren Buffett, we are in a class war. But only the capitalist class knows it. Robinson put it this way:

> Transnational capital and its political agents have been attempting to resolve the crisis by launching war on the global working class. (W. Robinson 2014, 172)

As revolutionaries, we seek strategically to unite the working class across race, gender, region, and nation. History teaches us that if we organize workers, the left will come. The class war is between the working class and the ruling class, rather than between the left and the right.

Today's upsurge in working-class struggle and political education is part of the motion toward developing working-class consciousness—to defeat the growing fascist threat at home and abroad. Protest is connecting across fronts of struggle—from labor to ecology and climate, to basic needs such as housing, food, and health care, to oppression based on race, nation, and gender, to state violence rooted in the police, prisons, militarism, and war.

The working-class movement is going through a shift in understanding and political practice. The trade union front of struggle is moving from representing just union members to representing the interests of the working class as a whole—a significant change in policy over the past fifty years. The UAW led the way during the 2023 strike wave, with UAW president Shawn Fain saying clearly at every picket line that the UAW represents the working class as a whole—not just its members. Earlier in the summer of 2023, Fran Drescher, SAG-AFTRA president, echoed this reality.

Huge and growing swaths of workers in all sectors of the economy—service workers, production workers, professional and technical workers—are struggling, are unionizing, and are striking for working conditions and wages. Many are forced to work more than one job just to survive. In this regard, the UAW Executive Board has called on trade unions to coordinate their contract endings on or before May Day (May 1) 2028, hoping to set the basis for a nationwide strike (general strike).

This awakening of working-class consciousness in the labor movement—among trade unions, across social struggles for living wages and safe working conditions, for basic necessities, and for wellness and bodily autonomy—is connected to the ecological movement to end fossil fuels, to address global warming and climate catastrophe, to protect the water, land, forests, and air, and to protect all life.

Indigenous peoples throughout the world have been at the front lines of the ecological struggle resisting settler colonialism and capitalist expropriation of nature for centuries and today are joined by other frontline communities and young people facing destruction from floods, fires, deforestation, pipeline construction, and so on (Estes 2019; Foster 2022). Today's movement links climate justice with human rights and a just transition—arguing that climate justice and ending ecological destruction require ending all forms of oppression and class exploitation (*Democracy Now* 2023a; Lakhani 2023).

In December 2023, climate justice activists gathered at the COP28 climate summit in Dubai, UAE, along with governments, oil capitalists, and lobbyists. Ruling-class representatives declared the final agreement as "historic" because it mentioned "fossil fuels" for the first time and called for "transition away from fossil fuels" to renewables. Climate justice forces rejected that claim, arguing that the agreement was full of loopholes—with no timeline and no mechanisms for enforcement—and had an escape clause for fossil fuels as "transition fuels." Beyond that, Indigenous peoples, frontline communities, and island states—those most impacted by climate change and most engaged in protecting nature, water, forests, and the land—had no real seat at the table. The ecological struggle is existential and ongoing (*Democracy Now* 2023a; Lakhani 2023).

The working-class movement against state violence is not new but has gained momentum in recent years in response to the intensification of ruling-class repression. The George Floyd rebellion, protesting the 2020 police murder of Floyd, was the largest and broadest demonstration in the United States in over fifty years. It was diverse across generations, race, and gender and went global. It was part of the expanding abolition movement against the prison-industrial complex and militarization of the police—including Cop Cities (A. Davis 2016; Gilmore 2022; Kaba 2021).

The Stop Cop City motion in Atlanta in 2023 brought together the anticolonial struggle of the Indigenous Muskogee people, the ecological struggle to defend the Weelaunee Forest—the home of the Muskogee and the site of Cop City—and the abolition struggle to end police militarism. Though the demonstration was peaceful, many protestors were arrested and charged with domestic terrorism, including sixty-one who were charged with racketeering under the Georgia RICO law. The effort to block Cop Cities in Atlanta and around the country continues (Lennard 2023).

The apocalyptic U.S.-orchestrated and -funded Israeli war against the Palestinian people has galvanized social motion throughout the United States to confront and stop the genocidal siege of Gaza and the legacy of colonialism, settler colonialism, and imperialism (*Democracy Now* 2023b). Jewish voices—in unity with Muslim and Christian voices—and young people from high school and college have been especially vocal and visible. When Palestinian trade unions called for trade union solidarity, several U.S. unions—the UAW, UE (United Electrical, Radio and Machine Workers of America), NNU (National Nurses United), APWU (American Postal Workers Union), and NEA (National Education Association)—stepped up to call for a ceasefire now. Dock workers blocked shipments of weapons to Israel (Schuhrke and Fletcher 2023; Vinall 2023). The movement at home demanded that Congress and the Biden administration support a permanent and immediate ceasefire, end funding and military support for Israel, and fund the needs of the American people.

This outpouring of solidarity for the Palestinian people has not been seen since the 1960s—when the LRBW met with and stood in solidarity with the Palestine Liberation Organization (PLO). This moment has affirmed historic connections between the Palestinian struggle, Indigenous struggles, and the Black freedom struggle around the history of settler colonialism and genocide (A. Davis 2016). The war to free Palestine is one of the last anticolonial projects of the capitalist epoch (*Democracy Now* 2023b).

Working-class forces are protesting in the streets, in the halls of power at the federal, state, and local levels, at the Supreme Court and courts at all levels, at state legislatures and city councils, at school boards, libraries, and college campuses. We are contesting at the ballot box—engaging the electoral process to support candidates, run as candidates, and shape public policy.

We are resisting schemes to disenfranchise voters—challenging purges of voter rolls, voter ID laws, and limits on absentee ballots—opposing gerrymandered electoral maps, and fighting for ballot access for returning citizens. We're using state and local ballot initiatives and policy struggles, especially in support of bodily autonomy and the right to control our health and reproductive choices.

Our democracy struggle is grounded in and asserts the truth, reality, science, and history of the American multiracial and multigendered working-class experience—rejecting ruling-class lies, distortions, and myths. We are actively opposing all forms of censorship and silencing—from the recent wave of book banning, to attacks on academic freedom and the criminalization of antisystem speech and protest. Our resistance embraces participating in the policy arena, creating spaces in schools, colleges, communities, and the media, and taking it to the streets.

NEXT STEPS

Going from the defensive to the offensive means more than protecting what we have and fighting for what we had and lost. Bourgeois democracy, at best, was not democracy for huge swaths of the working class. Taking the offensive is struggling for the future—for a cooperative, peaceful, and ecologically sustainable world. Robinson said it this way:

> The only chance that popular resistance forces have to beat back the threat of fascism is to put forward an alternative interpretation of the crisis based on working class politics that can win over the would-be social base of fascism. (W. Robinson 2022, 139)

This moment requires the American people to deeply understand today's capitalist crises—the interrelated crises of economy, ecology and climate, politics, and society—and to take the offensive to defeat fascism and win the world we envision, need, and want, to become fighters who think and thinkers who fight.

Centuries of struggle have taught us critical strategic lessons to guide our revolutionary path. We uplift many but emphasize three here. First, as conscious revolutionaries, our task is to study theory—collectively if possible—to understand the world as it is and the revolutionary process and to participate in the class struggle. Second, the U.S. South is a strategic battleground in the class war. Winning in the South is key to the well-being of people and the planet—throughout the United States and the world. Third, working-class unity in understanding the world and collectivity in political practice are essential—to become a multiracial, multinational, and multigendered force united in our struggle for transformation. We must gather the revolutionaries among the working class, especially among the "others," to forge a revolutionary organization rooted in the sections of the working class who are in motion and who can be united, to think and struggle together, to be a fighting force that can realize our vision for the future and win and hold our victory.

Survival of humanity and the earth requires all us to take up this revolutionary work. The revolutionary horizon is within our grasp. Make it happen!

APPENDIX

Methodology

Our methodology for this research project and book does not fit neatly into any social science category or literary genre. In the appendix we explain the various tools and types we used to bring this project to life in print, on the GBI website, and in ongoing political conversation and struggle.

For Jerome, huge parts of this project and book are autobiographical. He shares—as author and narrator, political actor, and interviewee—his politicization, joining the LRBW, and being part of the political journey to the LRBW and the current moment.

Walda joined the journey during the CLP days in the mid-1970s. She is co-narrator and political actor, as is Jerome, in the journey to the current moment and beyond.

For both of us, this project and book combine aspects of participatory action research and oral history and being authors, narrators, and political actors as part of the political journey we are all on.

Sampling and Interviews

In December 2015 several key LRBW comrades met at Marian Kramer's house. The group included Marian, Jerome, John Williams (a LRBW Executive Board member and an LRBW member today), and Darryl Mitchell (a member of the BSUF, the LRBW, and beyond). They/we brainstormed and used the snowball technique to identify and reach out to all the LRBW comrades we knew who were still living. Many were in Detroit, a few in Chicago, two others in Baltimore and Atlanta. We identified, connected with, and ultimately interviewed forty comrades. Our interviews with Nelson Peery, Mike Hamlin, Al

Gladyck, Jim Fite, Richard Fahoome, and Darryl Mitchell were their last before they died.

We also searched for and reached out to find video and/or audio of presentations of comrades no longer with us to include in our narrative. This included extensive video of General "Gen" Baker and a very short clip of Chuck Wooten.

Interview Questions and Process

Jerome and Virginia, who was part of the project from the beginning through the entire interview process, conducted all the individual and group interviews. By July 6, 2015, before we began the interview process, we developed this comprehensive list of questions and probes that provided an overarching framework laying out our collective purpose and the narrative for the project. We used these questions in all the interviews and adapted them depending on when and how folks became part of the LRBW journey from DRUM to the League of Revolutionaries for a New America (LRNA) today.

Questions

1. How did you get involved with the LRBW, and what was your work with the LRBW? Did you fall away from the League, or did you stay engaged through the transitions? For those who stayed through the transitions, what kept you in and going forward?
2. What is the role of Black labor in the industrial working class, in production, and in the revolutionary process post–Civil War to the current moment?
3. What is the role of women within these struggles?
4. How did the League get to the point of dedicating as much time as we did to political and theoretical study?
5. What happened to those who went through the study and the LRBW to the LRNA political journey?
6. What explains their/our longevity (from the LRBW, through the split, to the CL, CLP, and LRNA)?
7. How were they/we able to survive the ebbs and flows of the movement? The strategy and tactics of the social movement and the revolutionary process?
8. What are the lessons of this political journey and theoretical (scientific) study for today's generation of movement organizers and activists—some of whom think of themselves as revolutionaries?

Appendix

9. How can these lessons help address the ideology, political culture, and realities of this generation?
   - Lack of study and anti-intellectualism
   - Lack of willingness to join organizations
   - Thinking that social movement organizing and activism alone will get things done
   - Burnout
   - Lack of criticism and self-criticism (any real debrief and evaluation)
10. What happened to those who did not go through political and theoretical study?
11. How do League members understand the conditions, time, and place of the LRBW, the steps along the way, and the LRNA in the current moment?

Transcription Process

We sent interview videos (and audios) to https://scribie.com/, an online transcription service, for initial transcription. Walda and Jerome performed additional political editing and excerpting for this project and book.

BIBLIOGRAPHY

Ahmad, Muhammad (Maxwell Stanford Jr.). 2008. *We Will Return in the Whirlwind: Black Radical Organizations 1960–1975*. Chicago: Charles H. Kerr.
Allinger, Nancy. 2017. "Nancy Allinger Interview." Highland Park, Mich.: GBI.
American Civil Liberties Union (ACLU). 2022. "License to Abuse: How ICE's 287(g) Program Empowers Racist Sheriffs and Civil Rights Violations." April 26, 2022. https://www.aclu.org/report/license-abuse-how-ices-287g-program-empowers-racist-sheriffs.
Amin, Samir. 2008. *The World We Wish to See: Revolutionary Objectives in the Twenty-First Century*. New York: Monthly Review Press.
———. 2011. *Global History: A View from the South*. Cape Town, South Africa: Pambazuka Press.
Baker, General Gordon, Jr. 2015. "Letter to the Local Draft Board, Wayne County, Mich., September 10, 1965." *Viewpoint Magazine*, June 30, 2015. https://viewpointmag.com/2015/06/30/letter-to-the-local-draft-board-1965/.
———. 2016. "General Baker on the History of Struggle in Detroit (U.S. Social Forum, June 24, 2010)." Accessed August 8, 2016. https://www.youtube.com/watch?v=6SNGqz4FFGE.
Baker, Ilene, Kadesha Baker, and Yvette Baker. 2017. "Ilene & Her Daughters Interview." Highland Park, Mich.: GBI.
Baker, Valerie. 2017. "Valerie Baker Interview." Highland Park, Mich.: GBI.
Bastani, Aaron. 2019. *Fully Automated Luxury Communism: A Manifesto*. Brooklyn, N.Y.: Verso.
Bernard, Allen Ray. 2017. "Allen Ray Bernard Interview." Highland Park, Mich.: GBI.
Bish, Jim. 2017. "Jim Bish Interview." Highland Park, Mich.: GBI.
Black Alliance for Peace. 2023. "Bulletin on U.S. Domestic Militarization #3." October 19, 2023. https://blackallianceforpeace.com/bulletinonusdomesticmilitarization/edition3.
Black National Economic Conference. 1969. *Black Manifesto*. July 10, 1969. Accessed April 1, 2022. https://www.nybooks.com/articles/1969/07/10/black-manifesto/?lp_txn_id=1340710.
Boyer, Richard, and Herbert Morais. 1955. *Labor's Untold Story*. Pittsburgh: United Electrical, Radio and Machine Workers of America.

Brennan Center for Justice. 2022. "Voting Laws Roundup: May 2022." May 26, 2022. https://www.brennancenter.org/our-work/research-reports/voting-laws-roundup-may-2022.

Bush, Rod. 1999. *We Are Not What We Seem: Black Nationalism and Class Struggle.* New York: New York University Press.

———. 2009. *The End of White World Supremacy: Black Internationalism and the Problem of the Color Line.* Philadelphia: Temple University Press.

Caffentzis, George. 2013. *In Letters of Blood and Fire: Work, Machines, and the Crisis of Capitalism.* Oakland, Calif.: PM Press.

Chandler, Alonzo, Russell Jackson, Darryl Mitchell, and Abdul Roberts. 2017. "Thursday at Waistline's." Highland Park, Mich.: GBI.

Cockrel, Ken, Mike Hamlin, and John Watson. 1971. *The Split in the League of Revolutionary Black Workers: Three Lines and Three Headquarters.* Unpublished manuscript.

Consumer Guide. 2001a. *Cars of the Fabulous '50s: A Decade of High Style and Good Times.* Morton Grove, Ill.: Publications International.

———. 2001b. *Cars of the Fabulous '60s: A Decade of High Style and Good Times.* Morton Grove, Ill.: Publications International.

———. 2004. *Cars of the Classic '30s: A Decade of Elegant Design.* Morton Grove, Ill.: Publications International.

Davis, Angela. 2016. *Freedom Is a Constant Struggle: Ferguson, Palestine, and the Foundations of a Movement.* Edited by Frank Barat. Chicago: Haymarket Books.

Davis, Jim, Tom Hirschl, and Michael Stack, eds. 1997. *Cutting Edge: Technology, Information, Capitalism and Social Revolution.* New York: Verso.

Democracy Now. 2023a. "Phase Down, Not Phase Out: COP28 Deal on Fossil Fuels Disappoints Activists & Vulnerable States." December 13, 2023. https://www.democracynow.org/2023/12/13/cop28_fossil_fuel_phaseout.

———. 2023b. "'This Is a Colonial War': Historian Rashid Khalidi on Israel, Gaza & the Future of Palestine." December 20, 2023. https://www.democracynow.org/2023/12/20/this_is_a_colonial_war_historian?utm.

Du Bois, W. E. B. [1935] 1962. *Black Reconstruction in America 1860–1880.* New York: Atheneum/Macmillan.

Dutt, R. Palme. [1935] 1974. *Fascism and Social Revolution.* San Francisco: Proletarian Publishers.

Dyer-Withered, Nick. 2015. *Cyber-Proletariat: Global Labor in the Digital Vortex.* London: Pluto Press.

Dyer-Withered, Nick, Atle Mikkola Kjosen, and James Steinhoff. 2019. *Inhuman Power: Artificial Intelligence and the Future of Capitalism.* London: Pluto Press.

Engels, Friedrich. [1880] 1970. *Socialism Scientific and Utopian.* Accessed September 21, 2022. https://www.marxists.org/archive/marx/works/download/Engels_Socialism_Utopian_and_Scientific.pdf.

Estes, Nick. 2019. *Our History Is the Future: Standing Rock versus the Dakota Access Pipeline, and the Long Tradition of Indigenous Resistance.* Brooklyn, N.Y.: Verso.

Fahoome, Richard. 2017. "Richard Fahoome Interview." Highland Park, Mich.: GBI.

Fite, Jim. 2017. "Jim Fite Interview." Highland Park, Mich.: GBI.

Flammang, James M., and Auto Editors of Consumer Guide. 2000. *Cars of the Sensational '70s: A Decade of Changing Tastes and New Directions*. Morton Grove, Ill.: Publications International.

Ford, Cassandra "Cass" Bell. 2017. "Cassandra 'Cass' Bell Ford Interview." Highland Park, Mich.: GBI.

Ford, Martin. 2015. *Rise of the Robots: Technology and the Threat of a Jobless Future*. New York: Basic Books.

Foster, John Bellamy. 2022. *Capitalism in the Anthropocene: Ecological Ruin or Ecological Revolution*. New York: Monthly Review Press.

General Baker Institute (GBI). 2017. Website at www.revolutionaryblackworkers.org. Highland Park, Mich.: GBI.

Geography of Transport Systems. 2023. "Automobile Production, Selected Countries, 1950–2022." Accessed September 14, 2023. https://transportgeography.org/contents/chapter1/the-setting-of-global-transportation-systems/automobile-production world/.

Georgakas, Dan, and Marvin Surkin. [1975] 2012. *Detroit: I Do Mind Dying*. Chicago: Haymarket Books.

Geschwender, James. 1977. *Class, Race, and Worker Insurgency: The League of Revolutionary Black Workers*. New York: Cambridge University Press.

Gilmore, Ruth Wilson. 2022. *Abolition Geography: Essays towards Liberation*. Edited by Brenna Bhandar and Alberto Toscano. Brooklyn, N.Y.: Verso.

Gladyck, Al. 2017. "Al Gladyck Interview." Highland Park, Mich.: GBI.

Glotta, Ron. 2017. "Ron Glotta Interview." Highland Park, Mich.: GBI.

Gonzales, Beth, and JoAnn Capalbo. 2017. "Beth and JoAnn Interview." Highland Park, Mich.: GBI.

Gonzales, Nacho. 2017. "Nacho Gonzales Interview." Highland Park, Mich.: GBI.

Greenhouse, Steven. 2019. *Beaten Down, Worked Up: The Past, Present, and Future of American Labor*. New York: Knopf.

Guevara, Ernesto "Che." 1965. *Socialism and Man in Cuba*. Accessed October 3, 2022. https://www.marxists.org/archive/guevara/1965/03/man-socialism.htm.

Guttmacher Institute. 2023. "Interactive Map: U.S. Abortion Policies and Access after Roe." Accessed December 25, 2023. https://states.guttmacher.org/policies/.

Hamlin, Mike. 2017. "Mike Hamlin Interview." Highland Park, Mich.: GBI.

Heagerty, Brooke, and Nelson Peery. 2000. *Moving Onward: From Racial Division to Class Unity*. Chicago: People's Tribune.

Hersey, John. 1968. *The Algiers Motel Incident*. New York: Knopf.

Icarus Films. 1970. *Finally Got the News*. Accessed October 25, 2024. http://icarusfilms.com/if-fin.

Inner-City Voice. 1970. "Reuther's Dead: Black Struggle Continues." 2, no. 6 (June). Accessed November 2, 2024. https://freedomarchives.org/Documents/Finder/DOC513_scans/League/513.LeagueofRevolutionaryBlackWokers.InnerCity.June.1970.pdf.

International Center for Not-for-Profit Law. 2022. "U.S. Protest Law Tracker." Accessed October 18, 2022. https://www.icnl.org/usprotestlawtracker/.

James, C. L. R. [1963] 1989. *The Black Jacobins*. New York: Random House.

Joyce, Frank. 2017. "Frank Joyce Interview." Highland Park, Mich.: GBI.

Kaba, Mariame. 2021. *We Do This 'Til We Free Us: Abolitionist Organizing and Transforming Justice*. Chicago: Haymarket Books.

Katz-Fishman, Walda, and Jerome Scott. 2012. "Wage Labor." Pp. 2151–2154 in *Encyclopedia of Globalization*, edited by George Ritzer and Berch Berberoglu. Oxford: Blackwell.

———. 2019. "Race, Class and Revolution in the Twenty-First Century: Lessons from the League of Revolutionary Black Workers." Pp. 441–462 in *The Oxford Handbook of Karl Marx*, edited by Matt Vidal, Tony Smith, Tomás Rotta, and Paul Prew. New York: Oxford University Press.

Kramer, Marian. 2017. "Marian Kramer Interview." Highland Park, Mich.: GBI.

Kramer, Marian. 2016. LRBW *Extended Promo*. Accessed November 12, 2022. https://www.revolutionaryblackworkers.org/video/.

Lakhani, Nina. 2023. "Indigenous People and Climate Justice Groups Say Cop28 Was 'Business as Usual.'" *The Guardian*, December 13, 2023. https://www.theguardian.com/environment/2023/dec/13/indigenous-people-and-climate-justice-groups-say-cop28-was-business-as-usual.

League of Revolutionary Black Workers Education and Media Project. 2016. "Donate to General Baker Institute." Accessed November 30, 2016. https://www.revolutionaryblackworkers.org/.

———. 2017. "Video." Accessed September 28, 2022. https://www.revolutionaryblackworkers.org/video/.

Lee, Kai-Fu. 2018. *AI Superpowers: China, Silicon Valley, and the New World Order*. Boston: Houghton Mifflin Harcourt.

Lenin, Vladimir. [1902] 1961. *What Is to Be Done*. Moscow: Foreign Languages Publishing House.

———. [1917] 1976. *The State and Revolution*. Beijing: Foreign Languages Press.

———. [1920] 1964. *Left Wing Communism, an Infantile Disorder*. Accessed September 21, 2022. https://www.marxists.org/archive/lenin/works/1920/lwc/.

Lennard, Natasha. 2023. "Cop City Protesters Tried to Plant Trees. Atlanta Police Beat Them for It." *The Intercept*, November 15, 2023. Accessed November 3, 2024. https://theintercept.com/2023/11/15/cop-city-protest-police-atlanta-tear-gas/.

Mapping Police Violence. 2023. "Mapping Police Violence." Accessed January 2, 2024. https://mappingpoliceviolence.org/?utm_campaign=launch&utm_source=google&utm_medium=ad&utm_term=police%20violence%20statistics&gclid=CjoKCQiAhc-sBhCEARIsAOVwH.

Mauricio, Esther. 2017. "Esther Mauricio Interview." Highland Park, Mich.: GBI.

Marx, Karl. [1859] 1977. "Preface." In *A Contribution to the Critique of Political Economy*. Moscow: Progress Publishers. Accessed March 19, 2017. https://www.marxists.org/archive/marx/works/1859/critique-pol-economy/preface.htm.

———. [1861] 1973. *Grundrisse: Foundations of the Critique of Political Economy* (Rough Draft). New York: Penguin. Accessed June 17, 2017. https://www.marxists.org/archive/marx/works/1857/grundrisse/.

———. [1863] 1963. "Theories of Productive and Unproductive Labour." In *Theories of Surplus*

Value, pt. 1. Moscow: Progress Publishers. Accessed June 16, 2017. https://www.marxists.org/archive/marx/works/1863/theories-surplus-value/ch04.htm.

———. [1867] 1887. *Capital: A Critique of Political Economy*. Vol. 1. Edited by Friedrich Engels. Moscow: Progress Publishers. Accessed March 19, 2017. https://www.marxists.org/archive/marx/works/1867-c1/.

———. [1875] 1970. *Critique of the Gotha Programme*. Accessed September 21, 2022. https://www.marxists.org/archive/marx/works/download/Marx_Critque_of_the_Gotha_Programme.pdf.

Marx, Karl, and Friedrich Engels. [1845] 1968. *The German Ideology*. Moscow: Progress Publishers. Accessed May 29, 2017. https://www.marxists.org/archive/marx/works/1845/german-ideology/.

McAfee, Andrew, and Erik Brynjolfsson. 2017. *Machine Platform Crowd: Harnessing Our Digital Future*. New York: Norton.

Merriam-Webster Dictionary. 2023. "Workers' Compensation." Accessed October 10, 2023. https://www.merriam-webster.com/dictionary/workers'%20compensation.

Mitchell, Darryl. 2017. "Darryl 'Waistline' Mitchell Interview." Highland Park, Mich.: GBI.

Mitchell, William. 2017. "William 'Mitch' Mitchell Interview." Highland Park, Mich.: GBI.

Music, Marsha. 2017. "Marsha Music aka Lynn Battle Interview." Highland Park, Mich.: GBI.

Natanson, Hannah, Clara Morse, Anu Narayanswamy, and Christina Brause. 2022. "An Explosion of Culture-War Laws Is Changing Schools." *Washington Post*, November 10, 2022, 14.

Office of Energy Efficiency & Renewable Energy. 2009. "Fact #601: December 14, 2009 World Motor Vehicle Production." Accessed November 29, 2019. https://www.energy.gov/eere/vehicles/fact-601-december-14-2009-world-motor-vehicle-production.

O'Rourke, Anthony, and Wadie E. Said. 2023. "Terrorism Investigations on Campus and the New McCarthyism." *Portside*, December 14, 2023. https://portside.org/2023-12-14/terrorism-investigations-campus-and-new-mccarthyism.

Peery, Nelson. 1973. *The Negro National Colonial Question*. Chicago: Workers Press.

———. 1993. *Entering an Epoch of Social Revolution*. Chicago: Workers Press.

———. 2001. *The Future Is Up to Us*. Chicago: People's Tribune Speakers Bureau.

———, 2017. "Nelson Peery Interview." Highland Park, Mich.: GBI.

Peery, Sue, ed. 1977. *Outline for the Study of Marxist-Leninism*. Chicago: Workers Press.

Quintana, Chris. 2022. "In lawsuit over Student Loan Forgiveness, 6 States Slam Biden for Overreach." *USA Today*, October 25, 2022. https://money.yahoo.com/lawsuit-over-student-loan-forgiveness-215005756.html.

Randazzo, Pam. 2017. "Pam Randazzo Interview." Highland Park, Mich.: GBI.

Robinson, Cedric. [1983] 2000. *Black Marxism: The Making of the Black Radical Tradition*. Chapel Hill: University of North Carolina Press.

Robinson, William I. 2014. *Global Capitalism and the Crisis of Humanity*. New York: Cambridge University Press.

———. 2020. *The Global Police State*. London: Pluto Press.

———. 2022. *Global Civil War: Capitalism Post-Pandemic*. Oakland, Calif.: PM Press.

Robinson, William I., and Federico Fuentes. 2023. "Capitalist Globalisation, Transnational Class Exploitation and the Global Police State: An Interview with William I. Robinson."

Accessed December 10, 2023. https://links.org.au/capitalist-globalisation-transnational-class-exploitation-and-global-police-state-interview-william.

Roediger, David. 2017. *Class, Race, and Marxism*. Brooklyn, N.Y.: Verso.

Roediger, David, and Elizabeth Esch. 2014. *The Production of Difference: Race and the Management of Labor in U.S. History*. New York: Oxford University Press.

Rogers, Leah. 2017. "Leah Rogers Interview." Highland Park, Mich.: GBI.

Rogers, Wylie. 2017. "Wylie Rogers Interview." Highland Park, Mich.: GBI.

Schuhrke, Jeff, and Bill Fletcher. 2023. "Labor Demands a Ceasefire: UAW, Electrical & Postal Workers Call for Israel's Assault on Gaza to End." *Democracy Now*, December 26, 2023. https://www.democracynow.org/2023/12/26/us_labor_movement_israel_palestine?utm.

Schwartz, Sarah. 2022. "Map: Where Critical Race Theory Is Under Attack." *Education Week*, September 28, 2022. Accessed October 26, 2022. https://www.edweek.org/policy-politics/map-where-critical-race-theory-is-under-attack/2021/06.

Scott, Jerome. 2017. "Jerome Scott Interview." Highland Park, Mich.: GBI.

———. 2016. LRBW *Extended Promo*. Accessed November 12, 2022. https://www.revolutionaryblackworkers.org/video/.

Simmons, Charles. 2017. "Charles Simmons Interview." Highland Park, Mich.: GBI.

Srnicek, Nick. 2017. *Platform Capitalism*. Malden, Mass.: Polity.

Stalin, Joseph. 1934. *Problems of Organizational Leadership*. Accessed November 24, 2023. https://www.anesi.com/east/stalin.htm.

Statista. 2023. "U.S. Domestic Auto Production from 1994 to 2022." Accessed September 14, 2023. https://www.statista.com/statistics/184171/us-passenger-car-production-since-1994/.

Taylor, Maureen. 2017. "Maureen Taylor Interview." Highland Park, Mich.: GBI.

Tripp, Luke. 1969. "D.R.U.M.—Vanguard of the Black Revolution." *South End* 27, no. 62: 1–8.

———. 2017. "Luke Tripp Interview." Highland Park, Mich.: GBI.

UAW 2022. "UAW Membership 2021." Accessed April 9, 2022. https://uaw.org/about/.

UAW Research Department. 1998. "UAW Strikes at General Motors, Ford and Chrysler, 1967–1968." Received in email communication with Jo Matthews, UAW Research Department, October 1, 2019.

UAW Secretary-Treasurer's Office. 2016. "UAW Average Annual Dues Paying Membership 1936 through 2016." Received in email communication with Jo Matthews, UAW Research Department, October 1, 2019.

U.S. Bureau of Labor Statistics. 2022. "Employment, Hours, and Earnings from the Current Employment Statistics Survey (National), Series ID: CEU3133600101, All Employees by Thousands: Motor Vehicles and Parts 1990–2022." Accessed April 9, 2022. https://data.bls.gov/timeseries/CEU3133600101.

U.S. Department of Transportation, Bureau of Transportation Statistics. 2018. "Table 1–23: World Motor Vehicle Production, Selected Countries." Accessed November 29, 2019. https://www.bts.gov/content/world-motor-vehicle-production-selected-countries.

———. 2020. "Table 1–15: Annual U.S. Motor Vehicle Production and Domestic Sales, Passenger Cars, 1960–2020." Accessed April 9, 2022. https://www.bts.gov/content/annual-us-motor-vehicle-production-and-factory-wholesale-sales-thousands-units.

Valenti, Rita. 2017. "Rita Valenti Interview." Highland Park, Mich.: GBI.

Vinall, Frances. 2023. "Young Americans Are More Pro-Palestinian Than Their Elders. Why?" *Washington Post*, December 21, 2023. https://wapo.st/4ayz4jd.
Watson, Edna. 2017. "Edna Watson Interview." Highland Park, Mich.: GBI.
Watson, John. 1969. "To the Point of Production: An Interview with John Watson of the League of Revolutionary Black Workers." *Fifth Estate*. Accessed November 3, 2024. https://riseupdetroit.org/wp-content/uploads/2018/07/To-the-Point-of-Production-An-Interview-with-John-Watson-1969.pdf.
Wayne State Friday and Saturday. 2017. "League and Friends Large Group Conversations at Wayne State University." Highland Park, Mich.: GBI.
Wheeler, Linda. 2017. "Linda Wheeler Interview." Highland Park, Mich.: GBI.
Whitman, James Q. 2017. *Hitler's American Model: The United States and the Making of Nazi Race Law*. Princeton, N.J.: Princeton University Press.
Williams, John. 2016. LRBW *Extended Promo*. Accessed November 12, 2022. https://www.revolutionaryblackworkers.org/video/.
———. 2017. "John Williams Interview." Highland Park, Mich.: GBI.
Williams, Judy. 2017. "Judy Williams Interview." Highland Park, Mich.: GBI.
Williams, Robert. [1962] 1998. *Negroes with Guns*. Detroit, Mich.: Wayne State University Press.
Wooten, Chuck. n.d. "Interviews with Eldon Workers on James Johnson." Private communication, September 2, 2022. https://drive.google.com/file/d/1yAEHMnyreeHNMPR-V_lfKKnmw-ljCwig/view.
Wooten, Gracie. 2017. "Gracie Wooten Interview." Highland Park, Mich.: GBI.
Zuboff, Shoshana. 2019. *The Age of Surveillance Capitalism: The Fight for a Human Future at a New Frontier of Power*. New York: PublicAffairs.

INDEX

Abbreviations used in the index are listed on page xi.

activism. *See* revolutionary movement
African American workers. *See* Black workers
AI (artificial intelligence). *See* technology
Algiers Motel incident, 39, 44–45
Allinger, Nancy, 137
anti-imperialism: DRUM/LRBW and, 41, 46, 72, 103, 112; lessons learned, 165; of LRBW members, 32–33, 34, 35–36, 37–38; political education on, 115, 131, 145–146, 149; in revolutionary movement, 154, 180–181; U.S. rebellions as, 42. *See also* internationalism
auto industry: class struggle and, 7, 20–25; DRUM/LRBW struggle against, 46–54; employment in, 17–20, 164; race and racism in, 11–16, 22–23, 25, 38, 60, 133; reactions of, 51, 54, 60; UAW relationship with, 63–64. *See also specific companies*
automation. *See* technology
auto workers. *See* Black workers; Latino/a workers; UAW; white workers

Bagley, Don, 68
Baker, Carolyn, 81
Baker, General (Gen):
—analysis and commentary: on auto industry history, 20, 21, 22, 23, 24, 25; on Detroit, uniqueness of, 12; on Detroit Rebellion, 43, 44, 45–46; on James Johnson case, 66–67; on lessons learned, 159–160; on longevity in revolutionary movement, 152–153; on patience and kindness, 161, 166; on RUMs, 55; on working-class intellectuals, 100
—background, 11, 16
—relationships: with Fahoome, 138; with Gladyck, 133; with labor lawyers, 65; with LRBW women, 79–82; with D. Mitchell, 91; with Peery, 118; with Taylor, 135; with L. Wheeler, 132; with C. Wooten, 161
—as revolutionary: CCL, 121; CL, 125; DRUM, 47, 50, 51, 52–54, 55, 56–57; early activism, 29, 31–33, 36, 37, 39, 40, 41; League oral history project, 184; LRBW leadership, 58–59, 105, 106, 107, 110, 168; political education, 146, 148; publishing and resourcing, 68–69, 71; wildcat strikes, 60
Baker, Ilene, 79–81, 82–83, 86, 107
Baker, Jeanette, 81, 84, 85
Baker, Kadesha, 79, 80–81
Baker, Valerie, 81–82
Baker, Yvette, 79, 80–81

Battle, Lynn. *See* Music, Marsha
Bernard, Allen Ray, 12, 14, 40, 92–93, 145, 160
Bernard, Diane, 85
Bish, Jim, 129–130, 158, 168
Black Economic Development Conference (BEDC), 35, 69–71
Black history. *See* history; slavery
Black Jacobins (James), 54
Black liberation movement, 4, 12, 34, 42, 46, 56, 59
Black Lives Matter movement, 161, 169
Black Manifesto (Black National Economic Conference), 35, 69–71
Black nationalism, 129, 148, 149
Black Panther Party, 8, 73–77, 81, 122, 125, 129, 134–135
Black power movement, 144, 156
Black Reconstruction in America 1860–1880 (Du Bois), 42, 97
Black Star Publishing, 70, 71–72, 84, 85, 110. *See also* propaganda
Black Student Voice, 90, 91
Black Womens Committee, 82–83, 86
Black workers: as auto workers, 25, 38, 133; class struggle in auto industry and, 17, 20–25, 29–41, 60–61; Detroit Rebellion of 1967 and, 42–46; DRUM/LRBW and, 3–6, 10, 46–54, 103, 104, 107; economic exploitation of, historic, 69–70; at Frito-Lay, 89; importance of, 73–77, 131, 159, 169; Marx and Du Bois on, 42; migration to Detroit, 11–16; revolutionary spirit of, 7, 122; unions and, 145. *See also* DRUM; Latino/a workers; LRBW members; race and racism; white workers; *and specific individuals*
Boo, Betty (Betty Griffith), 83, 95
Boyer, Richard O., 110
BSUF (Black Student United Front), 13, 87–92, 95, 108, 160
Buffett, Warren, 179
BWC (Black Workers Congress), 12, 103–105, 108, 111, 131

Cadillac (GM), 91
Capalbo, JoAnn, 122–123, 158
Capital (Marx), 42, 120, 123, 129, 133
Capital Collective, 133–134
capitalism: auto industry and, 17–25; current crises of, 171; fascism as means to preserve, 174–178; LRBW revolutionary struggle against, 3–10; race and racism in, 69–70, 97–100; strategies and tactics against, 173–174, 178–182; technology and, 147–148, 173
car manufacturers. *See* auto industry; *and specific companies*
CCL (California Communist League), 113, 115–116, 120–124
Chandler, Alonzo, 40, 50, 56, 95, 110, 147–148, 161–162
Chicago, 118, 120–121
Chrysler: history, 20, 24; James Johnson case and, 66–67; LRBW members as workers at, 55–56; race and racism at, 25, 133; wildcat strikes at, 49, 50, 54, 61–64. *See also* Dodge Main plant; Eldon Avenue Gear and Axle plant
churches, 69–71, 165
civil rights movement, 14, 15, 16, 39–40, 144, 148, 156. *See also* revolutionary movement
CL (Communist League): development of, 105, 106, 116, 117–126; lessons from, 150–151; overview of, 113; political education and, 134, 137, 146, 156, 158–159
Clark, Mark, 73
Class, Race, and Worker Insurgency (Geschwender), 6–7
class struggle. *See* working-class struggle
Cleaver, Eldridge and Kathleen, 74
CLP (Communist Labor Party): Capital Collective and, 133; development of, 116, 117–126; lessons from, 150–151; overview of, 113, 138; political education in, 134
Cockrel, Ken: early activism of, 33–34, 35, 39, 40, 41; as labor lawyer, 53, 65; LRBW leadership and, 58–59, 104–105, 106,

111–112; MCLL and, 130, 131; movement resourcing and, 68; political education and, 149; southern roots of, 12, 16; *The Split in the League of Revolutionary Black Workers* (with Hamlin and Watson), 111–112

COINTELPRO. *See* FBI

Colectiva, 124, 125–126

Collier, Bob, 38

colonialism. *See* anti-imperialism

communism, transition to, 173, 178–179

Communist Labor Party. *See* CLP

Communist League. *See* CL

Communist Manifesto, The (Marx and Engels), 31, 118, 120, 122, 136, 169

Control, Conflict & Change book club, 128, 130–131

Cooper, Carl, 44

CP (Communist Party), 120, 123, 124, 129

Critique of the Gotha Program (Marx), 171

Cuba, 29, 31, 37, 38, 117

cultural work, 53–54, 72

Dearden, John, 69

desegregation. *See* race and racism

Detroit: as Black city, 23; postwar changes in, 24; Rebellion history suppressed in, 44–45; as revolutionary center, 7, 16, 34, 51, 120–121, 143, 146; worker migration to, 11–16, 20

Detroit (Georgakas and Surkin), 6

Detroit Forge plant (Chrysler), 56, 61–64

Detroit News, 33, 39–40, 41, 58, 70

Detroit Rebellion of 1967: Baker family experience, 79; DRUM/LRBW origins and, 46–47; lessons learned, 42–46; political education and, 110; significance of, 25, 39, 40

digital technology. *See* technology

discrimination, 168, 175–178. *See also* race and racism; sexism

Dodge Main plant (Chrysler): Detroit Rebellion of 1967 and, 43; DRUM/LRBW organizing at, 36–37, 51, 52, 56, 133; racial discrimination at, 25; wildcat strike at, 50, 53–54, 60, 79–80, 118, 155. *See also* DRUM; Eldon Avenue Gear and Axle plant

Dohrn, Bernardine, 74

Dowdell, Glanton, 68

Drescher, Fran, 179

DRUM (Dodge Revolutionary Union Movement), 36, 40; influence of, 125; LRBW and, 58–59; MCLL and, 128; origins of, 46–47; Panthers and, 73–74; propaganda, 51–53, 60; tactics of, 49–50; wildcat strikes by, 53–54

Du Bois, W. E. B., 42, 97

Earl (bar owner), 63

East Side Women for Peace, 137

economics. *See* capitalism; Marxism

Edelman, Mike, 65

education. *See* political education

Edwards, James, 56

Eldon Avenue Gear and Axle plant (Chrysler), 53, 58, 60, 65, 66–67. *See also* Dodge Main plant

Engels, Friedrich. *See also* Marx, Karl
—quoted, 6, 160, 162
—works of, 115, 147, 158; *The Communist Manifesto* (with Marx), 31, 118, 120, 122, 136, 169; *The German Ideology* (with Marx), 6

Entering an Epoch of Social Revolution (N. Peery), 117, 172–173

Ethiopian revolutionaries, 145–146

Fahoome, Richard, 137–138, 184

Fain, Shawn, 179

faith communities, 69–71, 165

Fanon, Frantz, 72; *Pedagogy of the Oppressed*, 131

Farmer, James, 86

fascism, 171, 172, 174–182

FBI (Federal Bureau of Investigation), 24, 36, 38, 81. *See also* infiltration; police

fighters versus thinkers, 152–153

Filo, Harry, 64, 65
Finally Got the News (LRBW video), 6, 72, 85, 133
Fite, Jim, 113, 119–122, 124, 158, 166–167, 184
Flint, Mich., 12, 150
Floyd, George, 180
flyers. *See* propaganda
Ford, Cassandra (Cass) Bell: on BSUF, 89–91; as leader, 95, 96; on lessons learned, 160; on LRBW split, 108; southern roots of, 15; on womens experiences, 78
Ford, Henry, 17, 19, 20, 23
Ford Motor Company: history, 17, 19, 20–21, 22, 23, 24; LRBW members as workers in, 11, 13, 80; worker organizing at, 55, 58
Forman, James, 69, 70, 106, 108, 152; *Making of a Black Revolutionary*, 71
Fraser, Douglas, 62, 63
Frito-Lay, 89

gender discrimination/oppression. *See* sexism
Georgakas, Dan, 6
German Ideology, The (Marx and Engels), 6
Geschwender, James, 6–7
Gladyck, Al, 133–134, 183–184
Glotta, Ron, 64–68, 129, 132
GM (General Motors), 20, 24, 25, 91, 120
Gonzalez, Beth, 123–124, 158–159
Gonzalez, Nacho, 124–126, 168–169
Gordy, Berry, 25
Griffith, Betty (Betty Boo), 83, 95

Hamlin, Mike: DRUM and, 52–53; early activism of, 33–34, 35, 40, 41; League oral history project and, 183; on longevity and lessons learned, 155, 170; on LRBW history, 93–94, 111–112; LRBW leadership and, 58–59, 105, 106, 108; MCLL and, 129, 131; on Panthers, 75; on political education, 143–144; propaganda and, 71, 79; resourcing and, 69, 70; southern roots of, 12, 13, 16; *The Split in the League of Revolutionary Black Workers* (with Cockrel and Watson), 111–112
Hampton, Fred, 73
Hamtramck Assembly Plant. *See* Dodge Main plant
Harding, Vince, 71
Head Start, 135–136
health and safety issues, 61–63, 66–67, 131, 145
Hewitt, Raymond (Masai), 125
Hinz, Gary, 66
history: Black, 149, 150, 177; fascist attacks on teaching, 177–178; importance of, 153, 154, 157, 162–163, 169–170; of slavery, 14, 16, 35, 40, 69–71, 87, 162, 170. *See also* League Education and Media oral history project

imperialism. *See* anti-imperialism
Indigenous peoples, 170, 177, 180–181
infiltration, 75, 111, 125. *See also* FBI; police
Inner-City Voice, 35, 40, 52, 71–72, 79, 130
intellectuals. *See* working-class intellectuals
internationalism: Israel-Palestine conflict, 35–36, 181; LRBW women and, 86, 94; political education on, 37, 115, 143, 145–146; strategic importance of, 41, 72. *See also* anti-imperialism

Jackson, Russell, 62, 95, 146–147, 149
James, C. L. R., 54
"James Johnson Needed a Thompson" (G. Jones), 66–67
Jim (auto worker), 60
Johnson, Charles (Charlie), 31, 37
Johnson, James, 66–67, 130
Jones, George, 66–67
Jones, Helen, 70, 83, 84, 85
Jones, Hugh, 66
Joyce, Frank, 127–129, 130, 157, 166

Katz-Fishman, Walda, 183, 185
King, Martin Luther, Jr., 39, 46
Kowalski, Joe, 66

Index

Kramer, Marian: on class and race, 98; early activism of, 40; influence of, 132, 168; League oral history project and, 183; on longevity and lessons learned, 151, 153, 159; on LRBW history, 3, 8, 9, 36–37, 82–83, 85–86, 105; on post-LRBW organizations, 115–117; southern roots of, 12, 14; vanguard debates and, 73

labor lawyers, 64–68, 129, 130, 131, 132, 155. *See also specific individuals*
labor movement: in auto industry history, 20–25; LRBW and history of, 3–10; strikes, 24, 179. *See also* wildcat strikes; unions
Labors Untold Story (Boyer and Morais), 110
Latino/a workers, 116, 135–136. *See also* Black workers; race and racism; white workers; *and specific individuals*
law enforcement. *See* FBI
lawyers. *See* labor lawyers
leaflets. *See* propaganda
League Education and Media oral history project: importance of, 3, 29, 31, 146, 159; methodology, 183–185; overview of, 6–10
League of Revolutionary Black Workers. *See* LRBW members; LRBW WOMEN
Leavell, Virginia, 184
Left Wing Communism (Lenin), 171, 178
Lenin, Vladimir:
—quoted, 103, 171, 178
—works of, 115, 120, 143, 144, 146, 147, 158; *Left Wing Communism*, 171, 178; *One Step Forward, Two Steps Back*, 129; *What Is to Be Done*, 31, 52, 103, 129, 131; *Where to Begin*, 31
Lerner, Josh, 132
literature. *See* propaganda
Los Angeles, 118, 120, 123, 124–125
—League of Revolutionary Black Workers: CL/CLP development and, 117–119, 121–122, 123; Detroit context of, 7; importance of, 3–10, 125, 169–170; labor lawyers and, 64–68; lessons learned, 150–151, 156–157, 168; origins of, 17, 25, 29–41, 42–43, 46–47, 58–59; other organizations and, 73–77, 127–138; political education in, 97–100, 134, 144, 148–149; resourcing, 68–73; sectarianism in, 163; sexism in, 82–86, 92–96; split in, 103–112, 116–117, 152; students in, 132–133; wildcat strikes as tactic of, 59–64. *See also* BSUF; DRUM; LRBW members; LRBW women; RUMS

LRBW members: CL/CLP development and, 121–122, 124; Detroit Rebellion of 1967 and, 42–43; early activism of, 29–41; families and children, 11–16, 79–82, 85, 87, 90, 93, 136; League oral history project and, 183–184. *See also* BSUF; *and specific individuals*
LRBW women: discussion of, 79–85, 92–96; internationalism of, 86; in LRBW publishing, 70–72, 85; overview of, 78–79; students, 87–91. *See also specific individuals*
LRNA (League of Revolutionaries for a New America), 113, 121, 158

Making of a Black Revolutionary (Forman), 71
Malcolm X, 79
male supremacy. *See* sexism
March, Ron, 47, 52
Marcus, Ben, 64
Marx, Karl. *See also* Engels, Friedrich
—quoted, 6, 42, 162, 169, 171
—works of, 97, 106, 115, 143, 144, 147, 157; *Capital*, 42, 120, 123, 129, 133; *The Communist Manifesto* (with Engels), 31, 118, 120, 122, 136, 169; *Critique of the Gotha Program*, 171; *The German Ideology* (with Engels), 6; *Value Price and Profit*, 133; *Wage Labour and Capital*, 122, 133
Marxism: as analytical framework, 5, 97–100, 103, 104, 121–122; importance

Marxism (*continued*)
of, 138–139, 158; lessons learned, 168, 170; longevity in revolutionary movement and, 152–155, 156–159; of LRBW members, 31, 33–34, 41, 43, 51; new form of, 154, 162–163; Peery on, 117; study of, 106, 107–108, 123–126, 133–134, 136, 137–138, 143–150; technological revolution as vindication of, 173. *See also* political education; revolutionary movement

Mauricio, Esther, 135–136, 161
McBecky, Nick, 71
MCLL (Motor City Labor League), 127–132, 158
means of production. *See* technology
MEChA, 124, 125
members of LRBW. *See* LRBW members
Mitchell, Darryl (Waistline): on BSUF, 91–92; on class and race, 97–98; League oral history project and, 183, 184; on lessons learned and longevity, 154, 162–163; on LRBW history, 9, 94, 95, 107; movement involvement, 51, 137; on new movement, 179; on Panthers, 75–76; on political education, 146, 148–149; on revolutionary process, 174; southern roots of, 15–16
Mitchell, Sandra, 83, 132, 137
Mitchell, William (Mitch): early activism of, 39–40; on James Johnson case, 66–67; on lessons learned, 162; on LRBW split, 109–111; on Marxism, 139; movement involvement, 71, 108, on political education, 145–146; on wildcat strikes, 60
MLWA (Marxist-Leninist Workers Association), 122, 123
Moore, Dave, 22
Morais, Herbert M., 110
Morales, George, 65
Motor City Labor League (MLWA), 127–132, 158
Motown. *See* Detroit

Motown records, 25
Muhammad Speaks (newspaper), 72
Murphy, Sheila, 130, 131
Music, Marsha (formerly Lynn Battle): on BSUF, 87–89; on Detroit Rebellion of 1967, 44; as leader, 95, 96; on LRBW split, 107–108; southern roots of, 15; on women in LRBW, 84

National Black Economic Conference, 35, 69–71
Nation of Islam, 71, 72
Negroes with Guns (R. Williams), 31
Negro National Colonial Question, The (N. Peery), 115
newsletters and newspapers. *See* propaganda
Newton, Huey, 73
nonviolence, 144. *See also* violence
NSM (Northern Student Movement), 128–129

One Step Forward, Two Steps Back (Lenin), 129
oral history project. *See* League Education and Media oral history project
Oughton, Diana, 74

Packard, 22, 24, 137
Palestinians, 35–36, 72, 181
Panthers. *See* Black Panther Party
patience, 154–155, 160–161, 165
Pedagogy of the Oppressed (Fanon), 131
Peery, Nelson
—analysis and commentary: on Marxism, 138–139; on post-LRBW organizations, 117–119; on revolutionary movement, current, 178–179; on technology and economic transition, 172–173
—as revolutionary: CCL, 120–121, 122, 123, 124; influence, 138, 158, 168; League oral history project, 183; political education, 9, 105, 146, 147, 149, 158, 168; post-LRBW organizations, 104, 113, 115, 116

Index

—works of: *Entering an Epoch of Social Revolution*, 117, 172–173; *The Negro National Colonial Question*, 115
Peery, Sue Ying, 120, 123, 124
Peoples Tribune, 120
Pitts, Iban (Aaron), 54, 89, 105
POC (provisional organizing committee), 124–125
police: fascism and, 176–177, 181; as Panthers target, 74; surveillance by, 52–53; violence of, 31, 35, 37, 39, 43–46; working-class struggle against, 180–181. *See also* FBI; infiltration
political education: of BSUF/LRBW members, 88–92, 95, 132–133; CCL and, 120, 121, 122–126; importance of, 6, 7, 99–100, 138–139, 143–150, 151, 174, 182; lessons learned, 158, 159, 161–163, 164, 165, 166, 167–170; longevity in revolutionary movement and, 152–155, 156, 158–159; of LRBW members, 31, 33–34, 35–41, 51, 59, 81; LRBW split and, 104, 105, 109–110, 115–117; of MCLL members, 128–132. *See also* Marxism; working-class intellectuals
practice and theory, 152–154, 157, 164, 165, 166–167, 174
propaganda: leaflets/flyers/newsletters, 51–53, 55, 60, 149, 166; as LRBW mission, 149, 163; newspapers, 31, 52–53, 71–72, 79, 120, 128; slogans, 160. *See also* Black Star Publishing; *and specific publications*
publishing. *See* propaganda

race and racism: antiracist struggle, 11, 31, 59, 107, 128; auto industry and, 11–16, 22–23, 25, 38, 60, 133; capitalism and, 3–4, 97–100; Detroit Rebellion of 1967 and, 42–46; DRUM/LRBW origins and, 47, 49, 59, 74–75; fascism and, 177; imperialism and, 32–33; life experiences of, 11–16, 55, 87, 89–90; political education and, 146, 148; religious institutions and, 69–71; revolutionary organizations and, 56, 116, 118, 127, 129, 130, 134, 156, 165; wildcat strikes and, 60–62; working-class struggle and, 97–100, 163. *See also* Black workers; Latino/a workers; slavery; white workers
Randazzo, Pam, 136–137, 157–158, 167
Ravitz, Justin, 35, 130
Rebellion, Watts, 43, 123. *See also* Detroit Rebellion of 1967
reforms versus revolution, 107, 112, 168–169, 173–174
religious institutions, 69–71, 165
revolutionary movement: analysis of, 56–57, 108–109, 165–166, 171–172; in Detroit, 7, 16, 34, 51, 120–121, 143, 146; leadership, 103–112, 159; lessons learned, 42–46, 159–170; longevity in, 152–159; LRBW and, importance of, 3–6, 46; Marxism and, 138–139, 155; political education and, 6, 7, 143–150, 157; strategy and tactics, 68–73, 178–182; unity versus division in, 67–68, 163, 165–166, 167, 169, 177, 182; vanguard, 73–77, 92, 131. *See also* civil rights movement; Marxism; working-class struggle; *and specific organizations*
Rhoades, Jim, 66
River Rouge plant (Ford), 21, 58, 80
Roberts, Abdul Donald, 54, 56, 95, 147
Robinson, Deanna, 125
Robinson, William, 174–175, 179, 182
robotics. *See* technology
Rogers, Leah, 38, 84–85, 150, 156, 169
Rogers, Wylie, 38, 39, 96, 99–100, 156, 169–170
Roosevelt, Eleanor, 22
RUMS (Revolutionary Union Movements), 42, 46–47, 55–56, 58–59. *See also* DRUM

Sams, George, 74
Sanders, Bernie, 144
Scott, Cynthia, 29, 37
Scott, Jerome: CCL and, 121; on class and race, 98, 99; family life, 81, 82; League

Scott, Jerome (*continued*)
    oral history project and, 183, 184, 185; on longevity and lessons learned, 153–154, 163–165; on LRBW history, 3, 7–10, 12, 55–56, 80, 93, 108–109; on Panthers, 76; on political education, 103, 144–145; on wildcat strikes, 61–64
Scott, Theresa, 81, 82, 84
Scott, Yolanda, 81
SDS (Students for a Democratic Society), 34, 39, 74, 104, 117, 119–120, 122, 124
segregation. *See* race and racism
sexism, 78–85, 91, 92–96, 168. *See also* women
Simmons, Charles, 31, 35, 37–38, 72, 150, 155–156, 165–166
Simmons, Larry, 135
Sims, Jordan, 65
slavery, 14, 16, 35, 40, 69–71, 87, 162, 170. *See also* race and racism
Smith, Carl, 71
Smith-Cook, Cassandra, 73, 85
SNCC (Student Nonviolent Coordinating Committee), 8, 38, 69, 108
South, U.S., 11–16, 178, 182. *See also* slavery
South End, 31, 35, 71–72, 73, 74, 76
Split in the League of Revolutionary Black Workers, The (Cockrel, Hamlin, and Watson), 111–112
Stalin, Joseph, 58, 146, 147, 149
Stapansky, Tom, 63
state violence: capitalism and, 4, 5; Detroit Rebellion of 1967 and, 39, 42–46; fascist, 175–178; working-class struggle and, 20, 21, 54, 100, 174, 180–181. *See also* FBI; police
Sterling Heights Stamping plant (Chrysler), 133
strikes, 24, 179. *See also* wildcat strikes
struggle. *See* working-class struggle
student revolutionaries, 51, 52, 84, 87–92, 125, 127–128, 160. *See also* BSUF; SDS; SNCC; youth
study. *See* political education

Surkin, Marvin, 6
synagogues, 69–70

Taylor, Maureen, 83–84, 134–135, 168
Teamsters Union, 22
technology: auto industry and, 17–20, 64, 103, 106, 122, 163; crises of capitalism and, 171; political education and, 168; in revolutionary process, 3, 5–6, 117, 147–148, 164, 172–174, 178; U.S. power and, 23–24
theory and practice, 152–154, 157, 164, 165, 166–167, 174
thinkers versus fighters, 152–153
Till, Emmett, 14, 15, 16, 39, 87
Townsend, Len, 50
trade unions. *See* unions
Tripp, Luke: on DRUM compared to Panthers, 73, 74–75, 76; early activism of, 31, 34, 37, 40, 41; on longevity and lessons learned, 165; LRBW and, 58–59, 143; on LRBW split, 105–106; on working-class intellectuals, 99
Troutman, Ronald, 56

UAW (United Auto Workers): DRUM/LRBW struggle against, 46, 47, 49–50, 54, 59; frustrations of working at, 157; history of, 17–20, 21; Metropolitan hospital and, 131; race and racism in, 22–23, 75, 109; wildcat strikes and, 62, 63–64, 65; working-class struggle and, current, 179–180, 181
UHURU, 31, 37, 38, 160
unions: analysis of, 145; in auto industry history, 17–25; at Cadillac, 91; at Frito-Lay, 89; Teamsters, 22; wildcat strikes and, 4; working-class struggle and, current, 167, 179–180, 181. *See also* UAW
United Auto Workers. *See* UAW
United States: auto industry in, history of, 17–20; Civil War, 162; imperialism/colonialism in, 32–33, 115; indoctrination in, 144; postwar global importance

of, 23–24, 25; race and class in, 11–16, 69–70, 97–100, 170; ruling class in, 159, 175–178; Vietnam War, 31–33, 55, 86, 87, 119–120, 128; working-class struggle in, current, 155, 162–163, 169, 178–182
University of Michigan, 38, 39
U.S. South, 11–16, 178, 182. *See also* slavery

Valenti, Rita, 130–132, 157, 167–168
Value Price and Profit (Marx), 133
Vietnam War, 31–33, 55, 86, 87, 119–120, 128
violence, 21, 44, 47, 49, 74, 75, 144. *See also* state violence

Wage Labour and Capital (Marx), 122, 133
Watson, Edna, 14–15, 16, 35–36, 70–71, 83, 130
Watson, John: on DRUM origins, 49; early activism of, 31, 33–34, 35–36, 37, 39, 40, 41; family, 12, 16, 83; LRBW leadership and, 58–59, 105, 106, 109, 111–112; MCLL and, 130, 131; political education and, 143, 148; propaganda and, 52, 71, 72, 79; *The Split in the League of Revolutionary Black Workers* (with Cockrel and Hamlin), 111–112
Watts Rebellion, 43, 123
Wayne State University, 31, 35, 37, 38, 41, 128, 129, 134
What Is to Be Done (Lenin), 31, 52, 103, 129, 131
Wheeler, Linda, 89, 90, 132–133, 156–157, 166
Wheeler, Terry, 89, 90
Where to Begin (Lenin), 31
white supremacy. *See* race and racism
white workers: in auto industry, 12, 21, 25, 89; Detroit Rebellion of 1967 and, 43–44; LRBW struggle and, 82, 98, 129, 133–134; Marx on, 42; in revolutionary organizations, 34, 104, 116, 127, 128, 130; unions and, 22, 23, 49; wildcat strikes and, 49, 60, 61, 62, 63. *See also* Black workers; Latino/a workers; race and racism; *and specific individuals*
wildcat strikes: Black and white worker experience of, 12; as Black working-class rebellion, 42–43; at Dodge Main, 53–54, 79–80; as DRUM/LRBW tactic, 4, 49–50, 59–64, 76, 155; labor lawyers and, 64–68; women and, 79–80, 82–83, 131
Williams, Carl, 63
Williams, John
—analysis and commentary: on class and race, 98; on Detroit Rebellion of 1967, 44; on longevity and lessons learned, 151, 154–155, 163; on LRBW, 9, 58–59, 92, 104–105; on Panthers, 73–74; on working-class intellectuals, 99–100
—background, 12, 13, 16, 82
—as revolutionary: DRUM, 50; early activism of, 31, 33, 38, 39, 40, 41; League oral history project, 183; LRBW leadership, 65, 106, 136; political education, 134, 143, 148, 149; publishing and resourcing, 52, 68–69, 70
Williams, Judy, 82, 84, 116, 134, 137, 167
Williams, Robert (Bob): Detroit revolutionary connections, 31, 37; *Negroes with Guns*, 31; political education and, 105, 115, 136, 145–146, 147, 148
women, 14–15, 70–72, 115, 159. *See also* LRBW women; sexism; *and specific individuals*
Wooten, Charles (Chuck): on James Johnson case, 67; League oral history project and, 184; LRBW leadership and, 59, 105, 108, 110; relationships, 82, 118, 161; revolutionary movement involvement, 36–37, 41, 54, 71; southern roots of, 12, 16
Wooten, Gracie, 36, 54, 71–72, 78, 82–83, 156, 161
workers. *See* Black workers; Latino/a workers; white workers

working-class intellectuals: importance of, 6, 7, 99–100, 149; in LRBW, 4, 5, 13, 43; LRBW split and, 104, 105, 109–110, 152; political education of, 146–147. *See also* political education

working-class struggle: analysis of, 97–100, 171, 172; approaches to, 73–77, 154–157, 160–161, 165, 167; in auto industry history, 20–25; BSUF as part of, 87–92; current, 168, 169, 177, 179–182; Detroit Rebellion and, 43–44; LRBW as part of, 3–6, 10, 46, 59, 64, 78–86, 92–96; political education and, 150, 152; RUMs as part of, 55–56; white workers as part of, 127–132. *See also* revolutionary movement

working conditions, 61–63, 66–67, 131, 145

X, Malcolm, 79

Ying, Sue, 120, 123, 124
youth, 159, 161–162, 165–166, 168, 170. *See also* student revolutionaries

www.ingramcontent.com/pod-product-compliance
Lightning Source LLC
Chambersburg PA
CBHW020815230426
43666CB00007B/1017